MW01087574

PRISON JOURNAL

an irreverent look at life on the inside

Joseph Timilty

ISBN: 1500137332
ISBN 13: 9781500137335

PRISON JOURNAL
An Irreverent Look at Life on the Inside

Joseph Timilty
with Jack Thomas

Northeastern University Press
Boston

Northeastern University Press
Library of Congress Cataloging-in-Publication Data
Timilty, Joseph F. 1938-
Prison Journal: an irreverent look at life on the inside/ Joseph Timilty
with Jack Thomas
p. cm
ISBN 1-55553-312-4 (alk. Paper)
1. Timilty Joseph F. 1938—Diaries. 2. Prisoners—
Pennsylvania—Schuykill County—Diaries 3.
Politicians—Massachusetts—Dorchester—Diaries
4. Schuykill County Prison (Pa.)—Social Conditions. I. Thomas, Jack
1939-
II. Title HV9468. T57A3
365'.6'092-dc21
[B] 97-10280
Printed and bound by Maple Press, York, Pennsylvania
The paper is Sebago Antique, an acid-free sheet
Manufactured in the United States of America
00 99 98 97 5 4 3 2 1

To Elaine,
my love, my light, my life's partner,
my best friend,
whose strength and fortitude
kept our family together

CONTENTS

ACKNOWLEDGMENTS

I t is truly impossible to thank everyone by name who helped in this publishing effort. Therefore, I will not trip over an attempt. For my alumni past and present, rest assured names have been changed to protect the guilty. To my lifelong friends who stood by me throughout this ordeal, a heartfelt vote of appreciation for your support. To Charley Sarkis, who believed in me from the first day of this debacle, my thanks for his tremendous support for myself and my family; he gives true meaning to the term "stand-up guy." I am also indebted to Ann Brian Murphy, who helped make greater sense of it all.

PRISON JOURNAL

PROLOGUE

Joseph Timilty grew up in Dorchester, an extensive working-class neighborhood in Boston, in the 1940s and 1950s. It was a world and a time that left an indelible mark on all who lived there. Boston in those years was a city of recent immigrants, living in uneasy proximity as separate clans—religious and ethnic tribes of Irish, Jewish, Italian, African American, Polish, and Yankee neighborhoods, and each fiercely guarded its cultural and physical boundaries. It was a world of "us and them," with the ethnic immigrants pitted intermittently against one another, and inevitably, essentially, against the powerful Yankee bluebloods who still ran the state.

Dorchester at that time was emphatically Irish, a neighborhood defined as much by parishes and the Catholic Church as by precincts and the rough-and-tumble world of Boston politics. It was also a world that still remembered the nineteenth century immigrant experience, and many grandparents and even parents vividly recollected (and resented) "No Irish Need Apply" signs. When Governor Endicott Peabody's wife visited the State House and complained about the lack of cleanliness in the bathrooms, the Irish of Dorchester were furious, remembering those long years—only then beginning to end—in which the Irish were the ones who did the cleaning, and the Yankees were the ones who owned the city and did the hiring.

Dorchester was a world in which loyalty and humor were paramount and essential values. You were loyal to family, to neighborhood and parish, to religion and ethnicity, and to political party, and you used humor to laugh at your own pains, to armor yourself against the world's injustices. It was a world that valued quick wit and a ready fist, in which people joked that they were born Democrat and five days later baptized as Catholic. Being Catholic and being Democrat were in those days virtually synonymous, and they were significant not only in saying who you were but in marking what you were *not*: not Yankee, not Republican, not Protestant, and not rich.

During and just after World War II, Dorchester was still a world of comparatively limited possibilities, in which the best and the brightest chose a career of public service, usually politics, while the other options included the safety of working for "the Edison"—the city electric utility company—or the telephone company or the excitement and further clan loyalty of the police or the military. For Joe Timilty, born to a political family, with a grandfather who was a state senator and an uncle who was police commissioner plus a campaign manager to James Michael Curley, politics was always a likely choice. The vital and feisty world of Boston politics combined the excitement of city street fighting with pragmatic idealism. Politics was a way to *live* your loyalty to your family and clan, by fighting the Yankees on their own territory, and it offered the hope of making the world a better place.

But if the possibilities in Dorchester were limited, they were still much, much greater than they'd been a generation or two earlier, and the people of Boston's neighborhoods, despite their clannishness and ethnic hostilities, were intensely loyal to the country that had so richly expanded their lives and their hopes for their children's futures. During the 1940s and 1950s, when Joe was growing up, the big events were the Memorial Day and Veterans Day parades, and what was really on parade was a fierce kind of grateful immigrant patriotism. The federal government, for Dorchester residents of Joe's generation, could do no wrong. The FBI was as respected as the parish priest, and parish priests were still the most respectable people imaginable.

Growing up in this world meant knowing who your friends were—and who your enemies were. It meant serving as an altar boy at St. Gregory's Church on Sundays and being able to hold your own, in both verbal and physical battles, during the week. It meant defending your turf against outsiders, defending your own family and friends against dangers, and never, ever, betraying a friend or "ratting" to the authorities. In subsequent years, Joe would lose the parochialism of Dorchester and develop a vision of the city that was profoundly multicultural and inclusive. But he never lost his belief in a code of honor that demanded loyalty first and above all else. And it was years before he lost his belief that the government was on the side of truth and justice.

As befitted a child of his neighborhood and generation, Joe opted to join the marines rather than go to college. At boot camp, at Parris Island, South Carolina, drill instructors reinforced the code of honor he'd grown up with: honor for the marines as for those Joe had respected in Dorchester, was simply not possible without loyalty. The marine slogan, *Semper fidelis*, was not just a slogan for Joe; it was a deeply internalized creed, a way of making sense of the world.

After the marines and a few years in the family laundry business, Joe entered politics, winning seats on the Boston City Council in 1967 and in the state senate in 1972. He served in the senate for six terms and built a reputation as an honest, hard-working, progressive, and innovative legislator. He chaired the Joint Committee on Housing and Urban Development in the 1970s, when urban issues were still influenced by the optimism and creativity of the 1960s. It was a time when some of the best minds in Boston were trying to devise ways to make cities safe, livable, and affordable. Joe used his political position in the senate to fight for the rights of gays and minorities, for the elderly and the physically and mentally handicapped, and for innovative new forms of affordable housing for all. And he did all this long before such positions were politically acceptable, especially to his constituents. But while the Boston Irish voters of his district often vehemently disagreed with him, especially in his vocal and unswerving opposition to the death penalty, but they also respected him, and they knew that he was voting his conscience and living by his code of honor. And so they kept reelecting him.

During these years, Joe was involved in three bruising and hard-fought campaigns against Mayor Kevin White, and many in Boston remember him especially for his political courage and integrity in the bloody, tempestuous days of school desegregation. In 1974, after long, protracted legal battles between the NAACP and an intransigent Boston School Committee, the federal courts finally ordered that Boston's notoriously segregated schools be integrated. It was a ruling that struck at the core of Boston's working-class identity: the cherished immigrant legacy of distinct ethnic neighborhoods.

In the subsequent busing battles (the term here is sadly literal) small children were escorted to school through jeering, violent crowds by heavily armed SWAT teams; blacks and whites across the city were subjected to terrifying violence (including the attack on Ted Landsmark, a black attorney, by an angry mob of white kids wielding a flagpole, carrying an American flag as a weapon); angry working-class whites felt they were being exploited by upper-middle-class policy makers whose own privately educated children were not at risk, and angry blacks felt they were once again being denied the right to an education and access to the American dream. Meanwhile, the mayor, the cardinal, and virtually every other figure of authority in the Commonwealth remained ominously, disgracefully silent.

Joe ran for mayor against Kevin White in 1975, and many political advisors recommended that he exploit the race issue by playing to his urban ethnic constituency and vocally opposing busing. Joe, however, steadfastly refused their advice. Had he followed it in the bitter, polarized climate of the time, he might well have won, especially since most ethnic Boston voters were seriously disenchanted with his opponent,

Kevin White. However, this kind of campaign would surely have exacerbated the already violent and dangerous mood of the city. Boston was constantly on the edge in those years; exploiting the race issue in such a context was worse than just sleazy, it was unconscionable and literally dangerous to the lives of the residents.

But Joe had another reason for refusing to throw gasoline on the fires of racial hatred: his own children were attending Boston's dangerous and volatile public schools and thus were far more at risk than the children of most elected officials. "I could continue to be a parent or a politician," he said after the election, referring to his determinedly moderate and responsible position on busing. "I chose to be a parent."

Choosing to be a parent in 1975 meant more than just refusing to exploit racial hatreds and fears. For Joe it meant being willing to appear on television with the African American state representative Mel King and plead for calm in the city. It meant spending time in his Hyde Park neighborhood helping to achieve and maintain calm instead of attending political functions. It meant insisting that the campaign literature be aimed at a multiracial, citywide audience, rather than playing (as Kevin White was doing) to specific neighborhood fears, anxieties, and even bigotries. And, ultimately, it meant losing the election by a very narrow margin to a candidate who had, at best, played it safe and remained silent while the city raged.

The following year Joe was tapped by presidential candidate Jimmy Carter to run his campaign in Pennsylvania. The victory in that state helped ensure Carter's election, and Joe was subsequently invited to the White House for dinners and served on two presidential commissions.

With college tuition bills looming, Joe decided to take a break from politics in January 1985 and went into private industry. He had long been interested in housing, as chair of the Joint Committee on Housing and Urban Development in the state senate and as head of Carter's US Commission on National Neighborhood Policy, so it was a natural step, in the real estate boom years of the 1980s, into housing in the private sector. But Joe hadn't lost his belief in community improvement or his commitment to the city. He sought a way to put his skills and experience to use in minority and working-class communities across the country. He started in East Boston, a working-class Italian neighborhood in the shadows of Boston's Logan Airport. There, Joe found a Roman Catholic school that had been closed for ten years. The archdiocese intended to sell the deteriorating, vacant building to a company that had plans to convert it into use for the airport—not a popular project among neighborhood residents who had long-standing grievances against the airport. In the late winter of 1985, working in a partnership with Philip Singleton, a successful real estate developer and a longtime friend and supporter, Joe persuaded the archdiocese to let them buy the building instead and convert it into condominiums.

Months later, in the late summer of 1985, the city solicited bids for the renovation of a nearby public school, which had been closed for fifteen years. Believing that the restoration of the public school building would make it easier to sell units in the Catholic school building and thus further contribute to the neighborhood's health and revitalization, Timilty and Singleton developed a plan, with the cooperation and approval of the neighborhood residents, to convert the public school into twenty-four residential units. They were awarded the project after a hotly contested competition because their project included such a high percentage of affordable units; eight of the twenty-four units to be marketed were earmarked for local residents.

Their next project also combined public service and potential profit. The worst eyesore in this East Boston neighborhood was a six-story brick building, called the gumball factory, which had been closed for over a decade. Neighbors feared the brick smokestack would topple at any moment, and its presence as an abandoned building damaged both the neighborhood's safety and its property values. In early 1986 Joe and Singleton drew up plans to convert the gumball factory into eighty-nine new housing units. Here, as in each of the buildings they worked on, 10 percent of the units were designated for low-income residents.

However, the real estate market was beginning to weaken, in part because of changes in the federal tax code, and in part as an early symptom of the dramatic collapse that would soon devastate the New England economy. The mad profligacy of the 1980s continued, but some banks were becoming reluctant to make loans, especially in working-class neighborhoods, and units in the two buildings were selling very slowly. By the end of 1986, Singleton decided to withdraw from the gumball venture, which left Joe facing a dilemma. The East Boston neighborhood had been enormously helpful in persuading the city to grant zoning changes that had allowed them to develop the two schools. Out of loyalty, therefore, Joe felt he couldn't just abandon these people and walk away from his commitment to restore the abandoned factory. But he couldn't do the restoration alone.

At this point, his former colleague in the state senate, Michael Lo Presti, of East Boston, who had been doing some of the legal work for the sale of units in the two schools, stepped forward. Lo Presti came from a long line of public servants in the East Boston community, and his family had been involved actively in the airport concession business and in state and local government. Joe and Lo Presti had never been close—indeed, Lo Presti had sided with Kevin White against Joe in their mayoral battle. But the men had set those differences aside, and Lo Presti brought to the real estate venture several important strengths: he knew the East Boston community intimately, he had close personal relationships with important and influential local people, and he was a lawyer who could handle the legal aspects of their real estate work.

On the down side, Lo Presti's legal work sometimes involved defending drug dealers, and he had been dogged by persistent rumors that he was associated with the Mafia. Joe, however, knew that most Italians in public life are plagued by such rumors, and he reasoned that the people Lo Presti defended were certainly entitled to a defense and that Lo Presti was a lawyer whose job was to defend them. On balance, he concluded, Lo Presti brought real strengths to the gumball factory project. Yet they still needed someone else, someone who could bring in the money.

Lo Presti introduced Joe to James De Cotis, a successful business-man who joined them as a partner and whose wealth helped persuade the banks that the gumball development project was viable. De Cotis insisted, however, that the partnership be expanded to include people with more knowledge of the specifics of actually selling real estate units. He suggested Michael D'Avolio, who local bankers thought might become another Donald Trump, and a man named Monte Marrocco, who owned a construction and development business and had a reputation for moving real estate units, even in a slowing market.

Joe had heard of D'Avolio, whose father was a judge in Salem District Court and whose uncle had represented East Boston in the state legislature. Marrocco, however, was a stranger. Finally, these disparate men agreed to form a partnership, the Gumball Realty Trust, based on a structure proposed by Lo Presti. Joe's responsibilities would be to handle issues involving the government and the neighborhood and to make sure construction work did not disrupt the residents' lives. D'Avolio would monitor construction day to day. Marrocco would sell the units, and Lo Presti would handle the legal responsibilities of the closings. Lo Presti and Timilty each owned 22.5 percent. The remainder was divided evenly among D'Avolio, Marrocco, and De Cotis—three men Timilty had never met before but who would change his life forever.

Problems arose right away between Timilty and Marrocco. When he discovered that Marrocco intended to award the construction contract to his brother, Timilty immediately vetoed the arrangement because it was a clear conflict of interest. Marrocco took Joe's action as a personal insult, while Joe saw Marrocco as exploitative and selfish for insisting on the exclusive right to sell the condominiums at a 7 percent commission, when previous realtors had only been paid 4 percent. Another dispute arose when Marrocco, who wanted to use nonunion help, was angered that Joe insisted on using more expensive union help.

However, these were comparatively minor issues, clearly negotiable, and a lifetime in politics had taught Joe how to work well with people he did not necessarily like or respect. What *was* eventually to create serious problems for the partnership was the complicated issues of second mortgages. During the wild real estate boom of the 1980s, many realtors and developers had resorted to providing second mortgages for their potential buyers, who then used that second mortgage to provide the down payment for the primary mortgage. This practice had been originated by the mortgage companies themselves in a time of soaring real estate prices, when even the lowly wood-frame, two-family houses in Dorchester were jumping in value from $25,000 to $90,000 or $100,000. Taking their cue from the mortgage companies, developers began to offer what was in fact a second mortgage by taking the down payment back "on paper" and deferring their own profits, confident in the rising value of real estate. Meanwhile, the mortgage companies had, on paper, equity in those increasingly valuable units.

Such second mortgages, of course, had to be disclosed on certain insurance forms, which usually asked about the existence of secondary financing. Yet during the boom market of the 1980s, when soaring property values and profits appeared inexhaustible, it seemed to be in everyone's short-term interest to expedite the loans and sell the housing units until the bottom fell out of the real estate market and the paper value of those homes became clearly inflated and unreliable. When the Massachusetts housing market did eventually fall apart in the late 1980s, loans went unpaid, banks foreclosed, and mortgage companies claimed, in the classic words of Claude Rains in *Casablanca*, to be "shocked, shocked" that so many first mortgages had been supported by second mortgages.

The implications of these second mortgages, however, were still far in the future. Joe was more concerned about Marrocco and about the viability of the East Boston project in the declining real estate market. Yet Joe remained in the gumball partnership for two reasons. First was his strong commitment to the working-class neighborhood and his reluctance to betray the trust of the people there. Second was his financial obligation; his name was on the three mortgage notes.

The situation worsened one day in early 1987, when Joe received a phone call from someone at city hall.

"Do you know you're in business with a drug dealer?" the caller asked.

"No," said Joe. "Who are you talking about?"

"Monte Marrocco."

Joe acted first to confirm this rumor, not wanting to react unfairly. Once he had confirmed the facts with the district attorney's office, he acted immediately. He set up a meeting with Marrocco at a coffee shop in Boston's Statler Office Building, where Joe had his office. As he descended in the elevator to the meeting, Joe reviewed his own goal for the encounter: to get Marrocco *out* of the partnership. He had decided that he would offer Marrocco an opportunity to resign and save face. If he refused to leave, however, Joe planned to threaten to force him out by having lawyers go to the registry of deeds and remove his name.

When he got to the coffee shop and saw Marrocco, Joe didn't mince words.

"It's been brought to my attention that you were involved in a drug offense that is the target of an ongoing investigation by the district attorney's office."

"Yeah, that's true," Marrocco replied.

Marrocco had clearly come to the meeting convinced that he could persuade Joe the offense was minor. He began to explain that his arrest had been a mistake but that it could be "fixed" by Lo Presti, who was his attorney and had defended other drug dealers.

"You don't understand," Joe said. "I've already talked to people involved. I know exactly what you were charged with, and it makes you unacceptable as a partner."

"This is important to me," Marrocco said. "I was brought up in a family that is strongly Italian. I'm the patriarch. I have brothers and a sister to take care of. They've looked up to me ever since I was an athlete in school. Being ejected from this partnership because of drugs would be embarrassing. I can't have this happen."

"You miss my point," Joe answered firmly. "I am not here to debate this. The only question is *how* it's done, not whether. Either you do it, or I do it. Now it would make more sense for you to do it, because then you could explain to everyone why you're doing it."

"This is a personal embarrassment to me and my family," Marrocco said. "We can never forgive you. Somewhere, sometime, this is a debt that will have to be repaid."

Removing Marrocco's name from the partnership at the registry of deeds was easy. What proved at first to be more difficult was assuaging the concerns of the bank, ComFed in Lowell, which had guaranteed the construction loan for the gumball renovation based on Marrocco's ability to sell. But Marrocco assured ComFed that De Cotis and D'Avolio would remain as partners, and the bank insisted that Marrocco remain responsible for the sales. That way, the bank was reassured that the loan was secure, while Marrocco, who subsequently pleaded guilty to the drug charge, still earned his 7 percent commission; Joe had to be satisfied that at least he was no longer a partner with a drug dealer.

Unfortunately, Joe's problems with the Gumball Realty Trust were far from over. The next ominous sign occurred one morning in late 1988, when Joe read a story in the *Boston Globe* about a real estate development in New Hampshire, an article describing second mortgages and indictments. By this time, the gumball factory was in serious trouble, as was the Massachusetts economy, and the prospect loomed that the venture might go belly-up. Only thirty of the forty-five units of phase one had sold, and the bank was becoming impatient and refused to invest further. In reaction, Joe's children began working at the site on the weekends, painting and repairing it, to make it more marketable. Joe phoned D'Avolio as soon as he saw the *Globe* article.

"Did you see the article in the *Globe* on second mortgages in New Hampshire?"

"Yes," D'Avolio replied.

"And the indictments?"

"Yes."

"Well," Joe asked, "what's the difference between their second mortgages and our second mortgages?"

"I don't think there's much difference at all."

This was definitely not the answer Joe had sought or expected. (He later learned that the very mortgage companies that had originally taught the developers the second mortgage arrangement had begun to complain to the legal authorities that they were being defrauded by those same developers. In claiming that the developers were responsible for fraud, many mortgage companies sought, successfully, to avoid being prosecuted for their own involvement in the arrangement.)

The mortgage situation was being further complicated by the fact that federal investigators were examining *all* the mortgages in which Marrocco had played a role, not just those in the gumball factory, as part of their ongoing investigation into his dealings. Their curiosity had been aroused by the fact that a striking number of his mortgages were going bad. When banks and mortgage companies went looking for the collateral in the loans Marrocco had handled, they found it did not exist, because the mortgage applications contained inaccurate information.

The gumball partners assumed that federal investigators would eventually ask about Marrocco's role in the gumball factory. Still, Joe knew he'd acted immediately to oust Marrocco as soon as he learned of the man's drug dealing, and it never occurred to him that he himself might be vulnerable. After all, lawyers on both sides had been checking and rechecking every number in their loan applications, while Lo Presti had presided as a lawyer over some of the gumball closings. Joe knew that Lo Presti was a smart lawyer who was unlikely to do anything to diminish his family's political reputation, nor to jeopardize his own career in real estate. The problem, as Joe saw it, was Marrocco's drug dealing—and the stagnating economy. If Marrocco or anyone was to be indicted for the second mortgages, Joe told himself, it might be politically embarrassing, but nothing more.

One day in early 1990, Joe's phone rang.

"Mr. Timilty, this is Agent Antoinette Craven with the FBI. We're investigating the sale of units at the gumball factory, and I'd like to talk to you."

"Sure, whatever you say," said Joe, raised to believe the FBI were the good guys and assuming the feds were looking into Marrocco's drug connection. "Do you want to do it at your office or mine?"

"I'll come to your office," she said, and they set a date to meet at the Statler Office Building. After this phone call, Joe went to see his attorney, Robert Murphy, who had worked in the Justice Department under Robert Kennedy and was a senior partner in one of Boston's most respected law firms, Casner & Edwards. Joe told Murphy that he believed the federal government had the goods on Marrocco but that he and D'Avolio had nothing to worry about. Joe then mentioned his conversation with the FBI agent.

"I don't want you to see or talk to her," Murphy said. Murphy knew D'Avolio and was instinctively suspicious of him. "You can't talk to them without understanding what they are looking for."

"I know what they want," said Joe. "They want to ask me about the gumball factory. They want to learn how those units were sold and why so many are going belly-up."

Murphy wasn't convinced. "Joe, let me get in touch with the US Attorney's Office and see if I can't find out what's going on."

A few days later, Murphy called back. "Joe, I have bad news," he said. "*You* are the target of this investigation. They've got you as the principal here."

"Why?" Joe asked, incredulous.

"I can only guess." Murphy replied. "But it's clear that it doesn't make any difference to them if they get your partners; they figure if they get you, they can go higher. They're using you for your political visibility, as a way to go after other people. They think you'll name names."

"I have no idea who they want," said Joe, stunned. "What do I do?"

"You need a criminal lawyer," Murphy replied somberly.

In 1991, not long after this conversation, Joe received a phone call from John Parigian, who had resigned as treasurer of the troubled Capital Bank and Trust Company in 1986 and had remained strikingly free of any subsequent prosecution. Many insiders believed Parigian must have been an informant. Whatever the truth of this rumor, Parigian was a man who prided himself on his knowledge of what was happening in the complex worlds of finance and federal investigation.

"I understand you've been in to see the US Attorney," Parigian said.

"No, I haven't," Joe answered, surprised.

"Then someone who represents you was in," Parigian insisted.

"You have good information," said Joe, impressed. "That just happened. My lawyer wanted to find out what they were looking for."

Parigian asked if Joe knew Marrocco had declared bankruptcy and dropped out of sight, trying to elude what most people saw as an inevitable indictment.

"No, but I'm not surprised," Joe answered. "My relationship with Marrocco is certainly not friendly, and I'm amazed they haven't caught up with him sooner, if not for drugs then for his other real estate dealings." Joe was thinking of information that had by then come out about Marrocco's phony mortgages.

"You know," said Parigian, "eventually Marrocco is going to get around to talking about you."

Joe immediately remembered that angry meeting with Marrocco in the coffee shop and the man's insistence that he would pay Joe back for ejecting him from the partnership. He was alarmed, because he knew Marrocco wouldn't let the truth get in the way of this opportunity for revenge. But he reassured himself that there wasn't anything that Marrocco could say that was *true*, and Joe still believed in the workings of the government and the fundamental justice of the FBI.

"You ought to know that D'Avolio has gone in and made a deal," said Parigian. "He's prepared to cooperate. I tell you, Joe, the first guy in gets the best deal. D'Avolio went in first, and he's telling them whatever they want to know, whether it's true or not."

After this conversation, Joe, with characteristic directness and honesty, called D'Avolio himself. "I heard a story that you've been to the US Attorney's Office, cooperating, and that you've implicated me."

"The only thing I can tell you is that you ought to get yourself a lawyer," D'Avolio replied.

Joe spoke again to Robert Murphy, his attorney, who recommended once more he hire a good criminal lawyer. In the spring of 1992, Joe went to see Diane Kottmyer, a former Assistant US Attorney and well-respected prosecutor best known for her successful conviction of a prominent Boston crime boss. Kottmyer, who had left the US Attorney's Office for private practice, was widely regarded as skillful and knowledgeable about the law. She suggested that she meet with Joe and Robert Murphy about the case.

The three of them sat down and reviewed the situation, with Joe and Murphy filling Kottmyer in on the background, including both Marrocco's drug dealings and the gumball factory's fiscal difficulties.

"Yes, Joe's involved with these guys in East Boston," Murphy told Kottmyer, "but I've represented him for years. I know his financial situation. I can assure you, he wasn't involved in the sale of the units, so he couldn't have been involved in any kind of fraud in putting together mortgages. His job was dealing with the city and being neighborhood liaison. And I know for a fact he hasn't made any money in selling units—with second mortgages or otherwise."

After reviewing the information, Kottmyer explained to Joe that the US Attorney firmly believed that Timilty had information that would help them bring in more indictments against people at the State House. She also explained that Joe's categorical refusal, not merely to cooperate with the feds but even to meet with them, was infuriating the prosecutors. She told Joe that the obvious option was to plead guilty to one count of conspiracy. She felt the US Attorney's Office wouldn't care what he pleaded guilty to, as long as he did so, since such a pleas would allow them to call Joe before a grand jury, giving him immunity, and ask him for information that would help them pursue other individuals in politics. She didn't know which they were really after, the East Boston businessmen or former political associates of Joe's, but it was clear his refusal to cooperate would only frustrate their investigation.

Joe remained adamant, however, in his refusal to name names. Everything he had ever believed in, the code of honor that shaped his entire life in Dorchester, in the marines, and in public life was violated and offended by this practice of asking people to testify against friends and colleagues.

Murphy, too, disagreed. "That won't work, because no federal judge will accept a guilty plea from Joe Timilty without forcing him to admit the specifics, and he doesn't know any. You *might*, possibly, be able to convince this guy, for the sake of his family, to plead guilty in return for a shorter sentence. But I know him, and he's never going to testify against anyone else, and he's never going to stand up in court and admit to something he doesn't believe."

After this preliminary meeting, Kottmyer visited the US Attorney's Office to find out in more detail what they were looking for. Then she met again with Joe and Murphy to report on what she'd discovered.

"They say you're involved in a second mortgage scheme," she explained to Joe. "They are convinced that you have information. I told John Pappalardo (the acting US Attorney) that you had nothing to do with the sale of the units, that you'd only been involved in the permitting process, and in neighborhood liaison, but they insist you were a trustee and that you signed some documents, which makes you legally liable. Furthermore, they have concrete evidence. Of the thirty units sold, they have your signature on five that say there were no second mortgages, when in fact there were, and these documents were faxed to New York, so there's the crime. In the use of a fax, you are now guilty of wire fraud. Pappalardo says he's not cutting you any slack, because you've shown no remorse and no inclination to cooperate.

"There is still an opportunity for you to cooperate, however," Kottmyer concluded. "They'll leave that door open. In fact, they urge you to talk, to show remorse and, above all, to name names. Frankly, I don't think they care that much about the mortgages. What they really want is information on possible corruption at city hall. They feel that shortcuts are being taken at various city agencies and that you received special treatment in getting the number of units you did at the gumball factory. They want to talk to you about that."

In other words, if he would rat on people with whom he'd worked at city hall, the feds might show some leniency over the existence of second mortgages, which Joe had always assumed were legal.

Timilty was stunned.

"This is absolutely, unequivocally wrong," he said. "It's like a bad dream. It has no bearing on reality. Marrocco and his assistant, Joseph Benoit, had exclusive rights. And lawyers were involved in all of these transactions. How could they possibly have been illegal?"

Kottmyer was trying to find an explanation, some way to account for the US Attorney's intransigence. "Have you met any of these people in the US Attorney's Office?" she asked. "Have you done anything to them politically?"

Again, Joe remembered Marrocco's promise to get back at him. But he knew of no one at the US Attorney's Office. "There are a lot of people I've done things to politically, who might enjoy roughing me up," he replied, "but I can't remember meeting any of these guys personally."

Kottmyer went on. "Well, they think you're nothing more than a criminal, just like the others. They figure that you were in business with people who were sleazy, so you're sleazy, too. And it doesn't help that you're a politician; these days people just assume that all politicians are corrupt."

"I can't believe this," Joe said. "When this appears in the newspapers, it will be embarrassing, and I'll be raked over the coals." He wasn't looking forward to explaining it to his children.

Kottmyer looked startled.

"Joe, it's much, much worse than that. We're talking mandatory jail time. They said to tell you that unless you cooperate with them, immediately, you're going to find yourself arrested as a common criminal."

That got his attention. "What are you talking about?" he asked.

"If you plead guilty to these conspiracy charges, I think I can get your sentence reduced to two years."

"Two years? For one count?" Joe couldn't believe it. "What's happening to the other guys?"

"They're all making deals," Kottmyer replied. "They're going to testify. And the US Attorney is offering you a deal, too, so that if you cooperate, and if you give all the names of people involved in these projects, *and* if you will attest to Lo Presti's involvement, I can probably get you a deal, but it will still mean some jail time."

Joe was silent. It was too much to take in.

"And if I don't cooperate? If I don't testify?" he finally asked.

"It will probably cost you $100,000 for legal fees if you go to trial," Kottmyer answered seriously, "and if you're convicted, you'll probably get more like five years."

Joe felt like he'd been struck by lightning. "I've seen men convicted of accessory to murder who got eighteen months," he thought, "and now, because I signed five documents I thought were legal, documents that were approved by a lawyer, I'm going to prison for five years?"

Kottmyer went on to review the prospect of arrest.

"There are two ways this is done," Kottmyer explained. "One, which is the more usual for someone in your position, is that if you are indicted, which they seem determined to do, then they will notify me when that happens, so I can accompany you and you can go in and surrender yourself for arraignment…"

Joe heard her words but was too numb to grasp their catastrophic meaning.

"…before a magistrate, and then we post bail, and you'll be released."

"My God," he thought. "I'm going to be taken in and arrested, photographed, and fingerprinted? Like a common criminal? When am I going to wake up from this nightmare?"

Kottmyer continued. "The second method is that they show up at your house one morning at dawn, when everybody's asleep. They will force open your door. They will arrest you forcibly and take you out in handcuffs, in front of your wife and children. Normally, they don't do this for white collar crimes, but I have to warn you, there are suggestions that if you don't cooperate, that's what they'll do: arrest you in your own home."

Joe was still struggling to assimilate it all. "So, what's the difference? What's the reason for doing it one way or the other?"

"That's something I'll bring up to them in a letter. The regulations specify that they are not allowed to use the threat of public arrest in order to intimidate you into cooperating with them. So, the only reason they'd do that is if you were at risk of escaping. I've told them you aren't going to do that, that you're entire life is here, and you're not leaving, but Pappalardo dismissed that. I don't get it, Joe. Have you ever had a problem with him?"

"No."

"Well, have you ever had any kind of relationship with him?"

"Not that I know of. As far as I know, I've never laid eyes on him."

"It's very strange. There's something there," Kottmyer said. "Where does it come from?"

"I don't know, maybe he just hates politicians."

When Joe walked out of Kottmyer's office he realized, for the first time, that the problem he faced was not one of public relations but of prison. He was facing disaster for himself and his family, not just emotionally but economically. He was facing the loss of a job, the loss of income, potentially even the loss of his house, certainly the loss of his reputation. It was unthinkable that he would be facing all this for reasons he didn't even understand, that he would be threatened by the agents of a government he had always respected and trusted.

The first thing he did was telephone his wife, Elaine.

"They're pursuing the investigation," he told her. "They're targeting me, and it could mean jail time."

None of this made any sense to Elaine, either. She, too, had trouble believing that the government would employ drug dealers to implicate her husband. Furthermore, she was the one who handled the family finances, and she knew how little Joe was making out of the gumball factory.

They agreed to tell their children right away, before the story broke in the press. So, that night, after dinner, the family, six of the seven kids, ranging in age from thirteen to thirty, gathered around the kitchen table. Joe told them all that the gumball factory project had become a serious problem and that an investigation was under way. He explained that false statements were being made about him and stressed that he was determined to fight them. Just as Joe had been, the kids were stunned that the father they'd grown up trusting and respecting could be indicted for conspiracy and that their government would go after him apparently in order to coerce him into testifying against others.

Whatever deal the feds claimed to want, they never offered Joe anything, probably because he utterly refused to talk to them. He made it clear, through his lawyer, that if they wanted to ask him anything, they could certainly do so. But he also made it clear that if they wanted to ask him to talk about anything else, if they wanted him to inform on colleagues, they had the wrong guy. At one point the US Attorney's Office told Kottmyer that they knew Timilty had information on other members of the senate (specifically Lo Presti) and that they wanted him to come in and give them that information. But Joe steadfastly refused to name names. His attitude was: "If you've got a case, and I don't think you do, then you'll have to prove it, but I will tell you nothing about myself and nothing about anyone else."

Weeks went by, and nothing happened. At times Joe indulged in the hope that maybe the nightmare was over, that the feds realized they had no case against him. Then one day in the early fall of 1992, Parigian called and suggested they meet, saying he had some information for Joe. The request was puzzling, since Parigian had never before seemed reluctant to use the phone for highly sensitive conversation. But Joe agreed to meet him at Legal Sea Foods in Park Square. Again, Joe was startled that Parigian had so much information from within the US Attorney's Office.

"I've got a scoop for you," Parigian began. "I got this today. I think you can be all right here. They're not after you now. They're really targeting Lo Presti."

"Does that mean they're going to forget me?" Joe asked.

"No, it doesn't mean they're going to forget you. It just means it's going to be helpful to you. Or it can be helpful. They're not after you. They think Lo Presti is involved."

"They're making a mistake," said Joe. "The only people who were involved in selling units are Marrocco, Benoit, and D'Avolio. Lo Presti never sold a unit."

"Did he close any of the units?" Parigian asked.

"Yes."

"Well, if it's not going to be Lo Presti, it's going to be you," Parigian claimed. "So, you ought to get in there and talk about it."

"I have no desire to go in there and talk to them at all about anything. None whatsoever."

Then the conversation took a surprising turn. Parigian wanted to know what role William Bulger had played in the gumball development.

"Bulger had nothing to do with it," Joe asserted in surprise.

"Well, how close are Lo Presti and Bulger?" asked Parigian insistently.

Joe thought about it. "Lo Presti is chair of the Senate Judiciary Committee. That's a position Bulger once had, and he appointed Lo Presti to it. They're friendly. I think they sometimes socialize with one another. But that's all."

"Joe," Parigian leaned forward. "Why do you want to take the fall for Lo Presti?"

Suddenly, Joe understood the bizarre quality of the conversation: Parigian was wearing a wire. So, Joe began to answer every question knowing it would play on a recorder in the US Attorney's Office. As their talk continued, whenever Parigian got an answer that might not please the US Attorney's Office, he'd repeat the question.

Once again, he asked, "Why do you want to protect Lo Presti?"

"I don't want to *protect* Lo Presti," Joe answered. "I don't have much use for him politically, but in order for me to help the feds with Lo Presti, I'd have to lie. If the US Attorney's Office wants me to lie then we ought to have a conversation about that fact. But only so long as they acknowledge that for me to 'give up' Lo Presti I'd have to lie."

Parigian quickly changed the subject. Joe was later to learn that Parigian had a lot at stake, for he was facing his own legal difficulties at the Capital Bank and had apparently evaded prosecution by serving as an informant for the feds. His assignment apparently was to get Timilty to implicate Lo Presti.

As it became clear that his legal difficulties were not going to be resolved, Joe and Elaine once again gathered the children around the kitchen table. The mood in the room was much more subdued.

"Look, guys," Joe started. "Here's the story. If I agreed to cooperate with the feds, if I were prepared to testify against other people, that would make things easier on all of us. But, on the other hand, if I don't cooperate, they're probably going to come in here at some point and arrest me. They'll cause a big scene, and they'll cart me out of here in bracelets and parade me in front of the cameras."

The kids were silent, listening.

"It's my feeling that we should not in any way allow this possibility to coerce us into doing something we don't think is right," Joe continued. "My position is that I do not care if they come in the middle of the night to arrest me. I'd rather not be a rat for the government or tell lies about other people to save my own skin."

Everyone at the table nodded in complete agreement.

Joe went on. "Look, Mother and I want to tell you that it is our strong feeling that if there is a hit to be taken, rather than implicate other people and act an informant, I'll take the hit. But you guys are all going to be effected by this, as well. So, you get to have a say in it. If you want to disagree, or if you have an opinion, this is the time to talk."

For a moment, there was silence. Then Gregory, a student at Boston College High School, spoke.

"The only thing I ask," he said, "and I know I speak for the rest of us, is that when they take you out and put you in front of the camera, you don't hold your raincoat over your head." The others agreed. They wanted to see their father walking tall, with his head high, not skulking around in front of the cameras, hiding his face or acting ashamed.

Joe looked at Gregory with pride and admiration and agreed.

The Timilty family got through the fall, through Thanksgiving, and through Christmas in 1992, all while waiting for the arrest, knowing it was imminent but not knowing when it would come. Elaine and Joe agreed after Christmas that if they could get to the February school vacation before the arrest, it would be easier for the boys, who then wouldn't have to return to school the morning immediately after a highly public arrest.

Meanwhile, the US Attorney's Office concluded that Joe was not going to cooperate. So, they moved quietly, on January 26, 1993, to indict Joe and several of his partners. Shortly after six o'clock in the morning of January 27, 1993, the FBI arrived at the Timilty home in suburban Boston. In the predawn darkness they pounded on the door, instead of simply ringing the doorbell, and yelled, "Open up, this is the FBI!"

The feds had clearly not done their homework, for, with rare exceptions, Joe left the house at five o'clock each morning to work out at the YMCA in Boston. The fact that he was home on this particular day was most unusual.

Upstairs in their bedroom, Elaine heard the commotion outside. No voices, just activity: cars in the driveway, then pounding on the door, loud, harsh, insistent. Downstairs, Joe's daughter Kara, still in her pajamas, opened the door, distressed at the pounding and the shouting. "It's the FBI. Open up!"

The lead agent, Richard Egan, immediately brushed by her into the house, followed by two other agents.

It was obvious to the Timilty family that the dreaded day had arrived. "This is it," Joe said. "Everybody just follow my lead. Take it easy. Let's do this the best we can." He headed downstairs, dressed in boxer shorts and carrying his robe.

"We're with the FBI," said Egan. "And we have a warrant for your arrest. You'll have to come with us."

Kottmyer had warned Joe, weeks earlier, that they'd try to rush him out of his home in his pajamas, if at all possible, so that he would look foolish and feel humiliated. "If they want to be sticklers, they won't let you use a razor blade," she'd told him. "So, go out and buy an electric razor. And they may follow you right into the bathroom. Make sure, though, that you get cleaned up. Take a shower. Do what you usually do. Don't rush. You'll already be under arrest, and once they tell you that you are, call me. I'll talk to them and tell them what I expect and what you expect. It will not be a pleasant experience, but don't do anything to make it worse. Get in for the arraignment as quickly as possible, and then get out."

Remembering her words, Joe spoke calmly to Egan, who looked nervous. "I'm going to get cleaned up, and I want to call my lawyer."

"That's not going to be necessary," Egan snapped.

"Oh, yes it is," Timilty said. "Which part of this don't you understand? I am going to call my lawyer, and then I am going to get cleaned up, exactly as I always do. I am going to shower and shave."

Egan looked annoyed and confused. "Then we're going to have to accompany you, and you'll have to keep the door open."

"That's fine with me." Joe walked out of the room and went back upstairs, asking Elaine to call Kottmyer and let her know what was going on. When the lawyer came on the phone, Joe spoke to her from the kitchen, in front of the three agents.

"There are three unwanted people here in my kitchen," he told the lawyer.

"They're there?"

"Yeah," Joe said. "They're here. One of them is named Richard Egan."

"I know him," Kottmyer said. "Put him on the line."

Joe handed the receiver to Egan, who explained that they wanted to leave immediately because they were in a rush to beat the traffic. Kottmyer sharply reminded him of Joe's rights, and Egan hung up the phone, contenting himself with pressing Joe to hurry.

Joe had just started down to the basement to shower, followed by two silent agents, when Kara spoke.

"Dad, do you want a cup of coffee?"

"No," Egan interrupted. "He doesn't have time for coffee."

The situation was threatening to become confrontational. Joe intervened and calmly insisted that Kara make the coffee, while Egan irritably insisted that they didn't have the time. Finally, recognizing that Joe was within his rights, Egan relented.

Joe then went down to the basement to shower and shave, with two agents lurking outside the bathroom door. He dressed carefully in his customary attire—dark blue suit, white shirt, conservative tie. It was important to dress appropriately, since Kottmyer had warned him the feds would certainly leak the news of his arraignment and that the press would be there. During the hour or so that it took to get ready, Joe and the agents had no conversation except when absolutely necessary. The agents, in fact, labored to avoid any eye contact.

After Joe had dressed he sat at the kitchen table, drinking the cup of coffee prepared by his daughter. He felt strangely calm, without fear, but at the same time powerless, caught up in an absurd situation. Finally, it was time to leave, and he said good-bye to the kids in the kitchen. Elaine accompanied him to the door. As they walked in the foyer, Joe overheard one of the agents whisper to the other that he had locked his keys in the car. To the first agent's relief, one of the partners had a spare. It occurred to Joe that these guys would have trouble catching a cold.

Joe kissed Elaine as she gave him his coat, and then turned and walked out the front door of his home, one FBI agent in front of him and two in back.

"We have to put on the 'cuffs," Egan said.

Joe held out his arms, and Egan clicked the handcuffs around Joe's wrists. It was a bitter moment. After twenty-five years in and around government, Joe had been arrested in his own home, in the presence of his family, and handcuffed in front of his wife. After a lifetime spent pledging allegiance to the United States, he and his family suddenly felt that the American justice system was anything but just. As the handcuffs were snapped onto his wrists, he turned to Elaine.

"You know, I never looked good in men's jewelry."

Ultimately, the US Attorney's Office indicted five people in connection with the gumball factory: Joe, Marrocco, Marrocco's assistant, Joseph Benoit, D'Avolio, and Ed Maccarelli, Marrocco's mortgage originator. Joe later learned that two of his codefendants, Marrocco and Benoit, had been telephoned the night before, in direct violation of the rules of the US Attorney's Office, and notified of the indictment. Despite the fact that they faced over twenty counts in their indictments, as opposed to Joe's one, they were offered an opportunity to turn themselves in, rather than face arrest. Yet while Kottmyer had sent three letters to the US Attorney's Office, saying that Timilty would surrender himself whenever and wherever they asked, the US Attorney chose to have him arrested at dawn in his own home.

The agents drove Joe to the basement of the Federal Building in downtown Boston, then took him in an elevator to an office where Joe was fingerprinted and photographed. He sleepwalked through the next few hours, numb with a combination of shock and anger. Still handcuffed, he was driven to the courthouse and placed in a holding cell until the arraignment at two o'clock that afternoon. At first, he was placed with Benoit and Marrocco in a traditional cell, with solid walls on three sides and floor-to-ceiling bars on the fourth. But Marrocco was afraid to be in Joe's presence, so Joe was moved to another cell.

At the arraignment, the prosecutor, Lon Povich, asked the magistrate to order drug tests for *all* the defendants, including Joe. Kottmyer immediately protested. "If you want drug tests because two of the defendants, Marrocco and Benoit, have a history of using and distributing drugs, fine," she said. "But Mr. Timilty had no history of drug or alcohol abuse, so what is the purpose of having him tested, except to embarrass him?"

The magistrate turned to Povich, who uncomfortably demurred, saying he had no intention of suggesting Joe be tested. He suggested it must have been a "clerical error." The magistrate agreed with Kottmyer, ordering drug tests for Marrocco and Benoit, but not for Joe. (Significantly, both men flunked the drug test, even though they had known in advance that they were coming in.)

What happened next was a disturbing revelation to Joe. Over the next few weeks, Benoit failed the drug test so often that, finally, on a day when the US Attorney's Office wasn't paying attention, a substitute magistrate who was unfamiliar with the case revoked Benoit's bail and ordered him imprisoned. The Assistant US Attorney had to rush the magistrate and persuade him that Benoit was an important witness who should be released. Finally the magistrate reversed his decision and allowed Benoit to remain free.

Meanwhile, after the arraignment, Joe headed downstairs, where the press was waiting. He'd heard the news of his arrest on the radio while awaiting arraignment in his cell, and he knew very well what was coming. Asked by the waiting reporters for a statement, Joe simply declared that he was innocent and that he expected a jury would believe him. Then he walked out of the courthouse and, realizing that he had no money, borrowed a dollar for the subway from Kottmyer. He wanted, more than anything else, to get the jail and its stench out of his system, so he headed over to the YMCA, where he worked out in the gym before his son picked him up.

When the story of Joe's arrest broke in the media, there were claims, especially in the *Boston Globe*, that Joe's indictment was a classic case of judicial overkill. Some articles blasted the US Attorney's Office for its pettiness, and a lot of people felt the feds were going after a high-profile real estate developer/politician in order to distract public attention from the fact that they had failed so miserably to provide adequate protection against the much more serious abuses in the savings and loan industry.

Feeling defensive and under attack, the US Attorney's Office contacted the *Globe*, suggesting the reason they'd been looking at Timilty, and had indicted him, was that Joe could lead them to Lo Presti, and Lo Presti could lead them to William (Billy) Bulger, the Massachusetts senate president. And, according to the feds' rather contorted logic, Billy Bulger could lead them to his brother, James "Whitey" Bulger, a noted figure in Boston organized crime. The feds implied that if the *Globe* continued running stories favorable to Timilty, it would end up being seriously embarrassed when the US Attorney eventually established connections between all these politicians and criminals.

Now, William Bulger was an erudite, articulate, witty, and colorful figure in Boston politics, a man who could quote Socrates in Greek one minute and sing Irish ballads the next. He was president of the Massachusetts senate for nearly two decades (until he was appointed president of the University of Massachusetts in 1995). Bulger was a formidable politician, smart, funny, and hardworking, who had ruled the senate with an iron hand. He had also spent his life despising and battling the press, which had returned the favor by consistently underreporting and demeaning Bulger. So, it was a smart move on the part of the feds to tell the *Globe* they were going after Bulger—one of the classic ways to curry favor with the press in Boston had long been to criticize Bulger.

William's brother, Whitey, was a dramatic contrast to his politician brother. Indeed, the two men exemplified the career choices formerly available to the Boston Irish: politics or crime. Whitey was said to rule the underworld in South Boston, the city's most notorious Irish enclave, and for decades he had played a shrewd game of cat and mouse with local, state, and federal law enforcement agencies. (Several years later, when word filtered through South Boston that a grand jury had finally indicted Whitey and that he would soon be arrested by the FBI, Whitey simply and conclusively disappeared to the enormous, ongoing embarrassment of the feds.)

Federal authorities had long sought to indict Whitey and would use anyone and anything to do so. But their frustration over their chronic inability to get him led them to neglect some crucial details about Boston politics and personalities. First of all, Lo Presti had not been involved in the day-to-day operations of the gumball factory development, and they therefore had nothing they could use to get at him. Furthermore, even if they *could* have gotten something against Lo Presti, they couldn't have used it to get to Billy Bulger, since no connection could be established. And finally, it was unthinkable that anything they found on the senate president could convince Billy Bulger to testify against his own *brother.*

The feds also seemed oblivious to the fact that Joe had never been particularly close to Bulger and would be extremely unlikely to offer any leverage the feds could use against the senate president, even if Joe had wanted to provide such information. The two men had historically not been political allies. What it came down to, finally, was that the feds never understood the intricacies of Boston's ethnic and political worlds.

The feds tried to convince the press that they were going after Timilty as a way to get to the city's most infamous unindicted criminal, Whitey Bulger. Ultimately, no connection was ever established between the gumball project and the Bulgers. Nor was Lo Presti ever indicted. So, was the feds' claim that they hoped to get to Whitey Bulger through Timilty the truth or just a story they figured would appeal to the Bulger family's archenemy, the *Boston Globe?* And if Whitey wasn't the federal authorities' ultimate goal, what *was* the motive of the US Attorney's Office in pursuing Timilty?

It might have been as simple as ambition. A. John Pappalardo was at the time simply the *acting* US Attorney, and he was desperately seeking recognition from the new administration in Washington. He may have assumed that his chances of winning a permanent appointment would be significantly enhanced if he went after a high-profile politician, pandering to the public's cynicism about all public officials.

The trial, which started in the late spring of 1993, was a profound shock to Joe. Throughout the long ordeal he had been convinced that the truth of his own innocence would inevitably become clear. He wasn't surprised to hear his three former "partners" lie on the witness stand—after all, they faced an average of twenty-five counts each, compared with Joe's one, and they would do anything, say anything, to stay out of jail. But he was also sure they wouldn't be believed. (Indeed, as it later turned out, none of these men *had* been particularly convincing to the jury.)

What he hadn't expected, however, was the testimony from the three mortgage companies: Citicorp, Prudential, and John Hancock. These were mortgage companies that Joe knew had been perfectly aware of the existence of second mortgages. Yet in court they claimed to have been completely ignorant. The people testifying for the first two mortgage companies were not local people; the woman from Citicorp, for example, was apparently based in St. Louis, and she had a history of testifying around the country. She knew how to present herself in court, and she made a very credible witness, essentially exonerating the mortgage companies of any culpability in the eyes of their stockholders by putting the blame entirely on the Gumball Realty partners. She insisted that Citicorp would *never* have accepted the mortgage applications if they had known that the down payments came from second mortgages. She'd never been to East Boston or seen the gumball factory, but she was an impressive witness.

Late one afternoon midway through the trial, Joe got a call from Kottmyer, asking him to come to her office to discuss some documents she had received from the US Attorney's Office.

"It's about a federal intercept," she said.

Joe had never heard the term before, but when he learned it meant a wiretap he was extremely interested, and he went over to her office. Kottmyer described the intercept as extremely significant. It was a fax, sent to her by the prosecutor, Povich. Apparently the federal government had maintained a long-standing telephone tap on John De Marco, a gangster in Revere who was reputed to be one of Boston's top cocaine dealers. The intercept contained information suggesting that Marrocco was not simply a casual drug user but a major dealer who was buying a kilo of cocaine a month. Until that meeting, Joe hadn't known what a kilo was, so he could only infer from Kottmyer's reaction that it was a significant amount. Joe felt a moment of hope that this information would conclusively reveal the moral bankruptcy of the man testifying against him.

When court convened the next morning, the jury was prevented from entering, while Marrocco's lawyer was summoned to the courtroom to protect Marrocco's rights, arguing that the jury should not be informed of his client's drug dealings. After a protracted discussion among the judge and lawyers, Marrocco took the stand, with the jury brought back in, and Kottmyer was permitted by the judge to ask only one question pertaining to Marrocco's drug activities.

"Do you know John De Marco?" asked Kottmyer.

"No," he replied without hesitation.

But the wiretap showed that Marrocco had been conversing weekly with De Marco and buying thousands of dollars of drugs from him. With her question, Kottmyer had conclusively proved that Marrocco was a liar: Kottmyer knew it, the prosecutor knew it, the judge knew it. Joe had always known it. But the problem was that Marrocco was legally protected from self-incrimination, and the jury never knew what Marrocco's answer meant.

Well before the end of the trial, Joe knew it was all over. When the jury came in to listen to the summation, the US Attorney had put on each juror's seat a copy of the indictment. The title was very short: "United States of America v. Joseph F. Timilty." At that point, Joe knew that if *he* had been on the jury, he would have been swayed by that wording, too, not Citicorp or Marrocco or the US Attorney's Office but the might and majesty of the United States of America.

Elaine Timilty, who attended the trial every day, was furious as she watched events unfold. She saw a US Attorney relying on the word of drug dealers to convict her husband. She heard a witness who had tested positive for drugs so often during the trial that a substitute magistrate had revoked his bail lying to implicate her husband. Ultimately, she learned that perjury was not a clear matter of telling lies but depended on prosecutorial opinion and need.

One day, for example, she watched Joseph Benoit leave the witness stand during the jury's coffee break. In direct violation of the judge's order that no one discuss the case with anyone, Benoit went around the corner in the courthouse hallway to the phone booth. When he resumed the stand after the break, his testimony was noticeably different. Elaine was shocked. But when she became aware that Monte Marrocco picked up Benoit after he had testified, and realized that they had gone to lunch and spent the afternoon together but never "discussed the case," she was sure their deception would be exposed. In her naïveté, Elaine really expected the prosecutor to say, in effect, "Ladies and gentlemen, we will excuse these witnesses. I did not expect they would lie. Please, pardon us."

"When does perjury cease to be a crime?" she wondered. "What happens to our justice system if everyone knows 'that's a lie' and nothing happens?"

But despite the government's fervent efforts to portray Joe as corrupt, the jury apparently had serious doubts. Another defendant in the case, Edward Maccarelli, had been charged with falsifying mortgage applications. The jury took only thirty minutes to decide he was guilty. But when Joe's case went to the jury, the situation was different. The jury had apparently mistrusted the evidence of his codefendants Marrocco and Benoit, regarding them as blatant liars.

The jury also had a hard time believing the mortgage companies, finding it difficult to believe how these companies could possibly have been utterly ignorant of what was going on. Finally, after a day and a half, the jury came back and told the judge they were deadlocked. The judge sent them back to deliberate some more. The jury went back out for another day. Three times they came back to the judge, claiming to be deadlocked on Joe's case. Three times, she sent them back, the last time with an additional explanation of the legal issues of both conspiracy and "willful blindness."

The fourth time they came back with a verdict of guilty.

In a letter to Judge Zobel, written after the verdict and before Joe was sentenced, one of the jurors said, "After listening to the testimony,

I was convinced that the chief reason Mr. Timilty…[was a defendant] in this trial and not [a government witness] rested on [his] reluctance to turn informer on [his] friends and colleagues. Even the lending institutions demonstrated a marked [laxity] in procedures designed more to accumulate loans than to promote good judgment or good ethics…As a juror who was impressed by the demeanor and dignity demonstrated by [Mr. Timilty], and one who was responsible for the impasse and [who] with great reluctance finally cast his guilty verdict, I ask the court to seek a most lenient sentence."

Charged with more than twenty counts, D'Avolio was allowed to plead guilty to one charge and sentenced to thirty days, which he served at home, wearing a leg bracelet. He paid no fine.

Charged with more than twenty counts, Marrocco was allowed to plead guilty to one count (his second conviction) and sentenced to 120 days at Allenwood. He paid no fine. He never lost his real estate license.

Charged with more than twenty counts, Benoit was allowed to plead guilty to one (his second felony) and was sentenced to ninety days in prison. He paid no fine and is still selling real estate with Marrocco, without a license.

The prosecutors asked Judge Zobel to sentence Joe to between forty-eight and fifty-one months. The judge, clearly surprised, asked them how they'd reached this recommendation when they had recommended that D'Avolio serve only thirty days for twenty seven counts. How, she asked, could they recommend more than four years for one count for Joe and only thirty days for twenty-seven counts for D'Avolio? The Assistant US Attorney explained that Timilty had demonstrated no remorse and had not cooperated with the prosecution in any way.

Zobel, however, wasn't willing to accept this recommendation. Suggesting that the D'Avolio sentence be used as a guide, she sent them back to recalculate their numbers. The Assistant US Attorney eventually returned and said the government was now asking for twenty-seven months, rather than forty-eight. Zobel once again said no. She asked Kottmyer if she had anything to add, and Joe's lawyer made a ringing statement on his behalf. Then Zobel turned to Joe and asked if he wanted to speak.

Joe stood. He looked at his lawyer and smiled at her, knowing Kottmyer had urged him strongly and repeatedly—had even asked Elaine to urge him—to keep his mouth firmly shut in this situation, lest his bluntness and anger make matters worse. He also remembered his kids asking him that he not leave the house covering his head. He remembered his years in politics, taking tough stands, and the code of honor that had seen him through tough days in Dorchester, the marines, and the State House.

And then he addressed the court. "When I leave this court I am going to address the press, your honor," he said. "And I don't want you to be surprised or blindsided by anything I say. So, I am going to tell you what I am going to say out there, and you can make your sentencing decision on that basis. I'm going to tell them outside that I am not guilty of this charge. That this was a charge fabricated by the federal government. I'm not guilty of conspiracy. I may be guilty of stupidity, for being associated with these people, but not of conspiracy. The real guilty people are the mortgage companies who were reckless and irresponsible in making loans and now are trying to blame someone else."

To Joe's enormous surprise, the judge responded, "I'm inclined to agree with you, but the jury has spoken, and I must abide by the will of the jury." And she sentenced him to four months in prison, two months at a halfway house, two years of probation, and a fine of $60,000.

Joe was originally sentenced to spend his jail time at Allenwood, but his codefendants complained to the Justice Department that they were afraid to be sentenced to the same prison where Joe would serve time. As a result, Joe was sent to the less desirable penitentiary at Schuykill, in Pennsylvania.

After spending most of his life working in government, after decades of evaluating other people's problems and searching for humane solutions, after years of living by a stringent code of honor, Joe Timilty was about to be incarcerated by the political system he had always admired and sought to serve and improve. After five decades of believing in the fundamental decency and justice of his government, Joe began to understand the value of questioning authority and the limits of patriotism.

Like a true product of Dorchester, however, Joe accepted the situation with humor. When asked by the press if he intended to appeal his conviction, Joe answered by quoting Kenny Rogers: "There's a time to hold them, and there's a time to fold them." When it was clear that he would be sentenced to four months in a federal prison in Pennsylvania, Joe, with vintage Dorchester humor, offered a timesharing plan to several of his close friends. (They very quickly volunteered to send their neighbors.) He told his family that if he'd survived four months with the marines at Parris Island, he could survive four months of federal prison. "Just do it, get it behind you," he thought, "and then come out and fight." Making the most of his situation, he kept a diary describing the ironies and inequities, the absurdities and tragedies, of life in prison, celebrating the characters that made him laugh or cry and what it meant to be a middle-class, fifty-five-year-old man thrust into prison life that changed forever the heart, mind, and soul.

JOURNAL ENTRIES

Monday, October 4, 1993

Outside, it is cold and dark and ungodly quiet.

In the house where I live in suburban Boston, in the second-floor bedroom, I am lying awake, unable to sleep. The only light in the room is the glimmer of green from the face of the alarm clock, the only sound the rhythmic breathing of Elaine.

Suddenly, from downstairs, I hear the grandfather clock as it strikes the familiar Westminster chimes, sixteen melancholy notes that remind me my time has come.

From its station in the foyer, the grandfather clock has tolled the hours of my life, celebrating the joys and mourning the lamentations. It has rung in jubilation through the years as my seven children grew into adulthood.

Now in solemn tones, like an old friend, the grandfather clock tolls the hour I have been dreading.

One...

Two...

Three...

Four...

1

Silence…

It's four o'clock in the morning, the loneliest of hours, the final moments before dawn on the worst day of my life.

I climb out of bed. Elaine wakes up the moment I move out of bed. I shower and shave. The house is dark and quiet and eerie in comparison to the activity here last night, for, in spite of my plight, the Timilty family enjoyed the night, as we always do when we're together—good food, festive music, and affectionate banter, lots of laughter and love.

In the kitchen, I flick the switch, and suddenly the room is flooded with harsh light. The only sound is the purring of Shadow, the cat. I fill the kettle with water and heat it. I feed Shadow. I spoon Taster's Choice into a cup, then add steaming water and, once again, I have made what may be the worst coffee in creation.

Tonight, when I fall asleep, I will not be in my home. Tonight, I'll sleep in another home, in another place, and who knows what the coffee will taste like?

Maybe I'll discover that my coffee is the second worst.

I have to watch the clock. It's 4:30 a.m., and I check my gear one last time. I've been packing quietly for days. I can't take much with me, but there are things I cannot get by without: two pairs of eyeglasses, two pairs of running shoes, two sweat suits, long johns, and of course, the rosary beads that were purchased for me a few weeks ago by Elaine.

She's something. Who else could have found, for my trip, a set of Irish penal rosary beads? That's a set of rosary beads condensed in size so Irish revolutionaries on their way to prison could smuggle them past the guards. I ponder for a moment how blessed I am to be spending my life with Elaine.

As I slice a banana for breakfast, the radio is on, so low as not to disturb anyone, and when I hear reports of the revolution in the Soviet Union, it occurs to me that I am not the only person in the world whose life is being turned upside down today.

Shortly after the clock tolls five in the morning, I climb the stairs to see Elaine one more time and to kiss her and tell her that I'll get word to her as soon as I can.

As I make my way out of the house, the rest of the family is still asleep. In the Timilty household, we believe that if you don't say good-bye, there is no good-bye.

I don't like this image, though. I don't like the fact that, instead of leaving the house dressed in a suit and carrying a briefcase, as I customarily do, here I am, leaving in a sweat suit and carrying a Duffle bag bulging with gear I'll need in prison.

I cannot count the mornings I have driven up the driveway, away from home, and invariably, like most people, I am so consumed by the day-to-day details that I take my blessings for granted and do not give a thought to what I am leaving—my wife, my sons, my daughters, my home, and everything I love most. On this particular morning, however, in the darkness, as I accelerate away from my family, my mind is busy, and my heart aches to contemplate what I am departing, and so, I cling to every image of my family, absorb every nuance, and try to memorize every word that has been said in recent days.

It will be a long time before I see them again, a long time before I come home.

The average person who rarely thinks about freedom may wonder what it feels like to leave home for prison.

What I feel this morning, in the darkness, as I drive away from my home and my wife and my children and head to prison, what I feel above everything else is deep sorrow.

In the car, I tune the radio to WBZ-AM for the 5:00 a.m. news, and I hear a newscast that is maniacally busy with murder and mayhem and with irrelevant traffic reports and irritating details about the weather.

Maybe it's just today.

Maybe it's just my predicament.

Maybe it's just me.

Driving toward Boston and listening to the news, it occurs to me that I have spent my entire life in politics hoping to be mentioned on the news. But in the past two years—has it really been two years?—I've been working hard to stay off the news.

That's what a federal indictment will do to you.

Here's a bit of irony. As I get close to Boston, a report comes over the radio about America's prisons and how the number of people incarcerated has increased in recent years. It's hard to believe that in the United States, we imprison a larger proportion of people per capita than any other nation in the world.

Since my conflict with the judicial system began, I have been surprised to note that so many movies and television programs focus on life in prison. Why did I not notice that before? And what is the fascination within all of us to know what goes on in prisons?

All I know is this.

In the federal prison system, there are approximately 100,000 inmates spread across the country at over sixty institutions.

Last night, more than a million Americans slept in prisons of all types.

Tonight, there'll be one more—me.

It's a little before 5:30 a.m. when I arrive at the YMCA. None of my friends expected to see me here today. As the Boston news media have reported on television, over the radio, and in the newspapers, today is the day that Joe Timilty goes to prison.

Among the familiar faces is that of my friend Sonny. I saw him walking yesterday in the Back Bay. Knowing that I was obliged to report to prison on October 4, he seemed concerned. Now he seems downright worried.

"Joe, what are you doing? Why are you here?"

"To work out."

"You got a talented lawyer, Joe. I mean the way she's managed to keep you here in Boston and out of prison and all, but be careful, Joe. You gotta watch out for your reputation."

4

Then it dawns on me.

Sonny thinks that I'm rebelling somehow and refusing to go to prison. I assure him otherwise.

"This is my last day here."

At the YMCA, the gym is busy with the usual cast of characters: Don, Frank, Bob, etc., all expressing concern that I'm going to be all right. I love the bond I've developed with these people at the Y: men, women, gay, straight, white, black.

My kind of crowd.

For me, however, on this morning, there will be no ninety-minute workout. I had to choose between the Stairmaster and Mass at Our Lady of Victories Church.

Mass wins out and with good reason: in the next four months, I'm going to need all the help I can get.

As I kneel for the start of Mass, I am mesmerized once again by the glory of Our Lady of Victories, a magnificent church of French architecture in a Boston neighborhood called Bay Village, which is a cosmopolitan community that features old brick houses, gaslit streets, and a reputation for welcoming a variety of people.

During my ill-fated career in real estate, I had an office nearby, and I came to appreciate the church for its beauty and also the neighborhood for its diversity and resiliency.

At Mass, people look at me strangely. Maybe it's the running suit. Maybe they wonder why I'm here at Mass in Boston when the newspapers say this is the day I'm supposed to be in federal prison in Pennsylvania.

After Mass, I drop off the car at a nearby gasoline station. Elaine will retrieve the car. By agreement, over the visor, I stash my driver's license and the keys to my YMCA locker. It is not yet eight o'clock. So far, so good. Everything is running smoothly. I am very well organized.

I hail a cab to Logan Airport, and at eight o'clock, although the arteries into Boston are clogged, I have an easy ride out of the city to the airport. Despite the bleakness of my situation, it is a beautiful autumn morning, the air clean, the sun bright, the wind soft.

The cab arrives at Logan Airport before 8:30 a.m., well in advance of my flight. It would not be a good idea to miss today's flight. I'm advised that when it comes to being a day late, the Bureau of Prisons has no sense of humor.

At the curb, a baggage handler recognizes me.

"Hey, Joe…how you doin'?"

"So far, so good."

"Everything's goin' to be OK, Joe. Good luck today."

At the US Air counter, the attendant is helpful but warns that the plane has not yet arrived in Boston and that when it does, the turn-around time for unloading, refueling, reloading, boarding, and take off is ten minutes.

"Ten minutes?" I say, astonished. "How big is this plane?"

"Oh, it's good sized. It's got a restroom."

Great!

I should have checked this out beforehand. I'm not a white-knuckle passenger, but I had experience in small planes when we'd fly over the Blue Ridge Mountains during Jimmy Carter's campaign back in 1976.

While waiting for the plane, I find a seat in the terminal near a window and gaze out across Boston Harbor for one last look at the city I love.

Then the plane arrives, and my first reaction is, oh-oh. It's smaller than I imagined, a thirty-eight seater, and even worse, the ground personnel are having trouble because the wind has picked up.

At 11:15 a.m., we are circling over Harrisburg, and the view is spectacular, blue mountains silhouetted along the horizon as if to cradle the farms that are ripe with the fullness of autumn. Most people seeing this terrain might think that Harrisburg is a sleepy farm community, but in my days managing the Carter campaign, I learned that the serenity of farm life disguises a people who play politics hard and fast.

Up with the tray table, advises the stewardess, and away with the notebook, I decide. Landing in mountainous terrain in a small plane on a windy day is every bit as nauseating as it sounds.

As always, it is disorienting to walk through a strange airport, but at last, I spot Nolan Atkinson, a prominent African American lawyer and a dear friend who offered to meet me here at Harrisburg Airport and drive me to Minersville, to Schuykill. I'm still uncomfortable using the word "prison," but I'll get over it, I'm sure.

Nolan has been meeting me at Pennsylvania airports since the 1976 campaign, which sometimes got nasty and, on one occasion, devolved into a fistfight alongside Philadelphia's Lotus Club.

For Carter, Pennsylvania's twenty-seven electoral votes were crucial, and we would not have won them if it had not been for Nolan's strength, his courage, and his integrity.

What made the difference in winning those electoral votes was our success in squeezing out a majority for Carter in Philadelphia, where a rebellious Democratic machine had pledged itself to the conservative mayor, Frank Rizzo, who had all the clout, all the patronage, and all the "walking around money."

What won the day for Carter in Philadelphia were the liberals and also the minority community. On election day, African Americans in Philadelphia turned out in record numbers, and we had one person to thank for that—Nolan.

Politics is a pyramid.

Jimmy Carter knew he could not be elected president without winning Pennsylvania. He knew that he could not win Pennsylvania without Philadelphia. He knew he could not win Philadelphia without winning African Americans. And I knew he could not win the African Americans without Nolan Atkinson.

That is why Jimmy Carter invited both Nolan and me to the White House on occasion and why he appointed us to serve on key commissions within his administration.

Politics in Boston and Massachusetts is tough, as it is in Chicago, San Francisco, Washington, New York, and from time to time in almost every city or state in a democratic nation.

But in Pennsylvania, the story has yet to be told of that 1976 campaign, of the threats, coercions, fistfights, and car bombings.

As the years passed, Nolan and I became family. I am the godfather to his youngest daughter, Aldyn. On this day, however, for Nolan as well as me, there is no joy.

We drive through Minersville, Pennsylvania, a symbol of Middle America, a small, tight, residential community of well-maintained homes and manicured yards. It's made up of people who have a strong sense of pride in themselves, in their values, and in America.

We stop for a cold drink, Poland Springs, wild cherry. This is a switch. I'm headed for a stretch in federal prison, and my last drink is mineral water. I've come a long way.

Nolan and I share a disturbing moment when we pass a section of subsidized housing, perhaps seventy townhouses, which are so run-down as to be depressing. How did housing under the care of the federal government deteriorate so shamefully?

The entrance to Schuykill is 300 yards off the highway; we then follow a winding road through a beautiful forest a half-mile long before we approach a massive and imposing prison, just the sort of place you can imagine Jimmy Cagney strutting into.

Both Nolan and I are struck by the glitter of the Pennsylvania reflecting off the walls of the prison, which are embroidered with row after row of rolled razor wire. The building looks new, the grounds are well kept. We follow the signs to the minimum security facility, Schuykill Farm, a group of new buildings made of cement blocks, some one story, some two.

The structure in front is obviously the administration building. It's surrounded by a lawn of Irish green that is dotted by two picnic tables with umbrellas.

For the next four months, this will be my home, this complex cut out of the Blue Ridge Mountains for the sole purpose of keeping people like me apart from everybody else.

The beauty of the place, the flowers, the lush grass, the outdoor furniture, all of it is an embarrassing contrast to the run-down federal housing we saw a few minutes ago.

It's a little after one o'clock, and for Nolan and me, it's time to part. On our ninety-minute ride, we have talked about everything but this.

"Let's do it," I say to myself. "Let's get it over with."

I'm not good at good-byes.

We climb out of Nolan's black Infiniti. I tug my Duffle bag from the backseat, and as I turn, I become aware that from every window, there are eyes staring at us, and something tells me they are not staring at Nolan.

We shake hands. He says he'll call Elaine. He promises to visit. To give me hope, I guess, he offers to pick me up when my sentence is over in February. As he talks, I cannot help remembering the better days we have shared, especially those at the White House.

Then, suddenly, Nolan is gone. I am alone. I turn to face Schuykill and my future.

I hoist the Duffle bag over my shoulder and head to the door. You know how a song rings in your head in a way you can't control? The lyric in my head at this moment is this: "I was a big man yesterday, but, boy, you ought to see me now."

From the White House to the Big House.

Welcome to the rest of Joe Timilty's life!

First impressions are important. The grounds are immaculate, the entrance unblemished, and although the floor is dazzling, nevertheless, it is being buffed by an inmate.

He winks, a sign of welcome. I find out later that his name is Robin and that he's from, well, nobody knows where he's from.

To the right are the offices. Inside, I see a receptionist. I walk in. She looks up and shouts.

"Wait outside!"

Robin approaches and whispers.

"Don't do anything until you're told to."

He looks around to make sure nobody is observing, then whispers again.

"Someone in uniform will be out soon to bust your hump."

He's right.

Alas, Robin is seen talking to me by a man in a shirt and tie.

It turns out to be Mr. Hurt, the deputy administrator, and in a stern voice, he reminds Robin of the rules, that he is not allowed to communicate with me. I am surprised that Robin took the chance, but I like him for it. Chastised, Robin goes back to buffing the floor that needs no buffing.

A man of slight build in his fifties is staring at me. He approaches.

"Are you Joe Timilty?"

"Yeah."

"I'm Jim Harris, from Peabody."

"How did you know I was coming?"

"I saw your picture in the paper. I've cut stories out of the newspaper about you, because it seemed to me you were getting railroaded. I know what you're going through, and I'll be as helpful as I can."

"Can you point me in the right direction to a priest or whoever would know about Catholic Masses?"

"Let me give you some advice. I'm not the best guy to ask about Catholic Masses. I'm Jewish. But I'm told that the priest who conducts services is an employee of the Bureau of Prisons, so his allegiance is not to your G-O-D, but to the B-O-P [Bureau of Prisons].

"So, if you go to confession or whatever, anything you say can and will be used against you. I don't know whether that's gospel, but that's what they say. If you want to know about Catholics, see that guy named Robin. He cleans up after Mass."

Now that my eyes have adjusted from the bright sunshine to the dim interior lights, I can see thirty feet down a corridor with doorways leading off. A crowd is gathered. What I see is people who have a job but who are not working. My guess is that there are not a lot of self-starters here.

Some of these guys are staring back up the corridor at me, and suddenly, it occurs to me. The population has been expecting my arrival.

Great!

Just what I need.

A short, heavy-set African American man approaches. He's dressed in clerical clothes, a white collar. He asks about my religious persuasion. I tell him that I'm a practicing Catholic. He says that he is the Protestant chaplain. He introduces me to the Catholic chaplain, who happens by Father Dene.

Fr. Dene is in his early sixties, five feet ten with thinning black hair and a sour expression.

"I'll see you at Mass on Saturday," says Fr. Dene, "and we can talk then."

As an afterthought, he tells me I am welcome to attend tonight's rosary and benediction service.

Even as a practicing Catholic, I haven't been to a rosary and benediction service in forty years, and I'll bet I'm not an exception.

"After the service," says Fr. Dene, "there'll be a movie."

From the administration office comes a woman guard in her early thirties, a chilly looking woman with frosty eyes and one of those marble, oh-no-you-don't chins.

Miss Personality speaks first.

"Empty your pockets!"

I'm anticipating a strip search. I dearly hope it's not by her. She proceeds to frisk me, and our relationship goes downhill from there.

On Robin's advice, I asked to be assigned to Unit One. Robin whispered to me that it is closer to chow hall and easier to get to in bad weather.

"Any chance of being assigned to Unit One?"

She glares at me.

"Why?"

"I have a friend there."

She assigns me to Unit Two.

I empty the contents of my bag. She takes away my watch, an inexpensive jogger's watch, and I take one last look. It says 2:15 p.m.

"You can buy one here," she says.

She tells me the Rick Snyder nylon running suit I wore from Boston has to be sent home, along with the watch, and that I can buy a similar outfit here. Next to go is a pair of the running shoes. I had brought two pairs, one on my feet, one in the bag.

"You need only one pair," she says. "If you need another, you can buy it here."

Also to be sent home are the three notebooks and four pencils I brought along to keep a daily log.

"If you need these things, you can buy them at the commissary," she says.

"And you have to send back these, too," pointing to the rosary beads.

"Why can't I keep my rosary beads?"

"You can keep them if you wear them around your neck at all times," she says, knowing that to be absurd. Then she says, "Well, you can keep this," referring to the crucifix. The rest will be sent back.

I refuse. I tell her the rosary will remain intact.

It is sent home.

At many prisons, the staff believes that crucifixes and rosary beads and other religious symbols may be used to signify membership or rank in gangs. Inmates who want such objects are required to purchase them from the prison to lessen the likelihood that they are designed as gang emblems.

Having been strip-searched by a male guard, I am once again in the icy presence of Miss Personality. More prisoners arrive, four in all, three from other institutions, and a fourth, Marty Donne, who, like me, is a self-report, which in bureaucratic lexicon is a prisoner allowed to show up on his own. Marty is my age, and by his accent, from New York or New Jersey.

For some reason, Miss Personality is going to great pains to keep the two new prisoners, Marty and me, away from the three transfers, which is not an easy task in this small room.

She turns and sees that I am talking with Marty.

"Do you two know each other?" she asks suspiciously.

"No," says Marty. "I never associate with criminals."

It's 3:00 p.m., and for the guards, time for a change of shift, which is why they are complaining about the lack of help in processing us. They are not paid overtime.

We are in a room with a window in the door, and as inmates walk along the corridor outside, they stop to peek in at us, the new prisoners. I'm beginning to understand what it feels like to be an animal in a zoo.

I meet the doctor, or more accurately, the PA, as he's called (physician's assistant), and we start off on the wrong foot. Having recently undergone surgery on my knees, I brought a letter from my doctor in Boston that describes the importance of my being assigned a lower bunk. This irritates the PA, who warns me in condescending tones that he wants me to return on October 13, so he can X-ray the knee to determine the real extent of my injury and whether I really need a lower bunk.

It's 3:45 p.m., and all I've seen of this place is the administration building. The hacks, as guards are called, are itchy to get rid of me, to drop me some place so they can go home.

I'm in no hurry. I'm here for four months.

They pick up a laundry bag, pillow, pillow case, sheets, blanket, and bath towel and escort me to one of two nearby buildings that look like military barracks. It's only one hundred yards to the front door of Unit Two, but under the circumstances, it's a long walk, and before we are halfway there, I see a gathering of about eighty guys.

"It looks like you're in for a welcome," says one of the guards escorting me.

I tense up, expecting the worst.

"They're not going to get a virgin," I reply.

I was in for a surprise I'll never forget.

Braced for trouble, for verbal and maybe physical abuse, I was astonished, because once the guards disappeared; it was as if I had brought news that all these inmates were getting early release.

Guys I had never seen before shook hands and shouted greetings.

"Hiya, Joe."

"Hey, welcome, Joe!"

I was given an extra sheet and an extra blanket.

By far the most helpful were inmates from the so-called Jewish group, and particularly the guy who had introduced himself in the lobby of the administration building, Jim Harris, a lawyer from Massachusetts who was fifty-three, funny, full of energy, and a decent human being. From the moment I met Jim, he helped make life bearable. Thanks to Jim, his group treated me as if I were Jewish.

He told me about the day he received word that it would be Schuykill where he'd serve his time.

"After I was sentenced, my daughter went shopping with me on what was a sad venture—to buy the things we thought I'd need in prison. I assumed I'd be going to Allenwood, and I was scheduled to report Monday morning. Late Friday afternoon, I got a call from my lawyer who told me I'd be going to Schuykill. I actually sat down and cried. And then my wife and I got out a map and spread it on the kitchen table to figure out where Schuykill was located."

At long last I am assigned. My new home is Unit Two, which is made up of four wings: *A, B, C,* and *D.*

B is the worst. It's called the ghetto because blacks and Latinos rule. It's made up mostly of young drug offenders whose idea of a good time is to stay up all night playing the latest raucous music. It is customary for a new inmate to be assigned to *B.* Then, after he is observed by various factions among the inmates, a decision is made that he will wither stay in *B* or move to one of the other "ranges," as the wings are called.

C and *D* wings are populated mostly by older guys who tend to be quiet, reserved.

I learn by word of mouth that thanks to the intercession of Jim, I escape the need to spend a probationary period on *B*, and instead I am assigned to *A.* It's a tough range, but I am promised that I will have an opportunity soon to move to *C* or *D.*

The reason that I escaped the ghetto is that Jim approached a fellow Jew.

"Joe Timilty's coming in," he said. "The guy ran for mayor of Boston and lost by a few votes. We don't want him living with the drug dealers."

Also, I learn that Jim telephoned his wife that night and arranged for her to telephone Elaine to let her know that I was OK.

From a personal locker maintained by the Jewish group, Jim makes sure that I have the basics—toothbrush, deodorant, shower shoes. The agreement is that I replace everything when I'm settled.

By late afternoon, the challenge is to find me a bunk in a cube, which is a cell that houses two people. It contains two bunks and two lockers. It's small. You have to step outside if you want to change your mind.

Fortunately, I end up in a cell with a guy from Massachusetts. Unfortunately, he is the single most disliked guy at the prison. We are opposites. This is a match made in hell.

The last thing I need, at this point, is a "mother" figure ordering me around.

"Pick up your running shoes." "Put that light on." "Put that light out." A year ago, if someone had told me I'd be sleeping in a three-by-seven room with this creep, I'd have laughed.

Having established a medical need for a lower bunk, naturally I draw the upper bunk.

Living on A are approximately sixty inmates, all blended ethnically, racially, geographically, mentally, and by age.

No one makes a more powerful impression than Polecat. Here's how I met him.

Word had passed among the inmates from Boston that I was arriving, and I was chatting with a number of them. Out of the corner of my eye, I could see a tough-looking guy, Polecat, as it turned out, and I noted that he was watching me carefully in my animated discussion.

After a few minutes, Polecat walked toward me and leaned in to whisper advice.

"Ninety percent of the people in this place are rats. I'll talk to you later."

Great! It's very reassuring to hear about the rats, seeing as that's how I got here.

Polecat didn't have to introduce himself. I recognized him right away. He not only grew up in South Boston, he was one of the toughest guys ever to come out of the neighborhood. His name is Paul Moore. I know his family.

Being alert in all such matters, he undoubtedly had followed my case and knew that I might be sent to Schuykill.

Oddly enough, though, he didn't want people at Schuykill to know how well he knew me. It was Polecat's way. He rarely spoke unless he wanted you to know something, and for good reason. Polecat awoke every morning assuming someone was out to get him, and maybe it would be an inmate, maybe a cop.

In Polecat's case, this is not paranoia.

As I learn, Polecat works in the kitchen as a pot cleaner. He used to box, and someone said he once sparred with Marvin Hagler. In any case, here at Schuykill, he works out every day for two hours, lifting weights outdoors, even on days when it's ice cold or snowing.

On occasion, he teaches young black guys how to box, how to hold their hands, how to lead with their left, how to hit the heavy bag, how to kickbox. He has all the physical strength anybody would ever need, but he rarely uses it.

At night, I hear two guys speculating about how difficult it would be to kill Polecat.

"If you were going to take him out," says one, "you'd have to do it quickly and with a shank."

That refers to a knife.

It also refers to how tough Polecat is.

It's 4:30 p.m., and I'm starved. I haven't eaten since I left the house at 5:10 a.m. The last thing I need is to miss another meal. I look like hell. I weighed myself this morning at the YMCA and tipped in at a whopping

160 pounds. Not a good weight for me. At six feet two, I should be at least 185. People had said I looked gaunt. They wonder whether I'm on my way to O'Brien's in Southie or O'Connor's in Dorchester, two of Boston's more popular Irish funeral homes.

Left alone for a moment with my thoughts, it occurs to me that there are three things I need to get through this, the three Fs.

First is family. I can't imagine going through this without the support I receive from Elaine and the kids. Couldn't do it.

Second, friends. There are not many stand-up people in life. And friends that remain friends at times like these are never forgotten.

Third is faith. Most important, when you are really alone, it is faith that comes into play, because it's true—there are no atheists in a foxhole.

It's 5:30 p.m. dinner call: chicken over noodles, soup, juice, cake, fresh fruit. Great food, all you can eat.

After chow, I walk through the administration building and look into the visiting room and see approximately thirty inmates, and then it dawns on me: this is the Catholic service the priest was talking about. It seems incongruous, but in that room, on their knees praying to God, are some of the toughest guys in the prison.

In many cases, their sleeves are rolled up over bulging biceps that are etched with tattoos. Some of these guys are serving ten years. And yet, here they are, heads bowed, reciting the rosary, and in their gnarled and powerful hands, they finger the plastic beads in order to keep count of their prayers to God for peace of mind.

It's seven o'clock. Unlike Mass, rosary and benediction is not a service Catholics are required to attend, and as I have confessed, I have not attended in forty years. It's ironic. After all that time, I find a rosary and benediction service that happens to be crowded, and where is it? In prison.

When I compare myself and my plight to these guys and their troubles, if they're attending rosary and benediction, I have no excuse not to, so I walk in.

The service lasts thirty minutes. Fr. Dene, referred to by inmates as the "Hack in Black," introduces tonight's feature film. It's *Robin Hood* with Kevin Costner, but it doesn't appeal to most of the guys, who head off to watch *Monday Night Football.*

Poor Fr. Dene. He's been working in institutions for so long, he's been institutionalized. He seems bored with his work. He's authoritative. He talks down to inmates. His attitude is less one of pastoral concern and more one of, well, you guys are here because you belong here. He never says anything funny. He rarely smiles. He never laughs. He'd never make it in politics.

I'm more interested in my new surroundings. The TV rooms are always packed. Laundry rooms are busy twenty hours a day. The library is a joke, consisting of little more than two bookshelves and a copy machine that doesn't work.

Back to Unit Two. Neighbors advise me never to get sick and never to ask another inmate how long he's in for. I must watch my sense of humor.

I encountered an inmate, and he asked me a question.

"What are you in for?"

"I'm a serial killer," I said.

I waited for his response.

He never cracked a smile.

It's quarter to ten at night, and I'm tired. My first day in prison. This is going to be challenging physically, but what will be more severe is the mental test. I must find a way to occupy every minute. My new friends whisper to me that those who do the hardest time are those who let the system get to them or those who feel sorry for themselves. Easy to do. And devastating on the mind.

At 10:15 p.m., I'm in my bunk, finally.

How odd to be sleeping so close to the ceiling. Not since the Marine Corps has this happened. I'm in suspended animation. I feel as though I may fall out at any second.

And the noise!

I am the father of seven children, ages thirteen to thirty, five boys and two girls, and I am certain that I would find it easier to fall asleep at home on the kitchen table with the entire family chattering away.

It's 10:30 p.m., and I'm exhausted when, at long last, the lights are turned off.

But the music isn't.

Forget it, Joe!

You're here for 120 days, 2,880 hours, 172,800 minutes, and if I remember the arithmetic taught by the nuns at St. Gregory's, 10,368,000 seconds.

The faster you get to sleep, the faster the days go by.

It's 11:00 p.m., and I'm still awake, still contemplating my first day in prison. I doze off, but then, no one warned me the hacks would be by two or three times a night with heavy boots, keys jangling, and worst of all, a flashlight shining in my eyes.

Who are these hacks? What kind of person would invest several decades of his life as a guard in a prison?

First, someone who needs to be in control. Second, someone who is incapable of doing anything more constructive or creative.

Midnight, and still I can't fall asleep. Too much noise. How long will it take me to get used to this? I lie here wondering what is happening at home with Elaine and the kids.

There's so much pain attached to incarceration, not all of it borne by the people incarcerated. A lot of it gets spread around. Many families go through a hell of a time. And it's odd, because so many people in America think there's a need for a political move to the right, that we need more prisons and harsher penalties. These people do not understand the prison system or the price that is paid by the taxpayers and by the inmates and their families.

Seventeen weeks before I can go home to Massachusetts. It's going to be a long haul...

Tuesday, October 5, 1993

At 5:00 a.m., I wake up automatically. Breakfast is served 6:00 a.m. to 7:00 a.m. Work call begins at 7:30 a.m. I shower and shave before chow. I must keep a routine to keep from going mad.

Having been to Parris Island, I know how to move in this environment. I know that if you want to fight the system, the system will win. You know by instinct that things are not going to get easier, and that is a fact of life. That's why I get up so early, my Marine Corps training; it gives me a chance to get squared away. You have to have been a marine to understand that.

One way to survive here, in terms of the administration, is to accept the sense of powerlessness. Now having come from politics, the journey from power to powerlessness might have been longer for me, but there is no more powerless experience than arriving as a Marine Corps recruit. I am able to reach back and remember that.

With that in my background, I looked around Schuykill. One thing that is clear is that Schuykill is not going to adjust to me. I have to adjust to Schuykill. That has been my mind-set from the moment I arrived.

I enlisted in the Marine Corps at age eighteen; I was from Dorchester. At Parris Island, they made me a marine.

It's 5:45 a.m. when I leave Unit Two for chow hall, which is located in the administration building. The day is beautiful, the sun coming up over the medium security buildings down in the valley.

What a great piece of property.

What a shame to waste it on 300 prisoners.

At breakfast, again, I am surprised: fresh fruit, plenty of eggs (fried), toast and butter, milk, a choice of cereals. Is there something wrong with this picture?

Breakfast is the only meal where you can socialize, and so I get a chance to meet other inmates, some of whom I saw at Catholic services. They seem different this morning. Gone is the image of pious men praying. By language and swagger, they are once again prisoners trying to act macho.

Latinos are the largest ethnic group, African Americans next, and then the white population. Although most facilities are integrated, ethnic groups stick together.

Back to *A* range to make the bed, clean the cell. It's not easy making the bed when it's the top bunk.

Work call, 7:30 a.m., and any inmate not up and ready with a clean cell is in trouble. I have not yet been assigned a job, so I take the time to locate the laundry room, where I am issued the rest of my clothing, underwear, socks, work clothes.

Jim mentions that the traffic in Boston is bad this morning.

"How do you know that?" I ask.

"I listen to WBZ all night."

"That's a Boston station."

"Yeah, but it has a 50,000-watt signal, and I have to tell you, if it weren't for the talk show hosts, Bob Raleigh and Norm Nathan, I don't know how I'd make it through the night. In fact, there are mornings when I hear traffic reports say Route 128 around Boston is all tied up, and I call my wife and tell her to take a different route to work."

Later in the morning, I start looking at potential jobs for inmates, but I realize quickly that virtually all of it is make-work. Everybody looks busy, but few people accomplish anything.

Kitchen duty is one of the few jobs in the prison that requires work. And inmates believe the legitimate work they have to do entitles them to help themselves to food, which they bring back to the units. We are not talking about one or two pieces of chicken a day. We are talking dozens.

After breakfast, I take a tour of the outside property. There are no fences. The grounds are beautiful, and with a great quarter-mile cinder track, an outdoor weight room, handball courts, football field, horseshoe pits, brand new bocce courts, the setting resembles a prep school.

The track is bordered on three sides by woods, and in the distance, less than a mile away, I can hear the sounds of a major highway.

There are no barriers, no guards, no one watching from those watchtowers so familiar in prison movies. As I walk the track, it occurs to me that the layout almost encourages thoughts of escape. It's tempting to forget the consequences and to dwell on how easy it would be simply to walk away.

But after you got out, then what?

Be careful, Joe!

If you let this place get to you, you'll become despondent.

One theme that emerges here is the waste. The waste of everything: food, money for education, money for recreation, and the $35,000 a year to keep each of us here in this serene setting.

I wander around, say hello to inmates I haven't met. Nobody asks me about my case. Everybody warns me to get a job before the administration assigns me to landscaping.

The most popular gathering spot for older guys is the track. It's lunchtime, and there are sixty guys, walking and walking, round and round, talking and talking and tallying miles.

It is the only safe place to talk. This is where I find out about other inmates, who's tight with the hacks, whom to trust (nobody), and whom to watch out for (everybody), and also which are the best jobs, where and to whom to apply. The track is the heart of Schuykill's social life, such as it is. If you want to learn about prison life, forget about the manuals. Walk the track.

Dinner tonight is lasagna, rolls, Jell-O, fruit. I can't remember eating so much in a single day; I'm stuffed. The food is great, but I can't help but thinking that in any direction from this facility, there are men, women, and children who, through no fault of their own, are going hungry. Yet here at Schuykill, we have more than we can eat. The food we waste in a day would feed a large portion of the homeless in Harrisburg. There is something wrong with this picture.

I have decided to write notes every day depicting what happens in a facility like this. I am told that keeping a journal is not allowed, so I must figure out a way to write without causing suspicion and also a way to get my notes out of Schuykill without being detected. Again and again, I am reminded not to trust anybody here. The best place for me to pen my notes is the library. There are six seats there, and although they are cramped, if I am writing in the library, I am less likely to arouse suspicion.

By the evening, word has passed quickly that I have arrived. More than twenty guys stop by my cell to welcome me and to engage in polite conversation or to ask a question about politics as it's played from

Washington all the way down to the wards. Visits from so many strangers make it difficult to focus on my journal.

It's 9:00 p.m. The music is deafening, and it comes out of Harlem. The night air is punctuated by laughter that is loud, raucous, overlapping. I had expected more sadness, more depression, more moping around. On the other hand, instinct tells me that the laughter is a mask disguising an explosive tension that permeates this place.

Wednesday, October 6, 1993

I'm up at 5:15 a.m., while most inmates remain asleep. Guards came around twice during the night. There is no way they have to make all the noise that they do, clicking boots, jangling keys, flashing lights.

It's a great hour to be awake and watch the glory of the sun rising over the Blue Ridge Mountains. This land should not be used for a prison. It ought to be the setting for, say, a campsite for the handicapped.

At breakfast, the coffee rolls are as good as I've ever tasted. As coffee hour ends, the chef comes out to take a bow. It's a guy everybody calls Doc, and he's liked not only for his skills in the kitchen but also for his personality.

In contrast to most people here, Doc is meticulously clean. He speaks in a booming voice. He's in his late forties, and conversationally, he's capable of anything, cracking a joke, talking seriously, or giving friendly advice about health. If anyone has a health problem, out of the goodness of his heart, Doc will examine him for anything from back spasms to ingrown toenails.

At mail call, Doc seems to be the most popular guy. His name is called a lot, but what he's receiving are medical journals.

As time goes by, we become close friends.

Why is he called Doc?

Because he was a real doctor, one of Pennsylvania's leading urologists, who was turned in to the federal government for prosecution for having prescribed steroids for Hulk Hogan and other members of the World Wrestling Federation. In many foreign countries, steroids can be bought over the counter without prescription for as little as five dollars. In the United States, they're illegal.

Unfortunately for Doc, one of the great big wrestlers got religion and agreed to cooperate with the authorities. He decided not to implicate the WWF, and Doc was found guilty.

But instead of sending Doc to a community where medical help is needed, the federal prosecutors got another pelt to hang on their wall by sending Doc to Schuykill, where he was assigned (where else?) to the laundry to stitch torn clothes.

Despite the absurdity of the assignment, Doc set about to reorganize the laundry. After a while, he realized that whether an inmate was a self-starter who worked hard all day to make life better in prison, he was treated no differently from inmates who simply slept all day.

So, Doc looked for a job more beneficial to himself, and he found it in the kitchen, where he became a baker and a damn good one.

Why did Doc not end up working on the medical staff?

He refused to have anything to do with the medical department at Schuykill. As he put it, based on what he saw at Schuykill, medical care in the BOP was often dangerously inadequate, and at times nonexistent.

All inmates, no matter what they're in prison for, are entitled to adequate food, housing, and the same level of medical care they would receive on the outside. That's the law.

Complaints have grown in recent years, not only among inmates but also among prison doctors who say that medical treatment in prison is woefully lacking. For example, there is an inmate here who fell on ice and was carried by other inmates to his bunk, where he has been lying on his cot for twenty days. Everyone believes he has a broken rib, but the administration says that if he wants medical attention, he has to go to sickbay for treatment.

The Doc says the inmate may suffer permanent damage.

It's hard not to wonder, is there no community in the country in need of a doctor? Is there no ghetto, no Indian reservation, no other place in the United States where Doc's professional skills could be put to use?

Wednesday is the day the warden inspects our quarters and gives each a grade from worst (one) to best (four).

This is taken very seriously.

If your cube is rated four, you rest easy for the week. If you receive the top mark for eight weeks in a row, you are permitted to receive a package of clothing from the outside that might include a running suit, sweatshirt, and running shoes.

If your mark is three, then you pass, but you are admonished to work harder to keep your area clean. That means the floor has to shine. No dust. Windows and bathrooms must be spotless.

If you receive a two, you are in trouble, and for the rest of the week you lose access to the commissary, telephone, and television.

At first, I thought this was petty. Later, after I saw the tendency of many inmates to live in filth, I came to think of inspections as a blessing.

My roommate, I discover, pays to have the cell cleaned, not with money but with the barter of goods bought at the commissary.

Also, they're passing out flu shots today. Inmates here the longest say no way, absolutely not, no flu shots. What they're concerned about, generally, is dirty needles and specifically, AIDS.

I decide to skip the flu shot.

After breakfast, I pick up clothes from supply. Three T-shirts, three skivvies, two long-sleeve khaki shirts and two khaki trousers, three pairs of white socks, and a pair of used boots that are as stiff as wood.

One item I'll miss is a handkerchief. They made me send mine home, and they don't distribute any. Odd.

At eleven o'clock, I'm waiting in line for lunch, which takes longer than lunch itself. But it kills one more hour.

On the menu today is a prison favorite, hoagies, or what we call in New England a submarine sandwich—cold cuts on a roll with onion, cheese, and tomato. One taste of today's chocolate cake explains why Doc is so popular. It's the best cake I've tasted in twenty years.

I'm still looking for a permanent job assignment. My first choice is the kitchen. Inmates working there get the best food, and I need to put on weight. But you cannot be assigned to the kitchen without a blood test, and that takes thirty days. I've checked out jobs from landscaping to orderly, and for what I want to have accomplished at the end of 120 days, in terms of my journal, my best bet is the library.

After lunch, I'm on the "list," what they refer to as the call sheet, to go to the medical department so they can establish how healthy I am. It's mandatory for new inmates.

The medic is from somewhere in Central America, and as I wait in line, I say a brief prayer that he was educated at a real medical school.

He is referred to by other inmates as "Dime Store Doc" and "Rent-a-Doc." He does not even look clean and certainly does not inspire confidence in BOP medicine.

Suddenly, I am in his inner sanctum. We go through the easy tests, blood pressure, etc., and then it is time for him to draw blood. From the finger, he does it easily. Probing my arm, however, he cannot find the vein, which is odd, because I am so thin the veins are plainly visible. After a number of stabs, at long last he finds it.

Then, he mentions something about a prostate exam.

"No, thanks, that's OK, I say, figuring that if he can't find a vein he can see, it's probably not in my best interest to have him behind me with a flashlight.

As dreary as this place is physically, and as tough as it is psychologically, it's not nearly as challenging as boot camp at Parris Island. I can still see the drill instructor striding up the middle of the barracks, hands behind his back, addressing seventy-five recruits standing at attention in our underwear and learning how to differentiate between our obligations to God and to the Marine Corps.

"God was here before the Marine Corps, so you can give your heart to Jesus," said Sgt. Guido. "But your ass belongs to the Marine Corps. Do you ladies hear me!?!"

After inspection, we are permitted to return to our cells. At *A* range, we have received some of the poorest marks at camp. My cell, A-9, got a three, which is tough to figure. My cellmate and I have paid five dollars apiece to a guy named Brutus to clean up for us, and we only scored a three?

It's 5:30 p.m., and the commissary is open. Items sold here are a major source of barter. Each inmate can spend up to $150 a week on commissary items that are then often used to gamble on sporting events or to negotiate with another inmate to do laundry or ironing, to type a letter or whatever. In the words of one inmate, "Like the outside, Bro, money talks and bullshit walks."

All of it is illegal. Money buys anything!

But as long as someone in the administration is making money off these activities, in this case the commissary, the administration is willing to turn its back.

My first trip is for necessities—toothbrush, hairbrush, dental floss, soap, shaving cream, razors, deodorant, jock strap, baseball cap (green), laundry soap, legal pads, master lock, stamps, and shower shoes. (Stamps are just like cash.)

Because they have sent home the running shoes I brought with me, I need to buy another pair. They'll cost me a lot more, and they'll be worth a lot less than the ones they made me send home.

I haven't been able to make telephone calls yet. I have to submit a list of telephone numbers for approval. This ensures, I guess, that I don't call John Gotti. I put $100 in my account so that I'll be able to make calls when my list is approved. I also purchase instant Maxwell House coffee and an insulated mug.

As with everything else here, it is a tedious process. The line is long and, at the end, waiting to be paid are the sharks from the Bureau of Prisons.

The only way for me to keep a journal is to write down as much as possible and send the information home to Elaine in letter form each night. If anyone asks why I'm writing so much, I tell them I'm researching my own conviction. I'm often asked about my case. Everybody knows about my trial because it was well covered in the newspapers and well circulated at Schuykill.

This robs me of the privacy I need to write my journal, and I have to be careful. If inmates think that they are being interviewed by me for a publication, they would clam up. And the rats would turn me in. Also, hacks open all incoming mail, but for some reason, they do not open outgoing mail. Still, as everyone warns me, you have to be concerned here with the rats. They're everywhere.

It's nine at night, and as I arrange my locker with my newly purchased goods from the commissary, I notice that my cellmate has purposely not divided our storage space evenly. He has kept extra drawer space for himself, as if he has seniority and is entitled to it. This is counter to the rules, but this is not the time for confrontation.

It is clear to me because of this and other observations that, for all the humor here, there's a lot of raw anger that bubbles to the surface from time to time. You can see it in the way inmates treat anyone who is weak or perceived to be so. Each range is a microcosm of society. Every racial group is represented, every age group, every culture. Living side by side, sometimes in the same cell, are drug dealers, bank tellers, car thieves, schoolteachers, and gang leaders.

As much as BOP tries to integrate the facilities, it just doesn't work, and it never will. At all meals, African Americans sit together, Latinos sit together, whites sit together.

Everything is done by race, from the selection of a bunkmate to the choice of partners playing football, softball, basketball. Even religious groups follow the pattern. No wonder the place is simmering with anger and animosity.

You may be able to guess the group held in the greatest scorn and more ridiculed than any other: college graduates.

You are wise here not to appear too intelligent.

The best organized, most cohesive bloc of inmates is the Jewish group, maybe fifteen guys who are always reaching out to help one another. I'm lucky that they adopted me.

The leader is Jim, the guy from Massachusetts who has been so helpful to me, and tonight, he was involved in a situation that demonstrates the tension here.

Jim was walking to my cell to bring me an extra blanket. En route, he had to pass a cell that is home to a thirty-year-old skinhead named Bruce, a self-described tough guy. As Jim walked by, Bruce yelled caustic remarks about a Jewish inmate from Florida.

"Fuck the Jews!" yelled Bruce. "They oughta get the fuck out of America."

Jim heard all of this, of course, and absorbed it, as Jews have for millennia.

"As I was walking back to my cell," Jim told me later, "I said to myself, fuck it; I'm not going to take that from him."

Now, Bruce is six feet two and a weightlifter. Jim is five feet seven and about 150 pounds. But Jim walked into Bruce's cell and looked him in the eye.

"I want you to repeat those remarks."

Bruce was stunned.

"I wasn't talking to you."

"Then why don't you shut the fuck up?"

Bruce screamed: "I wasn't talking to you!"

"Yes, you were, and besides, you're offensive to everyone here, so I'm telling you to shut up."

"I'm not talking to you."

"Whether you're talking to me specifically or not, I'm telling you now, shut the fuck up!"

A few days later, Jim was sitting outside the administration building savoring a rare cigar.

Bruce approached.

"I'm sorry," he said. "I didn't mean what I said."

Now, if the original encounter had erupted into a fistfight, Jim would have been severely beaten, and that was clear to everyone, including Jim. For standing up for what he thought was right, even at the risk of physical harm, I admired him, because I see in him the same courage that inspires Israeli freedom fighters.

Thursday, October 7, 1993

It's 5:45 a.m. I can't believe I'm getting up this early, because I am not sleeping well. I toss and turn most of the night. It will take a lot more time here before I get used to the noises, not to mention sleeping in the suspended animation of the top bunk.

The snoring is unbelievable. And so is—forgive me here—the sound of human gas. I'm not going to spend a lot of words on this indelicate topic, but the noise at night and the acceptance of it by inmates surprises me, especially having lived in a dorm in high school and in a Marine Corps barracks for three years. But I have to remember, after all, as they say here, "This is jail, not Yale."

Each building is assigned a counselor who also happens to be a hack, who is supposed to be the clearinghouse for all problems within the unit, whether it's bunk assignments, job assignments, phone lists, or visitor applications.

Our counselor is named Picasso. He's in his late thirties. Because he is aloof, arrogant, condescending, and often loses our written requests, he is despised by every inmate.

At 10:00 a.m. the commissary opens for what they call "open house items." I desperately need a watch since the hacks took mine and sent it home.

"Why?" I asked at the time.

"Because some of you try to smuggle drugs inside the workings of the watch."

Inmates say that's bull, that watches are taken away so that each of us will have to buy a watch from the BOP. The watch they took from me was a cheap Casio, twenty-nine dollars, but it kept perfect time. It had an alarm and numbers that glowed in the dark. But now, I have to buy their thirty-three-dollar special.

Also, because they sent home the running suit that I had brought with me, I now have to buy one from them. The cost is forty-seven dollars! And the only color available is (puke) green.

Good thing I'm not here to make a fashion statement.

Someday, I hope someone audits this operation. Profits from the commissary are supposed to go to inmate activities—movies, sports equipment, etc.

Fortunately, I have money with me, but what about someone less fortunate who arrives with no money or who has been here five years and has depleted his savings and has no family and no resources beyond his salary here, which is eleven cents an hour, or a net of twelve dollars a month? A haircut is four dollars, a third of your pay per month.

At lunch, a kitchen worker, a schoolteacher from Massachusetts, slips me a half-dozen bananas to take back to my cube. At any prison, bananas are a delicacy. As soon as bananas arrive in the kitchen, they are stolen by inmates who work in the kitchen. That is, if they have not been stolen already by the hacks at the warehouse.

The teacher, by the way, is a warm guy who becomes a good friend, but he makes me promise not to talk about him to other inmates.

"Joe, nobody here knows me, and I'd like it to stay that way."

By that, he means that nobody knows his background or anything about his offense or his trial.

I understand his feelings.

After lunch, I take a ninety-minute walk. I'm hitting stride on the track, a nice comfortable pace, just enough to break a sweat. And for the first forty minutes, a great conversation with Jim, the Israeli freedom fighter.

Then we are joined by others, among them Coach.

In *A* range, there are two inmates from Massachusetts, Paul and Coach, who are obsessed with working out.

Coach, who is a real coach, decides to coach me. He thinks I need help, not only in gaining strength but also in gaining weight. So, after my walk, he leads me in thirty more minutes of exercise, push-ups, sit-ups, and weight lifting.

I love running for the sake of running, which is why I have run eleven Boston Marathons, each a distance of twenty-six miles, 385 yards.

But I'm getting older. Today, I try to run one mile, just to see if my knee can take it. One mile, that's four laps. Roger Bannister did it in less than four minutes. It takes me eleven minutes and thirty seconds. Embarrassing. That's a long way from the days when I would race New England Patriots quarterback Steve Grogan.

He'd win, but at least I was running a 5:25 mile.

After dinner, I prepare to do laundry, but I find the washing machines busy, which they seem to be all day. Tonight, the lines are long. It's one more lesson in adjusting to prison life. It's an extension of life on the outside, except that even more important are the six Ps: "Prior Planning Prevents Piss Poor Performance." In prison, there is no room for error.

It's 6:30 a.m., mail call: for some the day's highlight, for others, the lowlight. Some guys get no mail and say they don't care. Nobody believes them. For even the toughest inmate, a letter can make the difference between a good night's sleep and restlessness.

I get no mail, but I don't miss it.

I can't make phone calls, but I don't miss them.

The only thing I miss is my family.

Like a lot of men my age, I get caught up in the seemingly important world that I work and live in and miss out on what's really important— the love and support of my wife and kids.

It takes getting sent to prison to appreciate them.

A subject of delicate nature that needs to be addressed is sex.

Among the oddest sights here are the inmates who walk around wearing lip-stick and eye shadow and carrying pocketbooks. As hard as they work to be noticed, for the most part they are ignored.

Tonight I am introduced to the second in command for the entire camp. His name is Mr. Hurt.

"What I really hope for," I say, "is that I can be assigned to the library."

"I have no objection to that," he says.

There seems to be something on his mind.

Later, I am told by other inmates that he once was taken in handcuffs out of Allenwood Penitentiary, his last assignment. The charge: stealing money out of the prisoners' candy machine account. I am told that because he was able to rat on several hacks, they let him off with a reprimand and transferred him to Schuykill as deputy administrator.

On my way back to my cell, I run into my counselor, Mr. Picasso.

"Has a decision been made about my job assignment?"

"You know," he says, "I think I misplaced that request. Could you put in another one?"

"Also, I can't make telephone calls yet?"

He invites me to the administration office and allows me to make a call home. Sensitive man that he is, he stands five feet away from me so he can hear the whole conversation. I should have waited until I could be alone. It made me uncomfortable, and my uneasiness was picked up by Elaine and the kids.

Actually, every phone call made by inmates is monitored by the guards patrolling the medium security facility in their vehicles. So, whatever you say can and will be used against you.

There is a problem tonight. It could have been an accident, but I doubt it.

It involved one of the least favorite characters here, Tom Thumb, who's five feet five, the kind of guy known in the Marine Corps as a "short round."

Tom Thumb had a girlfriend who used to come and visit, and hacks would have to break up their clinches. He was also suspected of being a rat.

Poor Tom Thumb.

Today, he had one of his letters opened, read, and then returned to the envelope. Unfortunately, it was from his lawyer, and worse, it outlined the case against him for sexually molesting an eleven-year-old boy.

The news about Tom Thumb is passed quickly, and soon everybody knows. The communication system here is as rapid as anything devised by the telephone company.

They don't like rats here. Even the rats don't like rats. One inmate who ratted on another for smoking returned to his cell tonight and found that someone had pulled back the blanket on his bed and soaked the sheets and mattress in ice water, then neatly folded the blanket back.

The inmate did not make the chilly discovery until he settled into his rack.

The only way for him to get a night's sleep now is to wait his ninety-minute turn for one of the driers.

Friday, October 8, 1993

Up at 5:30 a.m. Among the most dangerous habits to fall into in prison is napping. Some inmates here are yielding to a lifelong ambition to sleep all day. They fall asleep after breakfast. They sleep before and after lunch. They sleep before and after dinner. This cannot be healthy. I suspect it is part of the administration's overall plan. Inmates who are asleep are not likely to cause trouble.

I make a promise to myself. In the four months I am here, I am not going to take a nap during the day or even lie down.

At 8:30 a.m., I head for the library. This is a long weekend. It never dawned on me that holidays meant anything in jail. Some inmates love them because there are fewer hacks, and you can sleep late. Older inmates say that on weekends the time drags, and holidays are worse.

It's a beautiful morning, though. The fall foliage is in full show. What a view. I cannot shake the notion that rather than waste this land and the $35,000 a year it costs to imprison an inmate, America would be better served if a place like this was used as a haven for mentally ill people who are found on the streets of our cities, living on handouts.

At 10:00 a.m., there is a locker shakedown. Two hacks are going through each locker. I haven't been here long enough to know what they are looking for, but other inmates say they are searching for shanks.

Also, they are searching for food stolen from the warehouse or from the kitchen. Good luck to them. They shouldn't have a problem. There is more food here on our range than there is on the serving line in the cafeteria.

After lunch, I head for the track. It is such a glorious day. Where better to spend it than on the track, which is full of inmates walking in groups of two, three, four. The autumn sun shines more crisply here than it does on the coast of New England.

Later, at mail call, I'm hoping to receive newspapers from Boston. The good news is that I receive a *Boston Globe* and a *Boston Herald*. The bad news is that they're dated October 3. I was in Boston then, and I read both editions.

Tonight is fight night on television.

Each unit has two TV rooms. The upstairs TV is set aside for sports, the downstairs TV for movies, all of which are first run, by the way. Tonight's movie is *Unforgiven*, with Clint Eastwood.

Ten hours before the Friday night boxing matches, the TV rooms are staked out by various cliques who mark their territory by covering one or more chairs and sometimes a whole row with blankets.

The blacks sit together in one corner, Latinos in another, and whites in a third. No one is more possessive about TV time and militant in demanding it than Trekkies, that is, fans of *Star Trek*.

As the hour for the boxing match draws near, if anyone moves a chair or a blanket or otherwise encroaches on someone's space, there is a fight in front of the TV set that is sometimes more interesting than the one on screen.

It's true, as I'm told, that most of the fights here take place either in chow line or in the TV room. On the other hand, the potential for violence exists everywhere at every minute.

For example, there was an inmate here I had no use for, a fresh bastard who was always cutting in line. He used to clean up the superintendent's office, where he was a mover and a shaker. Turns out he was also a police officer in Washington, DC. They don't tell you who the police officers are. He was stashed here because he was a witness, but the inmates found out and gave him a beating that almost killed him.

Tonight, however, I'm interested in neither the fight nor the movie. What I want to do is finish my notes and send them home to Elaine.

Keeping the journal without attracting suspicion is becoming more difficult. Wherever I take notes, I attract attention. Tonight, however, everyone wants to be outside. The bocce court is busy, and there's a softball game going on. I have retreated to the library, where it is quiet, and I can catch up on my journal.

At 10:30 p.m., it is lights out, and one more day is over at Schuykill.

Saturday, October 9, 1993

By eight o'clock, visitors are lining up. We can see them, and they can see us, but we are not allowed to speak to each other. That is something not understood by the small children who cannot fathom a reason why, upon seeing their father twenty yards away, they cannot call out to him and run to him.

Or why dad doesn't speak to them or reach out to them.

It's difficult to rationalize the impact on young families wrenched apart by what we call justice.

As long as I am here, nothing will be more difficult to deal with emotionally than visiting hours and the sight of a three-year-old boy holding his father's leg, not understanding why his daddy can't come home with him.

Or elderly mothers visiting their sons.

Or the twenty-two-year-old who brings his girlfriend to visit his father in prison.

Guys serving longer sentences know these visits can damage inmate psychologically for days, so they discourage visitors. Some go years without a visit from anyone.

At brunch, it occurs to me that I am not a restaurant critic, but what they're serving here would match what you get at the Four Seasons Hotel in Boston: French toast, maple syrup, bacon, orange juice, rolls.

The only thing that's missing is a window seat overlooking Boston's Public Gardens and the Swan Boats.

I can't eat another thing. I'm going to explode. I've never consumed so much food in my life.

Afterward, all I want to do is take a nap. I feel like I could fall asleep standing up. The more they feed you, the more you want to sleep. And the more you sleep, the less effort it takes for them to watch you. I promised myself I wouldn't nap, but why am I so tired? Have they put something in the food?

Outdoors, in the center of the track, a softball game is under way. Thank God for four-letter words. Without them, Schuykill would be as quiet as a monastery.

Also, it seems, there is a high percentage of gentlemen whose first name is Mother.

As I move around the track, an inmate catches up to me. He's in his midsixties. His name is Pat, and he's the main man at Schuykill. He is what they call "connected." Everyone knows it, black, white, Asian, Latino, Middle Easterner, whatever.

Pat keeps to himself most of the time. On the outside, and on the inside, here at Schuykill, Pat is as tough as anybody I ever met.

Whenever there is a serious problem, people go to Pat to mediate and alleviate, and he is always successful. There seems to be nothing that comes up here that Pat cannot resolve. I later learn that Pat chairs a secret group of the heads of all ethnic groups to make sure there are no racial or ethnic wars.

Pat tells me that he walks the track on weekends, before the football games on television.

On Saturdays, it's the college games. On Sunday, the professionals.

At last, a light goes on in my head.

My cousin Jimmy has the same interest in football. He described it by telling people that he is a numerologist.

Pat came from South Jersey, spent a lot of time in Philly, Atlantic City, and Boston, and now, he's on the second half of a ten-year sentence. We talk about restaurants in Boston's North End, about the Parker House, and especially about Southie.

I must be homesick. Suddenly, I realize how pleasant it is to talk about Boston. Incidentally, my cousin the numerologist, telephoned one night, a week before I reported to prison.

"I've got to see you," he said.

"What's up?"

"I've got information that may help you in prison."

That got my attention.

Jimmy did thirty days in Massachusetts for operating a sports betting ring.

We arranged to meet Monday morning in the parking lot of a convenience store in suburban Boston.

Jimmy was his usual jovial self as he provided tips for me to survive in prison and also several telephone numbers in case there was any way he or his wife, Adrienne, could help Elaine.

"Thanks, Jimmy. I appreciate this."

"In return, I need one favor," he said. "It's the only favor I'll ever ask from you."

"I'll be in prison in a week, but anything, Jim. What can I do for you?"

"Please," he said. "Take Adrienne with you."

Later, at 6:30 p.m., Fr. Dene is offering mass.

For many inmates, religion in prison is a joke, a way to get out of work details, which is why some guys attend all four services, Catholic, Protestant, Jewish, and Muslim.

Inmates complain about Fr. Dene. They say conversation with him is strained, that the relationship he encourages is less one of pastor to communicant and more that of hack to prisoner.

Fr. Dene, oddly enough, enjoys horse racing. On Saturday afternoons, before Mass, Fr. Dene will be working in his room at the back of the chapel. As soon as the horse races appear on television, Fr. Dene comes out of his office with the speed of Cigar out of the gate.

Also, on the part of many Catholics here, there is a reluctance to go to confession. One reason is the lingering suspicion that Fr. Dene thinks of himself not only as a priest working for God but also as a hack working for the BOP.

A second is that, in this environment, a lot of Catholics are hard-pressed to think of any behavior as sinful. As a teacher from Massachusetts said to me, "What am I going to confess? That I had two extra fried eggs in the cafeteria?"

Fr. Dene has a knack for choosing hymns nobody ever heard of, and he is inclined to offer each Mass in memory of some obscure relative or friend that none of us knows. For example, today, Fr. Dene offers Mass on behalf of his deceased aunt and uncle.

Which is odd. Even if Fr. Dene's aunt and uncle had the misfortune to wind up in hell, they cannot have more problems than the thirty poor souls in this congregation, whose lives are in shambles.

What about a Mass dedicated to them?

Sunday, October, 10, 1993

Suddenly, I'm awake.

What time is it?

My God, it's three o'clock.

Something spooked me.

Something is wrong.

Someone is moving at the end of my bunk.

It's not a hack, because there's no noise, no boots, no keys, no light.

Then I recognize him.

It's Mac, who lives across from me. He's heading toward the rear door. He slips out, shutting the door behind him, and then, once again, it is quiet.

Since I'm awake, I decide to visit the latrine, thirty yards down from my bunk.

With all the windows open, it's ice cold as I head down the hall in my Skivvies and shower shoes.

Just as I get to the head, the main door opens.

Two guards appear with flashlights.

They are obviously on official business.

I realize that I look suspicious.

"Where are you going?"

"The latrine."

Suddenly, the back door opens, and Mac appears.

They move toward Mac, and one yells, "Freeze!"

They don't have to say that a second time to me.

I'm already freezing, and given the tension of the moment, not inclined to move a muscle.

They pepper Mac with questions. I'm too far away to hear answers.

The crisis is serious. The head count revealed an empty bed. An inmate is missing. The hacks are feverish to find him.

They leave Mac and me and return to their head count, using flashlights to check each bunk more carefully, and, in so doing, they wake up most of *A* range.

Then they leave for *B* range.

I head to Mac's cell.

"Where were you going?"

"To do a wash, but I ran out of soap powder, and I was coming back for more, but when I tried to return to the washing machines, the door was locked. I thought it was stuck and tried to go around through the front door, which set off alarms."

At 3:45 a.m., a hack arrives to open the laundry room for Mac, who is doing not only his wash but that of four other inmates.

40

Meanwhile, another hack whispers that they've found the missing inmate.

He was in bed with Pat, the gay who wears lipstick and carries the pocketbook. The two of them fell asleep, one on top of the other.

The inmate who was in the wrong bed was sent to solitary.

Pat was reprimanded and returned to the population, along with his pocketbook and lipstick.

Although it is now 4:15 a.m., because of the disruptions, I can't sleep. There are so many characters in this place that it would make a great screenplay. Amid the tragedy of wasted time, energy, money, and lives, there is plenty to poke fun at.

At 6:00 a.m., it is tough getting up. Feels like I've been up all night.

I make myself some coffee, Maxwell House instant, using the hot water nozzle at the drinking fountain near my cell.

If you're on the outside, that may not sound great. If you've been on the inside for a while, it tastes better than anything served at Starbucks.

I try to put in a wash, but everyone else has the same idea. For 150 inmates, there are two washing machines, three driers.

At breakfast, everybody's talking about last night's incident. There is no sympathy for either inmate. Nobody is surprised at Pat, but many are disappointed in the other inmate who, ironically, was recently married.

How do you suppose he'll explain this to the new wife?

When the subject of homosexuality came up, Jim told this story.

"The second day I was here, I was sitting outside with coffee, cigar, and a book, half-dozing, when this person walked by with a pocketbook, pink sweater, and tits. I couldn't believe it. Tits! I said to myself, 'Where the hell am I?'

There are homosexuals in every prison. They are a fact of life. They're tolerated but for the most part ignored. Some are in the closet, and some, like Pat, flaunt it.

As tough as prison is, it's tougher on gay men. Other inmates don't want to be seen with them, not in the cafeteria, not in the library, or anywhere else.

Having sex with gay inmates is frowned upon. It's just not accepted. There are inmates, macho guys who tease the gays so relentlessly that they themselves become suspect.

Gays in the closet somehow know by instinct which inmates are interested in sex with them, which are not. They're careful not to make a mistake. That would be dangerous.

After breakfast, the day's events are being organized. Because it's chilly, most are planned around TV, football, baseball playoffs, movies (*The Last of the Mohicans*), cartoons, music videos, pool, weight lifting, and cards, both bridge and gin.

In prison, cards are big. Some inmates play six hours a day, a waste of time guaranteed to shrink the mind as well as the body.

The goal, I guess, is simply to make it through another day in this warehouse full of brawn. Having consumed so much food, most inmates just want to climb into their bunks and sleep, which is a symptom of depression.

I can't let that happen to me.

This is visiting day, and shortly after 8:30 a.m., inmates are lined up in the administration building. Hearing the voices of children in these corridors in strange. Hacks who are processing the visitors and checking their identification get perverse amusement by delaying visits for trivial reasons. It may be that someone's name doesn't appear on a list. It may be that an inmate is not dressed properly.

In any case, it's a painful sight.

Later, walking around the track with Pat (the one without the pocketbook), I ask about the inmate everybody says was murdered.

"His name was Phil Kagan, and they killed him, just as sure as you and I are walking here."

His vehemence surprises me. Another inmate arrives, and the conversation turns to football. I have more questions about Kagan, but now is not the time, and in any case, I need to be careful with this issue.

It's midafternoon, and I'm walking the track, and although the temperature has dropped to forty-five degrees, the sun is bright. I like it out here, and I have devised a plan to preserve my sanity at Schuykill.

While I'm here, I'm going to walk home.

I'm going to spend as much time on this track as possible. At the pace I'm walking, I figure I do four miles per hour. That's twelve miles per day. Counting rain and snow days, I can average about fifty miles per week. So, I'm here for sixteen weeks. Boston is 750 miles away, and that will be my goal, to walk 750 miles.

Also, it will give me an opportunity to talk to people and get information for my journal. Then, I can write at night.

Now, all I need here is a job to occupy my days.

The danger is monotony. In fact, that's the real punishment here, to sit around and do nothing while you think of things that are important to you that you miss, like your wife and your children and your job.

The brooding—that's what causes people to lose their self-esteem and their minds.

At dinner, apples are served, and you don't need a graduate degree in chicanery to know someone has a deal involving the apples. These are apples you would not even pick up in a store. They're tiny, bruised, unsalable, and barely edible. Someone had to work hard to make sure all these bad apples ended up at this prison.

At six p.m., two things are going on at once.

In one classroom, a religious service draws about ten inmates.

In another, bingo attracts 150. The prize is a six-pack of Fresca.

Back in my cell, the atmosphere is cool. My bunkmate no longer talks to me. I saw him jump in the front at the chow line, which is the height of arrogance and ignorance, and I told him so. I'd rather go without a meal than jump ahead of ninety inmates. In other prisons, if you jump in line, you might find yourself stabbed.

I am reminded by another inmate that I have been here a week already. I hadn't thought of it that way. At four months, my sentence is short compared to guys serving nine years, and so I never talk about it with anyone. Privately, though, I have calculated every month, every week, every day, every hour, every second.

But now, it's time to try to sleep.

Monday, October 11, 1993

At 5:00 a.m., it's pitch black out and ice cold, and nobody is stirring but me. This is an opportunity to latch onto a washing machine before the others get up. With an armful of wash and a box of Tide, I balance a cup of instant Maxwell House and head for the washing machines.

One is already in use, but another is empty. As they showed me, I turn on the machine and let the water run until the machine is one-quarter full. Then, I put in detergent, then clothes.

There is no separation of colors. One wash does all.

And now, a twenty-five minute respite to shower and shave.

Once my clothes have gone through a cycle in the drier, I discover by the wrinkles that I probably overloaded the drier. And to judge by the new tint on my shirts, I overloaded the washer, too, with colors that never meant to be mixed.

I would never make it in one of those television commercials. All my whites look gray.

At 8:00 a.m., I get a chance to make some notes. If this journal is to succeed, I need a better system to deal with these notes. I'm carrying around three or four days' worth of notes, and that's dangerous. I don't trust my bunkmate. I can't keep them in my locker because the hacks conduct spot searches. The only solution is to mail notes home to Elaine each night in letter form.

Brunch is scrambled eggs, French toast, syrup, waffles, ham, turkey, salad, eggplant, milk, juice, and a great salad bar.

This is punishment? Most Americans don't eat this well. Maybe it's a trick. Maybe they know that if they feed us a steady diet this rich in starch, it will kill us.

Walking the track at midday, I ask Jim about the inmate who died before I arrived.

"Phil Kagan. The BOP murdered him." His voice was venomous. "Why are you interested?"

"I don't think the public realizes what goes on in prison."

"You're right," he said, "but you have to understand something."

"What?"

"The public doesn't care, and Congress doesn't care.

"Here's what happened. Kagan died despondent. Everything in life he held important had fallen apart. Kagan had been indicted, and although he maintained his innocence, he was convicted of bank fraud. His wife left him. He was disbarred. Bereft of resources and emotional support, he went off to prison. He was in frail health and gained an enormous amount of weight and was allowed to lie in his bed twenty-two days while his body swelled with fluids. When they finally took him to the hospital, it was too late, and he died."

As I discovered later, Kagan was forty-nine years old. He was five feet eight and he weighed 310 pounds. He arrived at Schuykill in August 1992, and he died on September 3, 1993.

Kagan's family, I later learned, filed a $15 million wrongful death suit against the Bureau of Prisons, charging that Kagan had complained to the administration and medical staff, beginning in June 1993, that his health was failing and that prison officials failed to take appropriate action until late August, when he was removed to hospital in Harrisburg, went into cardiac arrest, into a coma, and then died.

In the days that followed, inmates were stunned.

Greg, who was head of the born-again Christian group and ordinarily a quiet, unassuming gentleman, was so upset that he stormed into the administration office and demanded to know what happened. He was told to get out of the office, that he was overstepping his place. He raised his voice about it, and they threw him into a cell down in medium security for a few days.

It's 10:00 a.m., and from my top bunk, I can see all the nearby activities. Inmates are playing cards, writing letters, washing clothes, yelling at one another, laughing.

What a scene!

It reminds me of *Stalag 17, M*A*S*H*, and *Hogan's Heroes*.

I hope to get a permanent job assignment tomorrow.

One benefit of my stay here is that I have relearned the value of prayer.

Tuesday, October 12, 1993

Awake at 5:15 a.m., and boy is it cold. Winter's coming. I hope to find out this morning what my work assignment is. Every working morning, the hacks post a notice on the bulletin board in each unit. It includes job assignments, medical appointments, counseling sessions.

Reading this list and following it is a must. If you are listed to be someplace, and you're not, you are AWOL.

Bingo!

Timilty, J.F., Unit Two, is going to be an Education Orderly. I'm assigned to the library. Great!

Plenty of time to sit behind a desk and catch up on my notes.

The bet among the inmates was that because I had put in for the library, I'd be assigned to landscaping.

Walking back from breakfast, I have a recurring thought, that of a prison population, sleeping in warm, safe quarters and being served three good meals a day while who can say how many children in our country wake up cold, in homes, apartments, hotels, and even cars and then go to school hungry?

At the same time, in New York, the schools are more overcrowded than they have been in a decade, 91,000 more students than the system can accommodate comfortably, and as a result, students are crammed into closets, cordoned off in auditoriums, and plunked into locker rooms.

It's ironic, but I feel guilty being here, and it has nothing to do with my sentence.

As I begin my second full week, a clear picture of the process is emerging. It's not pretty. There are 280 guys here for various reasons and serving sentences of varying length. In virtually every case, each of us should be involved in something more productive.

We certainly ought to pay a penalty in some form for whatever crime landed us here.

In the case of inmates who held jobs, the $35,000 expense to taxpayers to house us does not include the potential loss to the labor force, the loss of tax dollars, and in some cases, the loss of businesses and homes, not to mention the cost of welfare that is sometimes required when the head of a household is incarcerated as a first-time offender for a nonviolent crime.

Even more important, perhaps, no one can put a price on the emotional scars on children whose families are torn apart, sometimes permanently.

Wouldn't it make more sense, from a public policy perspective, for the taxpayers to save the $35,000 a year cost and, instead, have nonviolent, first-time offenders serve their time on weekends, assign them to productive work in their communities, and have them turn over 25 percent of their income to the government?

Who wins in that equation? Everybody. The government, the taxpayers, the community, and the families, especially the children.

By 8:00 a.m., I've been briefed on my duties in the library. The floor has to be cleaned and buffed, a few windows kept clean, a small rug vacuumed, and a few chairs aligned.

My new job as a librarian will raise some eyebrows back in Boston, and maybe laughter. Growing up in Dorchester, if you patronized the local library, or even if you had a library card, you were suspect. I've come a long way.

At 1:00 p.m., I meet the manager of the education system and library, Mr. Heater. He's also in charge of the GED program, which stands for Graduate Equivalency Diploma, which means a high school diploma that can be earned by high school dropouts.

This is the biggest scam here.

Some rocket scientist in Congress decided that the root of crime in America is the lack of high school diplomas among so many people who then drift into crime.

And the answer? Require all men and women in prison to enroll in a GED program until they pass a test that proves they are educated to a high school level. When they pass, they receive a certificate at a small ceremony with cake and soda.

Meanwhile, for every inmate who passes, the BOP receives $2500 from the budget of the Department of Education.

Now, here's the scam: according to inmates who are teachers, the test is geared to a ninth-grade student. The result of this phony program is the waste of millions of dollars.

At 10:30 p.m., it's lights out. Tomorrow is inspection day, and guess what?

Tomorrow is my day off!

I can't fathom how you deal with a day off in prison.

Wednesday, October 13, 1993

Breakfast is oatmeal and Spanish hash. (What is Spanish hash?) Also, the BOP got taken again. If these apples were much smaller, they'd be radishes.

Inspection day. The most pressure-packed experience of the week. Most inmates are doing last-minute cleaning, swearing, buffing, swearing, dusting, swearing. A bad mark on the inspection day list means a bad week.

Today, my name is on the hospital list. They're still checking my knees. My knees qualify me for a lower bunk, but the doctors seem to be intent on getting an X-ray that will disprove that. I have not pressed the point on the lower bunk, simply because that would mean throwing another inmate out.

Other inmates tell me that, under ordinary circumstances, it would take four months to get a lower bunk. That means I won't qualify for a lower bunk until I'm scheduled to go home.

By 4:00 p.m., inspection is over, my cell gets a three again, and I'm not happy. If we're paying Brutus to clean the place, why isn't it clean? One look at Brutus tells me why. At six feet four and 300 pounds, Brutus is a slob.

He's twenty years old and serving time for computer fraud.

When Brutus walks, it takes a while for the rest of him to catch up. His fat just follows him around. He has a couple of earrings, little studs, that he slips into his ears to look cool during visiting hours.

Brutus, who resembles the cartoon character Baby Hughie, has a high school sense of humor. When he burps or farts, he thinks it's funny, and he laughs. No one else does.

They say opposites attract, and in the case of Brutus, that's true. Brutus rooms with a CPA from New Jersey who is impeccably neat, a hunchback in his midfifties whom everybody introduces as the Hunchback of Notre Dame.

The Hunchback would say things to Brutus, such as, "Don't worry; you'll never be as old as you look." Brutus would look at him, puzzled, not understanding precisely what that meant.

Brutus is one problem, my cellmate is another. I think he knows the string is running out between us.

Oh-oh. Tonight at mail call, my first infraction is recorded.

A friend arranged that a subscription to the *Boston Globe* be sent to me.

Instead of addressing it to: "Joseph F. Timilty, 194-00-038," he addressed it to "J.F.T., 194-00-038."

You wonder why that is a problem? So did I. Here's the answer.

At Schuykill, they forbid nicknames, and they have concluded that J.F.T. is a nickname. Strange, but they make a very big deal out of this.

By 9:00 p.m., I get the word. Now it's official, my bunkmate is leaving, and I'm to get the lower bunk. The upper will be empty until someone else is assigned, but it's the Jewish guys who are responsible for my reassignment to a lower bunk.

In one sense, they control this place. They know how it works. They know that the key to many day-to-day decisions is the inmate who works as an orderly. The hacks give the orderly great authority in such matters as the assignment of bunks. He and the Jewish group will be a factor in the selection of a new bunkmate for me.

Thursday, October 14, 1993

At work call at 7:30 a.m., I open the library and clean up after last night's activities. Emptying wastebaskets and straightening chairs takes fifteen minutes.

There are no books to put away.

Every afternoon at three, the newspapers are delivered, *Wall Street Journal, USA Today, New York Times, Philadelphia Enquirer.*

Within an hour, they are stolen.

Inmates tell me that every once in a while, a hack wants to see an article in one of the newspapers, and when he realizes it's missing, he goes berserk and orders a locker search—for yesterday's newspapers, no less.

That is why inmates never sign their own name.

Today's ledger shows that newspapers have been signed out by Bill Clinton, Janet Reno, and, of all people, the Rev. Billy Graham.

Today's the day for my meeting with the prison shrink.

Every inmate has to have a psychiatric evaluation upon entering the prison population. It takes place in a conference room with one large table and a number of chairs, one at the head and eight along each side.

As it happens, after my trial, my codefendants complained to the Justice Department that they were afraid to be sentenced to the same prison where I would serve my time.

So, it was recorded in my file that I am capable of violence, and now I have this shrink looking at me because he thinks—well, he doesn't know what he thinks.

You've probably seen this guy in a Stephen King movie. He's small, frail, wearing a sports jacket two sizes too big, and a dress shirt that would fit Arnold Schwarzenegger.

This thing is backward. I ought to be evaluating the shrink.

His eyes are magnified by thick glasses, and he glares at me as if the questions he is asking are meant to be piercing.

"Have you thought about killing anybody today?"

"No." (Not until now.)

"Have you thought about killing the president of the United States?"

"No." (We're both Democrats.)

"Are you angry with anyone?"

"No." (What a dumb question! Where do you want me to start? I'm in prison for having engaged in a common practice. I am here because a prosecuting attorney put witnesses on the stand he knew were lying, and then he tried to have me sentenced to four years in prison until a judge with common sense reduced it to four months.)

A couple of misplaced "yes" answers, and the shrink would jump out of his ill-fitting suit.

As the evaluation ends, I realize this guy could explode at any minute. Ironically, the most dangerous person I've encountered thus far at Schuykill is the shrink.

At 1:00 p.m., back to work. The library is a joke, a small conference room. There are shelves halfway around the room that offer a bizarre range of paperbacks left by inmates over the years, world atlases, a few English-to-Spanish texts, romance novels, and the like.

Congress mandates that every prison maintain a library, but the one here at Schuykill is pathetic. To aid in appeals, inmates are supposed to have access to legislation passed by Congress. Recent judgments by the courts are supposed to be available, along with regulations by the Justice Department.

In some cases, however, by the time documents arrive, they are outdated. In other cases, they're stolen.

Also, typewriters are supposed to be available for inmates who want to type legal documents. At Schuykill, there are four. One works.

Every year, prison programs, including the libraries, are audited, and reports are made to Congress. The problem is the audits are conducted by BOP employees from other prisons. So, the library at Schuykill is audited by librarians from other prisons. That ensures an honest appraisal, doesn't it?

Building prisons has become an industry that sustains itself.

As a correctional system, this place is misnamed. Whatever the federal government may tell you, and whatever you may read in the newspapers, Schuykill is not a correctional system. Nobody here is getting corrected.

Most politicians agree privately, but only those of courage will say so publicly, that this doesn't make any sense, that we might benefit by investing the money elsewhere.

Examples of the waste of taxpayer money are everywhere. For example, in the woods a half mile from the highway is what they call here a Wellness Center.

That's bureaucratic gobbledygook for an ultra-modern health club for the hacks. The reason it's called a Wellness Center is to disguise its true nature from Congressional watchdogs. I wonder if the mental giants in Congress ever asked the question, What is a Wellness Center, and why are we paying for one in the middle of a prison colony?

In the cafeteria at lunch, here's something that may surprise you. Before they touch their food, many inmates pause, bow their heads, and say grace, making the sign of the cross.

Nothing elaborate. It's very quick, very private.

But in prison, I never expected to see so many examples of individual faith. It's difficult to explain, not easy to capture on paper.

These are guys who, in spite of their circumstances and whatever their denomination, have not given up on God.

In many cases, these are men who have lost everything—homes, families, friends, jobs, reputations, and their freedom for as much as ten years.

And before their meal, they do not forget to thank God.

It's now 10:00 p.m. I've sent my mail again today, but Elaine told me by telephone that she had not yet received any. That makes me nervous. If anyone here in authority has opened any of my letters, I'm in trouble.

Friday, October 15, 1993

As usual, I wake at 5:15 a.m. I have to maintain discipline. Shave every morning and shower and clean the area where I live.

Based on what I see around here, once you start letting yourself go, the slide is quick. I've got to stay with it. Got to treat myself every day as if I were going home. I have a lot of people counting on me. Stay with it, Joe. One day at a time.

Wow! The fog this morning is so thick you can touch it, feel it, smell it. In a lifetime along the New England coast, I have never seen fog so heavy.

When it's this thick, inmates think "escape," and so the hacks shut down all operations and return inmates to their ranges for a lockdown. Most of the prison guards are then sent to the medium security facility next door to guard the extended perimeter of the facility. Schuykill is 3,500 feet above sea level, way up in the mountains. The biggest elevation near my home in Massachusetts is the Blue Hills Observatory, a mere 850 feet.

Throughout this facility, but especially in the dining room, the waste is shocking. Real resources lost every day in both dollars and labor. Why does Congress allow this? I'm not suggesting we close all prisons, but these camps are a flagrant waste of taxpayer money.

The latest figures I've seen show there are 90,000 in camps across the country. Calculate the cost at $35,000 per inmate. That's $3.15 billion. Imagine that money invested in other programs to provide food and medicine for the poor, housing for the homeless, education for illiterates, counseling for battered women and children, or perhaps halfway houses for mentally retarded adults who can work but have no families.

Maybe I'm a cockeyed optimist. Maybe you can't change a bureaucracy so entrenched. Especially when the reality is that there are those in high places with a stake in keeping the system just the way it is.

It's 4:30 p.m., and the lockdown is over.

The fog has burned off nicely, the sun is out, and it's cool.

The track is full, a softball game is under way, and the handball courts are busy. Bocce courts are a beehive of activity, and the weight room is alive with the sound of grunting. Over on the grass, a touch football game has drawn a crowd.

This looks like the kind of place you might read about in the *New York Times* travel section—Come to our summer camp for the rich here in the hills of Pennsylvania.

As I ready for bed, it occurs to me that my second weekend is coming up. Anticipating the weekend, most inmates take delight in what they don't have to do. By contrast, I want a lot to do. I'm trying to plan a weekend schedule with so many activities that I don't fall into this spider web of sleeping during the day.

Saturday, October 16, 1993

Although it is only 8:15 a.m., visitors are arriving. As I sit in the library, I hear the voices of children. At Schuykill, no sound will bother me more. Thank God my children are older—old enough, at least, to read news accounts of how I ended up here and make their own judgments.

But not these children coming to see their fathers, their uncles, their brothers.

This is a travesty: first-time, nonviolent offenders who should be productive members of society, paying taxes, being fathers and husbands rather than being stuck in this jail and being catered to by other inmates or catering to them.

It puts the federal government in the business of breaking up families.

At lunch, the Latinos, the largest group here, stay mostly to themselves. They not only eat together, they also work together, bunk together, hang together.

Many inmates believe Latinos stick together because they hate both blacks and whites. But I think the reason is not so callous. Many of them do not speak English. Here at Schuykill, I am catching on among them as a wordsmith, someone they can turn to if they need help writing a letter to a loved one or a legal paper to a judge, lawyer, or politician.

One young Latino was writing a letter to explain why he needed a transfer from Pennsylvania to a prison closer to his wife, who was ill, and to his two young children. He asked for my help. We worked on the letter together, and as a result, he saw me as a friend, and he spread the word among his Latino friends.

At Mass tonight, I am puzzled. Fr. Dene is delivering his sermon. I notice that he is reading from a typewritten page. Now, the topic chosen by Fr. Dene for the sermon is the gospel that urges us to contribute more to charity, to be more generous to the church. But Fr. Dene has been here three years, and he knows the men in his congregation here have no money to give.

Then, it occurs to me. Fr. Dene's sermon obviously was written for the parish that he preaches in on Sunday, and what he's doing here in prison on Saturday is rehearsing his sermon on us.

At 10:30 p.m., there is a major crisis. Prison life is brought to a halt. There's going to be a shakedown. This is unheard of on a Saturday night.

Whatever could warrant this?

It must be important.

Ten minutes later, it is clear. What the hacks are searching for is a tape recorder that was stolen from the library.

Among a group of inmates, I ask what proves to be a stupid question.

"Why would anyone want to steal a tape recorder?"

The inmates laugh.

It seems one of them has figured out a way to disassemble a tape recorder and use the parts, including ink, to print tattoos on his fellow inmates.

Think about it.

If someone applied that kind on ingenuity in corporate America, he might become another Bill Gates.

Sunday, October 17, 1993

At breakfast, Doc's banana bread is terrific. Orange juice is on the menu but in the dining room. Where is the orange juice? Speculation is that one of the hacks in the warehouse is running a "still" and needs the oranges.

After waiting in line for twenty minutes and then eating for twenty, we sit at the table and talk for forty.

I pick up this week's schedule.

At the library this week, I'll be working Sunday and Monday from five to eleven, and then I'm off Tuesday and Wednesday, after which I work Thursday through Saturday, 7:30 a.m. to 3:30 p.m.

After breakfast, I head to the track.

My walking mate this morning is Stephen, who works in the warehouse, where, I've been told in whispers, there is widespread stealing by hacks that they cover up by phony inventories.

Here's a story that captures the insanity here. There is an inmate who complained that his job at the warehouse is 90 percent make-work. He says he is so bored that when he sits down on the job at the warehouse, he falls asleep. As the days went by, he was getting so much sleep at the warehouse that he couldn't sleep at night.

But the hacks warned him sternly not to sleep at the warehouse. So, in order to stay awake, he took to playing cards. One day, when the guards conducted a surprise inspection, they found him playing gin, and they were angry.

He did not understand why they were upset.

At least he was awake.

At 11:30 a.m., I bump into Pat, who is on his way to Unit One, to the television room to watch the Philadelphia Eagles football game. Pat's sixty-five years old. When he gets out of here, he'll be seventy. This is the man who keeps the lid on trouble before it starts.

Convicted of manslaughter, his oldest son is serving twenty years at a maximum security facility. In addition, Pat's wife is sick, and his daughter has problems with her business. He's five feet six, 160 pounds, but when Pat talks, people listen, whether it's a Hell's Angel or a skinhead.

Watching football games on television here is quite a ritual. It's not one of those spur-of-the-moment afternoons when a few guys get together to watch TV and munch potato chips. On the contrary, this is a catered affair.

On this day, one chef has pilfered a brisket of beef from the kitchen, and so everybody has hot corned beef sandwiches.

As luck would have it, days later, when that same corned beef was on the menu in the cafeteria, inmates would wait an hour for a slice.

But if you fit in here, you eat the same food days earlier in fresher and more flavorful condition than when it is eventually served in the cafeteria.

It's 6:00 p.m., and I am back at my cell.

There are 280 stories in this place.

Take my friend, Camel. He's from Egypt. Camel roams the place at all hours of the night. He goes to bed at seven and gets up at three.

He opened a trucking firm in New York's garment district. One day, federal agents, acting on a tip, stopped Camel's truck, and lo and behold, what did they discover but an impressive stash of cocaine.

Camel claimed the cocaine had been planted by competitors.

His lawyer worked out a deal with the prosecutor: if Camel pleaded guilty, he'd get nine months in jail.

An indignant Camel rejected the offer, saying he had confidence in the American system of justice. He said he wanted a trial by jury because he was convinced his peers would find him innocent.

Well, as luck would have it, Camel's peers found him guilty.

Camel was stunned and furious. At sentencing, Camel used the *F* word imaginatively to tell the judge the disdain in which he held the prosecuting attorney and the hatred he held for the jury of his peers. He then called the judge a motherfucker and a cocksucker, and he went into detail as to precisely where the judge could stuff his American jurisprudence.

Instead of nine months, Camel was sentenced to six years.

Monday, October 18, 1993

One inmate is being discharged today. He owns a trucking company in upstate New York. He arrived weighing 354 pounds, walked ten miles a day, lost 152 pounds and left weighing 202, a new man.

My new cellmate, Bill, has served time in Pennsylvania and Connecticut and is now doing ten years here.

He's five foot eight and weighs 185. He has a ruddy Irish complexion, reddish-brown hair, and on his upper left arm, a Marine Corps tattoo in the form of a caricature with a hat that says USMC.

Bill is married and has a small child. He's a Clint Eastwood guy. He doesn't say much, keeps his own counsel. But I like him. He doesn't smoke, and he's not a rat. He and I will get along fine.

He works in the kitchen, and if corned beef is going to be on the menu, I'll find three pounds of it wrapped on my pillow at night.

He is a disabled marine veteran who was found guilty of making and distributing speed. I'm stunned at the amount of time he has to serve. I find it difficult to comprehend the reasoning that justifies ten years for a nonviolent offender.

At 6:00 p.m., it's time for rosary and benediction. (I'm given time off from the library to attend religious services.) As I said, I haven't attended these services since I was a teenager, but if inmates serving five years think it's worthwhile, then I ought to make the time, too.

As a carrot, after the service, Fr. Dene shows a movie. Tonight, it's *Lethal Weapon*. I've seen it, but I'll watch again. The room is quiet, smoke free, and a lot quieter than back in Unit Two.

Tuesday, October 19, 1993

As much as the government tries to integrate these facilities, it's amazing the extent to which it doesn't work, because, after all is said and done, everybody hangs out with his own kind. It's a fact of life, I guess. I find myself migrating to the white population, to the guys from New England. At meals, I often sit with the Jewish group that adopted me when I arrived.

This morning I was confronted with a ticklish situation. I had filled my tray at the serving line. When I turned to face the dining room, I looked toward my customary table and saw there was no room. In fact, there were only two tables that had an open chair. At one table was Herb, a black guy from Florida with whom I had talked often about long-distance running and about his hopes of running the Boston Marathon. At the other table was a former assistant to a Democrat who was an elected official in the Northeast, a white guy who is a braggart. Recognizing my consternation, he beckons me to his table in such grand gestures that he attracts attention.

So, what does Timilty do? Does he choose white? Does he choose black? What would you do? There are often these tests in prison.

I walk toward my white political friend, and I joke about a recent news event, but then walk over and sit down with Herb. The decision is not lost on anyone with eyesight. Leaving the cafeteria, I fall into step with another inmate.

"I'm glad you didn't submit to the loudmouth," he says.

The lesson: in prison, nobody misses anything.

After breakfast, I head for the track. Winter comes early here in the mountains, and these days, walking the track, you can glimpse a young bear cub going through the trash or in the evening, a bobcat racing among the trees, and often deer and even wild turkey.

What a setting for inner-city kids instead of old jocks worried about weight control!

Also, you do not need to be here long to notice two problems that drain this place of efficiency. One is the nepotism, which is rampant. On the payroll, the administrator has placed his brother, his sons, his wife, and a couple of gal pals.

Another is the charge that inmates are to blame for everything that's stolen. Now, it's true that inmates are responsible for some of the pilferage, but there is theft taking place here on such a grand scale that inmates cannot possibly be responsible for all of it. The charge here right now is that inmates have stolen 100 gallons of frozen orange juice concentrate, 1000 pounds of sugar, crates of chickens, and hundreds of pounds of frozen fish.

That is absurd. Where would inmates store all of it? How could they possibly refrigerate hundreds of pounds of frozen fish?

The problem of theft also extends to office supplies and building supplies. The Achilles's heel here is the warehouse. That's where most of the goods are stolen. Millions of dollars are lost to theft as well as waste, and for some reason, nobody seems troubled by it. Year after year, the BOP budget comes before Congress and is approved without much challenge, without even much question.

Congress can drone on in speeches for hours over a few pennies in the food stamp program, while, at the same time, their ignorance of what goes on at a place like Schuykill is almost criminal. The largest growth industry in the country is prisons. For the BOP to perpetuate itself is no small feat. They must have a powerful lobbying group, although none of this says very much that's flattering about Congress.

On the track this morning, I meet Manny, a young Latino from Spanish Harlem who speaks broken English. This morning, however, he has additional difficulty. Manny's face is swollen, and he tells me he's having trouble with his teeth.

"Why don't you go to the dentist?"

"I did go to the dentist. That's the problem."

"What do you mean?"

"The dentist said I had to have a tooth pulled. So, he pulled the tooth."

"And it hasn't healed?"

"No, he pulled the wrong tooth. I had to go back the next day and have another tooth pulled. Now I have two teeth missing."

Lunch today is meatball subs, French fries, cake, ice cream. The subs were good, but I thought they tasted funny. I find out after lunch that the meatballs were actually processed turkey. You wonder what they mean by processed turkey.

Or maybe you shouldn't wonder.

On the track, I am joined by the teacher from Massachusetts who works in the kitchen. As we stroll along, he points out the greenhouse that is used each day for the classes in horticulture.

Each day, a teacher who is well liked comes in from the outside to teach horticulture. The program has two purposes. One is to take care of plants on the grounds, and the other is to teach the art of planting.

The assignment, he says, is great from May 1 to October 1 but cold as the Arctic Circle the rest of the year.

Wednesday, October 23, 1993

Here's something that amounts to a crisis at Schuykill.

One inmate who has always received a perfect score of four on inspection today received a three, and he's livid. The reason his score was marked down was because the hacks found a dust ball behind his locker.

Before he came to Schuykill, he earned $500,000 a year as a senior partner in one of Pennsylvania's most prestigious law firms. Today, his life has been ruined by a dust ball.

By 5:30 p.m., the fog has burned off, and I head to the track to walk off cabin fever. It is drizzling, and the only other person on the track is Jim Tayoun, a political colleague from Philadelphia, a Lebanese, and a member of the city council who was found guilty of accepting payoffs. He's five feet ten, 185 pounds, with black hair, a dark complexion, and strong features, desert forged.

He pays me a compliment.

"In the two and a half weeks you have been here," he says, "you have proven yourself to be made of fine leather."

"Fine leather" is a reference in the Middle East to the very best of leather, which is used in the making of pouches to carry water or wine in the desert. Only the toughest, purest leather can survive the rigors.

Jim Tayoun was the perfect ethnic pol. He knew how to handle people. He knew how to get along. He knew where the best jobs were.

Having owned a restaurant in Philadelphia, he was assigned to the kitchen here at Schuykill. He knew how to prepare food, but (more important) he knew who should get the food first- the hacks, the administration, Fr. Dene.

When I arrived, we had an affinity. We were both urban, both ethnic, and, as I have said, we both had been city councilors, he in Philadelphia, I in Boston.

I met with him in the Carter campaign, but he was not with us. Although he was a Democrat, he was a pro-Nixon conservative who was allied with the hard-nosed mayor, Frank Rizzo. They all maintained they were Carter people, but in reality they didn't like Carter or anybody associated with him. Nevertheless, in spite of them, Carter won Philadelphia and Pennsylvania.

Even though it violated the rules, the hacks permitted Tayoun to keep a typewriter, and he used it to write a book on how to prepare for prison. That is, what to pack, how to get ready mentally, and so forth. I didn't think much of the book, and, to be honest, he's too cozy with the hacks.

Call it instinct, but in prison, no one does well. If somebody appears to be doing well, the assumption is that he's swapping information with the hacks.

As inmates, we don't need proof. In prison, these things are not driven by democracy.

Tonight, I walked by what may be the most bizarre character here, an inmate from *A* group who has the Howard Hughes phobia.

Everyone calls him Hand Washer because he washes his hands twenty times a day. Hand Washer refuses to shake hands. If you stick out your hand to shake his, he withdraws.

He's forty-five years old, six feet two, with jet black hair cut in the shape of a cereal bowl. He looks like Stan Laurel of Laurel and Hardy, but without the smile.

He thinks everything has germs. He throws up a lot and takes serious doses of medication. He was convicted of something to do with stealing family funds.

Hand Washer is like the walking dead. He's tall, thin, gaunt, stooped over. He keeps his head down, and his eyes, too, rarely looking at anyone. To see him, you'd think he just lost his best friend. The truth is, he's probably never had a best friend.

Hand Washer demonstrated a weakness in washing his hands compulsively, and as a result, the sharks were all over him.

The first time I met him, I tried to strike up a conversation.

"How's it going?" I said.

He stared at me and said, "How's it feel to talk to a serial killer?"

Everybody makes fun of him because this is a cruel place and the rule is survival of the fittest. He doesn't belong in prison. He's dying a thousand deaths.

When he walks by, inmates yell, "Hey, go wash your hands, asshole" or "Stop making so much fucking noise."

He makes no response.

His face is like ice. If he smiled, it would crack.

Thursday, October 21, 1993

This morning, I'm on the call sheet to go to the doctor to have blood drawn. I'm being tested for AIDS. How sensitive of the hacks to test for AIDS. How intelligent of them to wait three weeks. How much damage could have been done in that time?

Later in the morning, while I'm waiting to see the dentist, a young inmate comes in and sits next to me.

"Is the dentist in?"

"Yeah."

His face is swollen, and he's in obvious pain. When the dentist emerges, the young man jumps up to complain of his pain.

"Do you have an appointment?" asks the dentist.

"No, but I have a lot of pain."

"Make an appointment through normal channels."

The inmate knew that meant a wait of seven days.

I interjected.

"He can have my appointment. I'll reschedule."

The dentist looked at me.

"Mind your own business."

At lunch, my companion is Jacob, a Hassidic Jew from Brooklyn, whom I respect. He made the administration toe the mark on his religious beliefs. He made sure his meals were 100 percent kosher. He was not afraid to telephone his people in Brooklyn to put on the pressure, knowing the last thing the BOP wants is the entire Hassidic community on its back.

Walking the track, I am advised by inmates that my behavior in the dentist's office was ill-advised, that I run the risk of what is called "Diesel Therapy."

It's a form of BOP torture. Your feet are manacled in irons. Your hands are cuffed, and you are seated three abreast on a bus called the Silver Bullet, then driven north or south for up to thirty hours without the opportunity to use the bathroom.

This punishment is saved for inmates the hacks hate or from whom they are trying to elicit information. Some inmates who have been through it find it painful even to discuss.

This afternoon, in the bathroom, I saw Hand Washer. He was scrubbing his hands. It's a warm day, but he's dressed in extra clothing, as if the temperature were thirty degrees. He thinks that will ward off germs.

His job here is in the mechanical house, where he sits by himself from three to eleven, monitoring dials for water pressure and the like. His face is ice.

When I saw him, I said hello.

He didn't answer.

Friday, October 22, 1993

At 7:30 a.m. work call, I head to the library. It's 100 yards away, but it takes thirty minutes to get there because of the frequent stops to talk to inmates.

I open the library. It's become a different place. It's fun now. It's turned into a political hangout, where I get a chance to dispense political theory, along with advice on legal, marital, and medical matters, and even counseling for budding revolutionaries.

It's a lot like a neighborhood barbershop.

After lunch, a crisis develops.

As it happens, the staff of six who are assigned to keep the library clean is also responsible for cleaning the Wellness Center, that expensive workout facility for hacks. The advantage to the administration in having the library crew clean the Wellness Center is that there will be no record that inmates are cleaning up after guards.

On this day, when I arrive at the library, I am told to go to the Wellness Center to clean it. That surprises me, because I know three of our crew already had been assigned to the Wellness Center.

And so, I ask about them.

"What happened to the guys already assigned there?"

"They're on light duty," says the hack.

Now, "light duty" is a term that means an inmate is disabled for one reason or another, and therefore not obliged to exert himself so much as to empty a wastebasket, buff the floor, or even walk the one mile to the Wellness Center.

The news angers and frustrates me, and I demand to know who these light-duty patriots are. This place is crawling with fakers. And as the day goes on, I become more and more infuriated.

Dinner tonight is lobster Newburg over rice, beef barley soup, French garlic bread, ice cream, and cake. What do you suppose they're serving at your local homeless shelter or state school for the handicapped?

It's eight p.m., the movie hour, and this is a big weekend. *Unforgiven*, *Black Rain*, and *The Last of the Mohicans*. My Jewish friends invited me to Jewish services, after which they are showing *Yankee Doodle Dandy*, the story of George M. Cohan, staring Jimmy Cagney, a great flick. It is common for a religious group to invite nonmembers to view a movie before or after service, but as with the Catholics, a guest is not expected to attend services.

These are especially tense days.

Matters are complicated because of the World Series. I am reminded of one of the first rules I learned when I arrived, that the two worst spots are the chow line and the TV room, which is so volatile tonight that the hacks show up to referee.

I had planned to write anyway, so I passed on Jimmy Cagney and the World Series. My cellmate likes TV, especially *Star Trek*, and so that helps our compatibility. While he's watching TV, I'm writing.

Saturday, October 23, 1993

After yesterday's incident, my blood pressure is at the boiling point. For any inmate to claim light duty while working in the library is ludicrous.

We had a guy on medical dispensation. That excused him from being required to lift anything heavier than seven pounds, and yet I'd see this guy in the gym, pressing 350 pounds.

What irritates me it that every inmate knows that whatever work he doesn't do is passed on to the next inmate. In this case, that's me! This time, the goldbricker is from New England. He's part of a motorcycle gang, Hell's Angels or Hell's Devils or some dumb name like that. He was convicted of growing and selling pot, and he looks the part—pony-tail, ragged beard, dirty clothes.

He is on light duty because of a bad back, I'm told, but I saw him playing basketball yesterday, with plenty of body contact. And later, he walked by me on the track at a fast pace.

And I'm doing his work?

Well, I'm determined to confront Ponytail and anyone else in the library who claims he's on light duty.

There are so many problems within these walls.

One inmate named Marty, an ophthalmologist serving sixteen months for medical fraud, is deteriorating before my eyes. He's stopped shaving. He shows symptoms of hypochondria. His shoes don't fit. The flu shot made him ill. Food has caused him to break out in a rash.

At one point, we thought we were going to lose him. He slipped into a serious depression. He let his facial hair grow. He didn't comb the hair on his head. On days when he shaved, he'd miss big patches, and he'd cut himself while shaving. He was a psychological basket case.

Today, I had a talk with him.

"You've got to straighten out, Marty. You've got a long time to go here. Don't let these guys beat you down."

He talked of problems at home, how defenseless he was, and how he no longer seemed able to cope. He was in despair that his daughter was about to get married and that he would not be permitted to attend her wedding.

Another inmate in trouble is Bob, who is eating himself into an early grave. He came in fat. He's put on twenty pounds. And he's still at it. When not in the dining hall, he fills his face with junk food—chips, popcorn, candy, soda. I'd like to reach out to Marty and Bob, but these issues are individual, and a guy has to help himself.

Every one of us here is going through his own hell. Some of us disguise it better.

Walking the track, I chat with Stephen, who was a gardener until he was assigned to the warehouse, and he feeds me information about missing merchandise.

He's about forty-eight years old. He has sandy hair and a light complexion. He's five feet ten and 175 pounds, most of it baby fat that rings his stomach. He's so soft he seems never to have worked a day in his life.

From his shirt pocket, he pulls a piece of yellow legal paper with notes in longhand that list missing goods, TVs, lawnmowers, computers, clothes, washing machines.

Then he whispers, "There are real crimes going on around this place, but the real criminals are not in the prison. They're guarding us."

Steve maintains the inventory they take at the warehouse is phony, that goods are simply stolen and then, on inventory sheets, the hacks will list thirty-two TVs, for example, when there are none in the warehouse. The same with other equipment, even sit-down power mowers.

He said that sometimes, the goods inmates sign for never come in, and the people in charge know it.

Later, I'm walking with my friend Jim, who says that Polecat is the toughest white guy he's ever met. He's about forty-five, six feet one, 200 pounds, and he is in exceptional physical condition. Coming from South Boston, he trusts no one. He's here for nine years.

Tonight, I was going through chow line with Polecat.

Now, chow in prison is like chow in the Marine Corps boot camp. It's one of those rare moments in the day when you have a modicum of control over your life, when you are less subject to the whims of petty bureaucracy, the petty drill instructor, the petty hack.

In prison, food is important. On a bad day, it's the only enjoyment, and because you spend a lot of time in line for a meal (sometimes and hour) it's important to make sure you're in line with someone you like.

That's why I was in line tonight with Polecat, a frequent companion and, as Jim says, without challenge, the baddest guy in the place. Age did not matter, or skin color, or ethnicity—nobody at Schuykill was beyond Polecat's influence.

Usually, he avoids trouble, but going through chow line today, Polecat was involved in an incident that shook everybody and served as a reminder that for all the humor here, there is violence lurking beneath the surface. Day or night, there is never a moment when the threat doesn't hang in the air. It can break out at any moment. It's pervasive.

After filling his tray, Polecat went back to the salad bar because he had forgotten utensils.

Then, he forgot something else. He forgot one of the most important rules, and so he reached across an inmate's tray, something that is never, ever done in prison. It's a violation of space and a health hazard. Who knows, for example, what's on someone's sleeve?

At any rate, the guy across whose tray Polecat reached is among the meanest characters at Schuykill, a black guy from New York who has served time at several prisons and is here now serving ten years for pushing heroin.

He's not racist.

To be sure, he hates white guys.

But he also hates black guys.

At the time, the dining room was crowded with maybe 200 guys, some at tables, some in line.

Suddenly, the air is split by the voice of the black guy, screaming at Polecat.

"Hey, you dumb, white motherfucker, you ever go near my food again, I'll cut your heart out."

Everybody heard. All other conversations stopped. Everybody was waiting to see what Polecat would do. When Polecat spoke, his voice was soft, his words menacing.

"Make your move," he said.

"Stay the fuck away from my food."

"There's nothing between us now but your hot air," said Polecat, icily, and then leaning in so they were face to face: "No matter how this comes out, you're gonna lose an eye. Now, put that fuckin' tray down and come outside."

In the end, other inmates, some black and some white, stepped in to separate them, and to everyone's relief, the threat of immediate violence subsided.

We need a lot of things at Schuykill.

More racial tension is not one of them.

After lunch, I am approached by Jimmy and a few others in the Jewish group. Some guys resent the Jewish group because, although there are only a few of them, they have gained a great deal for themselves. I don't resent them, though. I congratulate them for their fight. If you're an inmate here, you don't get anything unless you fight for it. The Jewish guys are tough and decent, and what they want from me now is help in trying to arrange a classroom for a bar mitzvah.

Working with other library personnel, we fix up a classroom, buff the floor, and set up the tables for refreshments.

A social note: the guy being bar mitzvahed does not have to worry about his brother attending the ceremony. His brother is here doing time.

Tonight, Catholic Mass is offered by Fr. Dene for his mother and father.

It's 10:00 p.m., and when the music is blasting, this place reminds me of the movie *One Flew Over the Cuckoo's Nest*.

On the other hand, it's hard not to laugh at what goes on here.

Where else will you find a Korean obsessed with singing "Danny Boy" one minute and then "Hava Negilla" the next?

Sunday, October 24, 1993

I wake at seven, which is late for me, the longest I've slept in months. When I get home, I'll have to hire a three-piece band to play in my bedroom so I can fall asleep.

At brunch, I'm looking for Ponytail, the jerk on light duty. I spot him sitting with two guys from New England. There's an empty seat. I sit down and get right to the point.

"Listen, you may have fooled the administration with that bullshit about a bad back and light duty, but as far as I'm concerned, when I come to work at the library at four o'clock, I expect the place to look as good as it was when I left it, because I'm not picking up after you or anyone else."

He looks like he's ready to say something, but I beat him to the verbal punch.

"And if you have a problem with what I'm telling you, let me tell you this—I'll throw you and your bad back and your fucking pony tail right out that window over there."

The other two guys grab their trays and disappear.

As I leave, it occurs to me that too many rats in the dining room have witnessed the confrontation and that within the hour, they'll squeal to the hacks and the administration that I had threatened Ponytail.

Every time you think that this place is as nutty as it gets, sure enough, it gets nuttier.

Stephen, who works at the warehouse, was given a weed whacker and told to trim around the flower garden. Never having used a weed whacker before, or any other power tool, for that matter, he managed to whack down the weeds all right, but in the process, he also managed to whack down quite a few flowers.

Having failed so conspicuously with the weed whacker, he was then graduated to the power mower and blower. Because of his inexperience, he manipulated the machine in such a way that it flung a rock the size of a baseball through the windshield of a car owned by a hack.

Stephen, as a result, is being congratulated by other inmates.

"It's amazing," Stephen says. "They make sure no one leaves the warehouse with a pencil, lest we turn it into a weapon, and then what do they give us crazy inmates? Chain saws."

At 10:30 p.m., it's lights out. Another week gone by. I expect to hear tomorrow about my altercation with Ponytail. But I should note that he got the message, apparently, because when I reported for work tonight, the library was spotless, floor buffed, and even the wastebaskets were emptied. Maybe he's not as stupid as he looks.

Monday, October 25, 1993

My friend Camel is a regular now at waking me up, and sure enough, he comes by at 5:15 a.m. As a friendly gesture as this is, the odd thing is he never sits with me at breakfast. No special reason. He has his group, I have mine.

At breakfast, there is plenty of food, and there's also plenty of speculation about what is likely to happen to me for threatening Ponytail. There's no question, apparently, that I'll pay a price.

After breakfast, on my way to the track, I stop at the latrine, which, by the way, is filthy.

Prison is bizarre, but within a prison, the latrine is even more bizarre. One reason for rising early is to be among the first in the latrine, because (there's no delicate way to say this) guys in prison don't have the best hygiene. Toilets go unflushed. The sink might be encrusted with nasal excretions.

If you get there early, though, and you avoid lines, you get a longer shower, you might find a clean sink, and you won't have guys hovering over you while you brush your teeth.

Today, in the latrine, the inmate on duty has heard about my confrontation with Ponytail, and he's speculating that I might be transferred out of the library as punishment. He has a suggestion.

"You ought to think about the latrine," he says. "I'm on my way to a halfway house, and so they'll be looking for somebody. At least you're your own boss here."

Later, at the track, I mention to Jim my conversation about going to work at the latrine.

He's surprised.

"Joe, that's the dirtiest job here," he said, shocked that I would even consider such an idea. "On the other hand, the guy who does it sure has a lot of time off."

At noon, I am summoned by Mr. Heater, the head of the education department.

"What happened over the weekend?" he asks.

Without using names, I tell him.

"Some of my fellow inmates who work with me in the library are on phony light duty, and they feel that's an excuse for not cleaning the library, which is light duty anyway!"

"Well, I'm sorry, but I agree with them. If they're on light duty, they're not to do any of that work, and that includes even walking to the Wellness Center."

His attitude is clear.

So are my options.

If I remain in the library, I'm liable to throw that lying, lazy Ponytail right out a window. And so, to ensure that my four-month sentence isn't turned into a year, I suggest a change in jobs.

Mr. Heater agrees.

"I'd rather work with books than urinals," I said, "but I'd like to request a transfer to latrine duty."

He thought I was joking.

I wasn't.

After the one o'clock count, I search out the latrine worker who first suggested I apply for his job, and oddly enough, where do I find him but in the library.

In a walk around the track, he gives me twenty reasons why I should not apply for latrine duty and one reason why I should, and that is that I would be my own boss. After my encounters with Ponytail and Mr. Heater, being my own boss sounds mighty attractive.

At 6:30 p.m., at Catholic services, it's an awakening to me how much strength I draw from these services and from the inmates who attend.

After service, one of the toughest-looking inmates here, who is serving eight years, gives me a copy of the "Prisoner's Prayer," and he urges me, for peace of mind, to do what he does—read it daily.

After service, Fr. Dene announces that the movie will be *Lethal Weapon II*, which I have seen a number of times. Still, the ambience here in the visitor room is calm by comparison to the rest of the prison, and so I stay.

It's 10:30 p.m., and as I lie here waiting to fall asleep, I can't shake the picture in my mind of Andy Griffith in the role of PLO (Permanent Latrine Orderly) in the movie *No Time for Sergeants*.

That's me.

And so, Joe Timilty, who has gone from the White House to the Big House, is now on his way to the outhouse.

Tuesday, October 26, 1993

On my way to breakfast, I am worried that I'm not putting on weight. I never miss a meal, and I eat fattening foods that I haven't touched in twenty years: eggs, pancakes, French toast, doughnuts, ice cream, cake, milk.

Polecat says I spend too much time on the track walking.

On the track, after breakfast, I see Jim.

"What have you decided?"

"It's the latrine," I tell him. "The pluses outweigh the minuses."

So, say hello to Schuykill's new PLO!

The latrine is located in the administration building between the library and the dining room. In recent months, it's become a problem spot, and so it gets a lot of attention from the administration. On occasion, it has been used for every illegitimate activity imaginable in prison.

The latrine is open twenty-four hours a day, seven days a week. There are five sinks and five urinals in one room, four toilets in the second, and there are mirrors and chrome that need cleaning. Also, the stock has to be replenished regularly.

So, this is my new role in life, and I still can't believe it.

Joe Timilty, Permanent Latrine Orderly.

Newspapers back in Boston would have a party with that tidbit.

Tonight, at nine o'clock, Polecat comes into my cube after his kick-boxing exercises. He's done the math. The cost of keeping us here is $35,000, compared to the cost of an electronic bracelet for the leg that would enable the BOP to monitor a convict's location to ensure that he never left his home.

As we look around *A* range, the waste of resources is stunning. Across the nation, there are 90,000 people in these camps, many of them first-time, nonviolent offenders who enjoy the best of food, the best of movies.

This is what alternative sentencing was meant to correct.

Some examples are more obvious than others. Take my friend, Sam the Colostomy Man. He's seventy-one years old, an Italian built like a fire hydrant. He has a head full of wavy hair, and if Francis Ford Coppola were looking for a stand-in for Marlon Brando as the Godfather, he'd want Sam the Colostomy Man.

Sam had a major operation for cancer that requires him to carry a bag permanently, and as a result he requires frequent visits to the hospital. His medication is expensive, and worst of all, life here, in the most intimate sense, is horrendous for him.

He will shower only after other inmates have gone to bed or else he gets up to shower at 4:30 a.m.

Sometimes, he cannot get to the bathroom on time, and the result when he gets there is an impossibly dirty situation. We are very protective of him, though. When Sam has an accident, the supposedly hardhearted guys here take care of him, help him clean up.

Everybody's supposed to have access to the latrine, but when Sam's in there, having a problem that results in the sinks and the walls being dirty, Sam's friends secure toilet paper across the door to signal that temporarily the latrine is closed while they clean up the latrine to save him the embarrassment.

Occasionally, an inmate will challenge the lockout, saying what's the story with the shithouse, and the answer is, "Don't ask any questions. Go somewhere else."

Every once in a while, a new inmate arrives and complains about the stench, but he is quickly brought into line.

Now, why wouldn't Sam the Colostomy Man be a prime candidate for home confinement? Instead, the BOP does everything it can to keep him here.

It's clear the BOP is protecting its job base, that it sees alternatives such as halfway houses and home confinement as a threat.

And so, the BOP falls back on the tired pitch that law and order is the issue. Keep the criminals locked up. Throw away the key. Three strikes, and you're out. Congress, meanwhile, is toothless, and either cannot see the waste, or does not want to.

In the end, who is gouged for the costs?

The taxpayers.

Wednesday, October 27, 1993

Today is my first day on the new job.

My friends call me Permanent Latrine Orderly. This job is looked upon as the worst in the system, and I must confess, I never thought that, at age fifty-five, I'd be consumed with coming up with a better methodology for people to go to the bathroom.

As I survey the scene, the most important weapons are latex gloves and plenty of Lysol. Before I'm through, they'll be calling this the Lysol room.

As my predecessor learned, this is not an easy task.

In an effort to get inmates to clean up after themselves, he'd put out a small dish of candy that he had purchased at the commissary with his own money.

On the dish, he attached a note.

It said, "If you clean up after yourself, please help yourself."

It was run on the honor system.

Naturally, the first inmate into the bathroom stole all the candy.

Other inmates tell me that previously, the administration had assigned the latrine to Jacob the Hassidic Jew, but that did not work out.

Jacob never left the latrine.

But he never cleaned it, either. Sometimes he'd be standing ankle-deep in discarded paper towels.

The administrator would yell at the deputy who would yell at Jacob who would shrug his shoulders and say that it was against his religion to clean somebody else's bathroom.

It's 5:30 p.m., and time for a meeting of my team.

Each inmate has a team of administration personnel that, according to the BOP manual, are supposed to assemble on a regular basis to check on his progress, his good time, and any requests pending for transfer to another facility or to a halfway house.

These meetings are a prime example of the disdain administrators have for inmates.

Because the BOP, the Department of Justice, and ultimately Congress expect these meetings to be held, the administration here goes through the motions, barely.

They schedule inmates fifteen minutes apart, then cut five minutes off that.

The cruel part is that these transfers are crucial to inmates and their families. Halfway house time is of paramount concern in terms of not only morale but also mental health.

After waiting months for these meetings, inmates are disappointed to discover that they last about eight minutes.

I had been warned that if I had questions, I should limit 'em to two, keep 'em, short, and write 'em down.

My team consisted of Mr. Hurt, Mr. Heater, and my coordinator, Miss Personality.

She hates me, but I'm in good shape in spite of that, because she hates everybody, and so, I was confident that what she held against me was no more than what she held against every other inmate.

And in every case, she held everything against everybody.

I was in the room for ten minutes. Miss Personality read off my sentence.

I was asked if I had any questions.

"Yes, I have a question. In regard to my transportation home in February, do I have to go on the BOP bus, the Silver Bullet, or could I take private transportation?"

No one knew what to say.

"We'll get back to you, but for now, you're excused."

Thursday, October 28, 1993

I wake up at 5:15 a.m. and head for the shower. Since I started my new job, I find myself washing my hands more often and taking more showers.

At breakfast, a new inmate is wiping tables. He's not likely to get a hernia here. He's from Brooklyn, Italian, one of John Gotti's lieutenants on the street, and he reminds me of Joe Piscopo.

Danny T., as he's called, is doing big time, finishing seven years on a thirteen-year sentence. This guy is straight from central casting. I can see him on a street corner in Manhattan, tanned, duded up, and flicking the ash from a big cigar as he climbs into a Caddie with fish tails. If you watch closely, you can see older inmates from New York, New Jersey, and Philly go out of their way to pay Danny T. respect.

This morning, he's sitting at our table, and he's on a roll, talking politics, welfare, homelessness in such steady chatter that nobody can get a word in edgewise.

"Nobody should be homeless. Nobody should be selling pencils. Nobody should be at the intersections of New York washing the windows of your car. In fact," he says, "I used to give 'em ten dollars with a request that they not wash my windows."

Everybody laughs.

"I've got a friend in New York," he says. "He was intrigued to watch the night deposit business, wherein successful gentlemen would pull up and drop bags of money into a night deposit slot. So, my friend, he puts on overalls, walks across the street, and puts a sign on the slot that says it's out of order. Then he places a metal box on the floor with a sign that says, 'Place Deposits Here!' Then, he waits across the street. The first car pulls up. A person steps out, reads the two signs, drops his deposit in the temporary metal box and drives away. My friend walks across the street, retrieves the package, and then retreats to his hiding place. He does this for one entire night, and in the morning, he's made a year's pay. The man had Brooklyn imagination."

This afternoon, I notice the bulletin board has me listed for "A&O," which stands for admission and orientation. It's an eight hour briefing every new inmate has to go through.

"Bring a good book," says Paul.

"I'd rather have a root canal," says my cellmate. Billy.

Friday, October 29, 1993

I'm on time for the "A&O" meeting, and so I'm able to get a seat in the last row. I see Danny T. from Brooklyn with his *Sports Illustrated*.

Everybody's here, Pat, the gay, and Marty, who's shaved and got a haircut and is getting his act together.

"What is the purpose of this meeting?" asks Billy.

"Routine," says Danny T.

"They're going to issue us guns, knives, and brass knuckles for the day we go home."

Into the room walks my friend Walter, who is now retired as a motorman for the New York City transit authority. He's frail but a funny bastard who tells the story how he was traveling through a southern community with a young date. Walter was arrested, and they took his crack pipe. That's what upset him, that they never returned his crack pipe.

Walter's five feet five, weighs 135, has rotten teeth, and speaks in an exaggerated black dialect.

He's seventy, but it's not a well seventy; in fact, it looks as if he may expire at any minute. The gray hair that remains is hidden under a red baseball cap. The hacks are always trying to get him to go to work, but he insists that he needs a hernia operation and that he can't work until he has it. They try to give him easy duty, but he won't buy in to it. The reality is that for all his frailty, Walter has never been sick, and when he utters the word "work," he winks at us. He's at Schuykill for only sixty days. They got him for transporting drugs over the state line. I don't think he's been in another institution.

Unlike the rest of us, as the "A&O" meeting begins, Walter insists on sitting down front. As he puts it, "I want to be able to fall asleep in the man's face."

At 8:15 a.m., Mr. Grille arrives, the first speaker. He gives us a schedule. Twenty people will talk to us at thirty-minute intervals over the next two days. Grille wants us to sign a paper stating that we have heard all the speakers and understand all the issues. Otherwise, he says, we'll have to attend the next session.

I say in an Irish whisper that the reason I landed at Schuykill is that I signed the wrong papers, and everybody laughs.

The next speaker is Mr. Hurt, whose public-speaking coach must have advised him that dropping a verbal bomb would wake up the audience.

"If you escape from here," he begins, "we'll find you and bring you back, and we will add a minimum of eighteen months to your sentence."

Then he gets solemn.

"And we *will* find you," he intones, "even if it takes twenty-five years."

Inmates don't like Hurt. As he talks, we laugh, and he thinks we're laughing with him, when in reality, we're laughing at him.

"I must remind you that you are not permitted to make business phone calls," he says. "If you are caught, you will lose all phone privileges. Once we caught an inmate on a call trying to sell a 727 aircraft for a drug deal in Central America for two million dollars."

From the audience, someone yelled, "The cheap bastard."

Saturday, October 30, 1993

In the late morning, an inmate asks whether I'll be putting out a dish of candy.

"No, but we are going to install pay toilets."

In line for lunch, I overhear two guys talking about the inmate who was murdered, Phil Kagan. Murder is a strong word, maybe too strong. But the Kagan story keeps coming up. Every time I open my notebook, I think of him. Phil, I'm told, was a loudmouth, an obnoxious New York lawyer who hated everyone. He had been found guilty in some sort of stock fraud case, and he was bitter, and he was angry.

My friend Jim put it best. "There's no excuse for what the officials didn't do for him."

In the two weeks prior to his death, Kagan rarely came to the cafeteria. On one occasion, when he did, he pointedly thanked Big John, a Mafia character in the kitchen, for having sent over dinner when Kagan couldn't get to the chow hall. After Kagan left, several inmates needled Big John, saying that he was a softie after all and not the two-bit leg-breaking Mafioso he pretended to be. Big John shrugged.

"He's a prick," he said of Kagan, "and I don't like him. But what am I supposed to do? Let the poor bastard starve?"

Ordinarily, I do my push-ups and sit-ups in my cube. Today, after lunch, I head for the weight room, but it's wall-to-wall muscle, and there is no room for a newcomer in Testosterone City, where forty iron-pumping bodies are grunting and groaning in a room meant for twenty.

At Mass tonight, Fr. Dene dedicates the service to his dead uncle.

Sunday, October 31, 1993

It's 5:15 a.m., and my man, Camel, is right on time. He enjoys telling people that he wakes me every morning. Today is another dark, dreary, rainy day. I had planned a walking weekend, but not in this rain, not with one pair of shoes.

It's noon, and I am working out inside today, three hours. Polecat tells me there used to be three state-of-the-art stationary bikes, purchased by the recreation department. Unfortunately, the units were assembled by in-mates who didn't know what they were doing, and so the bikes soon broke down. The inmates were blamed, and the bikes were stored, unrepaired, in a room across the hall. Paul got a key to the room and showed me the bikes—very expensive, virtually new, and now sitting idle, covered with cobwebs.

It's 8:00 a.m., and I'm on the cell block.

My neighbor from New York has a talent for poetry. It's a way for him to express himself, his life, his family, his being black, and the blood that has been shed by his brothers.

His name is Kiester. He shows me writing samples, and I encourage him. He's smart. He's aware that I ask a lot of questions and that I write a lot. He has good instincts. He knows that something is going on. Now in his late thirties, Kiester grew up in Harlem, a career criminal. He's lost most of his immediate and extended family to violence, and he alludes to that in his poetry.

He has all the black mannerisms that Eddie Murphy makes fun of. In terms of vocabulary, he is the master of malapropisms, often using the wrong word, or, when he does have the right word, mispronouncing it. He is very funny. I lie in my rack and listen to him banter and laugh aloud.

I don't know whether his poetry is any good, but I like it. He writes from the gut about sleeping in the streets and what it's like to wake up and see your small son sleeping on a box top.

Here's one he gave me today:

Sign of the time.
Another day,
Same old crime.
A young man is killed,
'Cause he don't have a dime.
Day after day, new mothers cry,
Another son killed,
Another drive-by
Time after time,
Same old crime.

It's 9:30 a.m. The forecast is for five inches of snow. It's the last night of October, Halloween. I feel as if I have been here forever, but it's been only a month. Or as the long-termers say to me, "You just got here." In the rack, I'm reading. The Boston Police Athletic Association has sent me a series of three novels by Nelson DeMille. I thoroughly enjoy his writing style.

Monday, November 1, 1993.

It's 3:00 a.m., and the hacks come by. They roust the landscaping crew out of bed to go out and sand the paths and shovel the snow. It's freezing outside. This is what other inmates meant when they said, "Stay off the landscaping crew." Arriving at the latrine at 7:00 a.m., I'm stunned. How can a place get so dirty in one short weekend?

At 9:00 a.m., it is the second day of "A&O," and the crowd is getting tougher to control. While one dweeb is at the front of the room lecturing us about something or other, there is considerable talking at the back of the room. Hoping to establish his authority, the dweeb addresses an inmate at the back of the room, Mad Dog, who's carrying on a private conversation.

From the stage, the dweeb sneers at Mad Dog. "Do you wish to say something?"

From the back of the room comes Mad Dog's sneering reply, "Who the fuck's talking to you?"

Silence.

The dweeb stares at Mad Dog.

Mad Dog glares at the dweeb.

The dweeb thinks better of his momentary experimentation with macho behavior and goes back to delivering his boring speech.

The next speaker is Mr. McCarthy from food services, who looks like Mr. Peepers. He starts off on a shaky foot:

"I must tell you, there is not enough money in the budget to feed all of you properly because so many of you are stealing salt and pepper shakers, paper plates, and plastic utensils."

The audience lets out a moan. He tries again.

"I myself," he says in a whining voice, "would not eat the food, because I have seen how it is prepared."

On and on he drones, and then, realizing that he has lost the attention of the audience, he seeks to regain it with an apology.

"I am not very good at public speaking."

The auditorium erupts into thunderous applause.

He asks if anyone has a question. From the back of the room, an inmate asks, "Why do they serve the vegetables cold?"

"Well," says Mr. McCarthy, "that's so they won't screw them up by cooking them."

Next is the shrink who interviewed me several weeks ago. He's wearing the same ill-fitting jacket, and in a room full of guys with problems, he still appears to be the one in the most difficulty. Up and down the aisle he walks, staring at the inmates, appearing as if he is about to explode, and outlining the reasons why inmates might want to avail themselves of his staff.

In listening to the shrink, there is one consolation. No matter how little of his meaning you grasp, you know you're not missing much.

His favorite topic is suicide.

"Although we do not realize it," he says, "we are all prone to suicide. Watch your cellmates, and report it immediately if you see any signs of depression."

One inmate points a finger at the inmate beside him. Another hollers a name. Soon, everybody in the audience is pointing fingers and yelling out names. Among the names being yelled out are Mr. Hurt and Mr. Nye, the superintendent and his assistant.

Eyes twitching, the shrink then goes on to a topic of painful concern to everybody here—"Dear John" letters, that is letters from wives, girl-friends, or significant others that end a relationship and are, says the shrink, a potential contributor to suicides in prison. From the front row, in another Irish whisper, Walter R., the retired transit worker from New York, mutters that he'd like to get a couple of "Dear John" letters because he's caught between his wife and a couple of girlfriends, all of whom live in the same neighborhood and know one another.

Next is Rev. Brown, the black Protestant minister, who is well liked by inmates and who has just returned from his honeymoon with his new wife, who is, of all people, my coordinator, Miss Personality.

I promise to say some prayers for Rev. Brown.

Recognizing that he is the last person to speak in a program that runs two boring days, Rev. Brown is brief, and for that, we all thank God.

Tuesday, November 2, 1993

After a weekend and two days of "A&O," the latrine needs extra atten-tion. It's pretty nasty. Inmates who are in the administration building stop by to say hello, crack a few jokes, and move on. It makes time go by faster. As I am replacing toilet paper in the stalls, I notice one is occupied, although I didn't see anyone come in. After a considerable length of time passes, I check again. This time, I see no shoes under the door. Thinking perhaps the door is stuck, I push it open.

What a surprise!

There sits my man, Winslow, who cleans the floors just outside the latrine. Winslow is six feet five and weighs more than 400 pounds, and he's sound asleep.

"Oh, hi Joe," he says, waking up.

"Winslow, what are you doing here?"

"This is where I hide out mornings. It's a good place to get sleep."

How Winslow manages to hide that huge body in that tiny stall so as not to be seen is a mystery to me and a challenge to the laws of physical science.

Late morning, I am walking the track with Steve, who has cancer and needs medicine on his person at all times. Without it, he might die of an attack. The physician's assistant refuses to fill the prescription, saying that Steve has to see the doctor. (But it takes days for the doctor to arrive. Then, when the doctor finally writes the prescription, the wrong medicine arrives. Two and a half weeks pass before the proper medication is delivered.)

It's 7:00 p.m. I try to do my writing each night at this hour. I had to stop taking notes during the day. It was attracting too much attention. There is no way I can remember everything unless I make notes at night: a few well-chosen words recorded now will stimulate total recall later.

I've been in here thirty days now. I've settled into a pattern, and I'm glad to be out of the library. For me, that place was a danger zone.

At 10:30 p.m., it's lights out.

Wednesday, November 3, 1993

At 7:30 a.m., it's latrine call.

Wow!

Cleaning this place is like cleaning the men's room at Boston Garden after a Bruins game. We need some practice sessions here, guys. You're hitting everything but the urinal. What I need is a strategy to deal with inmates whose aim is awry.

Here's an idea. Why didn't I think of this before? I need tape, masking tape. I'll cut up Boston newspapers, the sports page, comics, political stories (all small print) and place them above the urinals. Because of the small print, guys will have to stand closer, and they'll be more likely to hit the urinal. Prison ingenuity: we aim to please, and your aim will help.

It's my second week at the latrine, and I haven't had an argument yet. The commodes don't talk back, and now the latrine has become the place to be in the morning, a social hangout. The kitchen help appreciate a clean latrine, and they bring the food that they're preparing in the kitchen: steak, chicken, pizza, all the good stuff.

That presents a problem, though. Where do I eat this food? I can't take it out into the corridor, because the hacks would see me. So, I have to exercise the other option and learn to eat in the latrine.

After lunch, I'm obliged to attend another meeting.

Now that Miss Personality is back from her honeymoon with the Protestant minister, she's meeting with all her wards, and today it's my turn. While I'm waiting, a secretary asks her for whom she'll vote in November.

"I never vote," she answers in a voice meant for me to hear.

Great. Here's a woman getting her salary from the federal government, married to someone who's making his salary from the federal government, and she can't find time to vote. Why do I suspect she's among the first to complain when government doesn't work?

"The last time I voted," she says, "was when I lived in Massachusetts."

Oh-oh, I say to myself. I'm in trouble. Sure enough, Miss Personality tells me that I'll be lucky to get out on my due date. Fifteen times, she addresses me as "Senator," and you don't have to be a mental giant to know that she means it negatively. It's clear she's baiting me, and it takes all my self-control not to say something nasty to her.

At 7:00 p.m., it's picture time.

The boxing team from *A* range lines up for photos, and as coach, I'm included. One thing is certain, if I run for office again, this photo may well be circulated by my opponent, because we all look like prisoners of war.

Among the profit-gouging enterprises in this institution that ought to be audited is the business of photographs. What does it cost to make a print, ten cents? Twenty? And what do they charge inmates? $1.75.

Thursday, November 4, 1993

My latrine is looking better and better. But now, I have a different problem. It's becoming a hangout. Inmates are coming and going, hanging around outside. It's beginning to draw attention, which is precisely what I don't want.

Here's an example of the internal workings of a prison. The place is buzzing today. Everybody's talking about the inmate who left here on a "writ," which means he went to testify for the government against someone.

Occasionally, that kind of information is speculative. In this case, it is authenticated by a newspaper article that says the inmate testified at a trial in Connecticut where five men, two of them elected officials, were found guilty of bank fraud. The underground network here spares no effort in identifying him as a rat. Although our copier is broken down, somehow, from somewhere, someone manages to produce fifty copies of the newspaper article, which are taped all over the camp.

Upon his return, the inmate involved complains to the administration that he has been exposed, and he asks for a transfer from *A* to *C* range, thinking he'll be safer there. The reality is that for the rest of his time here, his life will be a misery.

From the warehouse, inmates have been giving me advance copies of menus, and I notice more and more discrepancies between what the menu promises and what is actually served. Inmates working at the warehouse tell horror stories about missing food, stolen equipment, damaged goods, phony inventories.

Two items that leave the warehouse and rarely make it to the kitchen are cheese and ice cream. The hacks, naturally, accuse the inmates, but it is absurd to assume that we could possibly steal hundreds of gallons of ice cream, for example, as they charge. Where would we store it? How could we keep it from melting?

The camp at Schuykill could not survive a legitimate audit. When inventory is taken, the hacks in charge tell the inmates what to write down.

The hacks insist that the audit count boxes they say are full of food, but which inmates know have long been empty.

In the early afternoon, walking the track, Scott tells of the night he arrived. He had been in a county jail in Washington, DC. They cuffed him, shackled him, and bussed him to Schuykill. He arrived after midnight and climbed into an upper bunk. When he woke in the morning, he was shocked to see his cellmate.

At breakfast, he asked if Schuykill was co-ed, and everybody laughed.

Scott had spent the night sleeping above June Bug, a transsexual who had undergone surgery that gives him the appearance of being a woman, and he loved to flaunt the success of the surgery.

June Bug, who is way out of the closet, is referred to by many inmates as "she." He has bleached blond hair. He's six feet one, 145 pounds, and someone said he has a relative who's a federal judge somewhere. He irons clothes for inmates in return for cigarettes.

Once, June Bug had a boyfriend who used to hang around with him, or go out with him, as other inmates described it. He was Spanish, came from Philadelphia, and he was a weight lifter who worked in the kitchen. Because of his romance with June Bug, Weight Lifter was persona non grata among the straight guys.

Someone asked Weight Lifter what he saw in June Bug.

"Fuck it," said Weight Lifter. "If June Bug wants to act like a woman, then there's nothing wrong with it."

Among straights, this conduct is utterly unacceptable. Many straight guys are on the lookout for guys whose behavior is suspect, who might be seen coming out of the shower together, or wandering into the woods a few minutes apart.

June Bug, by the way, is no longer at Schuykill. He was causing too much friction. The administration decided that he had too many relationships going at the same time.

At 10:45 p.m., it's lights out. Another day on the mountain.

Friday, November 5, 1993

At breakfast, Danny T. is telling jokes. He should be on *David Letterman*, because even if the jokes aren't funny, the way Danny T. tells them inspires laughter.

"In this one neighborhood, all the young guys played baseball. One said, 'Whatever else happens in heaven, I hope we can play baseball.' Another predicted that in heaven, the baseball fields would be perfect. They make a pact. The first one to die would come back and describe the baseball fields in heaven. Twenty years later, the first death occurs, and that night, the dead player appears to his friend in a dream. They talk baseball.

"'So what are the baseball fields like in heaven?'

"'There's good news and bad,' says the dead player. 'The good news is that the fields are perfect, the equipment never breaks, and the skies are always clear.'

"'Great! But what's the bad news?'

"'You're pitching tonight.'"

Everybody walks out of the cafeteria laughing.

At 9:00 a.m., Mr. Hurt comes by the latrine on a surprise inspection. He looks around, says nothing.

"It's difficult to keep this place clean," I remind him, "because it's open twenty-four hours a day, seven days a week."

"Yes, I know," he replies. "It should never have been built in this location."

Without another word, he turns and leaves. I still don't know what he was talking about.

On the bulletin board, I note the movie schedule for the week: *Indecent Proposal*, *King of Kings*, and *Passenger 57*, all first-run movies. Nothing but the best for us dangerous criminals.

It's dusk, that blue hour, sad and melancholy, and despite the cold, John C. and I are walking the track. He's about fifty years old, as near to an intellectual as you are likely to find here, and, as a result, he is tormented by other inmates. Because they treat him badly, I treat him well. I befriend him. He borrows books from my growing library (thanks to the Boston Police Athletic Association). I have no idea why John's here, and I have no intention of asking, but he is a walking example of the need for alternative sentencing.

Saturday, November 6, 1993

It's 5:15 a.m., but already, both washing machines are in use by inmates, who hire out to do the wash for other inmates. The cost ranges from $2.50 to $5.00, depending on how dirty your clothes are. It's not a bad deal. Your clothes are washed, dried, folded, and delivered to your cell. The washers are paid in the form of commissary chits, which they can use to buy everything from stamps and clothing to junk food.

These deals are illegal but essential to the financial and even mental health of the inmates with no family outside. Otherwise, inmates are paid eight to eleven cents an hour for a forty-hour week, about four dollars a week, or sixteen dollars a month. That figures out, after deductions, to a net of twelve dollars a month.

There are other opportunities to make money. The warehouse pays extra, and inmates who are licensed tradesmen are compensated at a higher rate. A master plumber might make twenty-five dollars a month.

In terms of compensation, the best job is Unicore, a private corporation here that makes equipment sold by and used in penitentiaries. It's a moneymaker for the BOP, and inmates who work for Unicore make as much as $1.50 an hour. Jobs there are highly prized. Inmates who owe a lot of money in fines to the federal government are assigned there without requesting it, and up to three quarters of their pay is applied to their fines.

By six, I've showered and shaved, and I'm still waiting for the washing machine. This is throwing me off schedule. I'm agitated. In prison, the little things get to you. This morning, I had the impression that another inmate had jumped ahead of me to the washing machine, and I was ready to fight him until a third inmate persuaded me that, in fact, the guy had been ahead of me.

At breakfast, I am greeted by the sweet aroma of coffee rolls, which means that Doc is on duty in the kitchen. Hacks assigned to the cafeteria make sure that no inmate gets more than one roll. One hack even follows one inmate to his table to take back an extra roll. At the same time, I can see the kitchen help going out the side door, back to their rooms, their coats bulging with coffee rolls for inmates who were too lazy to get up and come to the cafeteria.

Now comes my man, Camel. He's been watching the scene from the other side of the dining hall. He finishes his coffee roll and starts up to the serving line for a refill of coffee. He waits for the hack to be distracted, then grabs a plate with a second roll and heads for his table.

The hack spots him!

"Hey, put that back!"

Camel pretends he doesn't hear, takes the roll off the plate, and holds it in his hands. The hack strides to Camel's table.

"One roll to a customer," he intones.

Camel, looking hurt, says, "But I've already touched it." Meaning, of course, that it cannot be returned uncontaminated. The hack grabs the roll from Camel's hands, plunks it down on the plate, and returns the roll to the serving table.

Hoping to suggest even further contamination, Camel yells, "And I just went to the bathroom!"

Congratulations to the hack. He's done his job. From Camel he has rescued one roll that will be thrown away because now it has been handled by the guard as well as Camel. Meanwhile, I counted ten dozen rolls that were pilfered out the back door and delivered to Units One and Two.

On my way back to the unit, I hear young voices at the end of the hallway, which means that visiting hours will be starting soon. It's so incongruous here, the sound of children.

Elaine has been wanting to visit. On my last call home, she told me that a friend. Bob Kuehn, with a private airplane wanted to fly her down to see me.

I had made up my mind that for only four months, I would discourage visitors. They remind me too painfully of what I'm missing. But I'm advised that visitors have feelings, too, and people would think it strange if Elaine had to explain why she never saw this place. The truth is, though, that I'd rather serve an extra month than have her visit.

At noon, I'm on the track, with lots of time. If I were working in the library, I'd be working all day today, and if I tried to sneak out for a couple of miles, Ponytail undoubtedly would drop a dime on me.

What a guy!

Fr. Dene leaves a lot to be desired in what I have come to expect from clergy, but I find myself warming to him. Tonight I told him that the administration had taken away my Irish rosary beads. He laughed and gave me a pair someone left behind.

Now, I often wonder. Who had these rosary beads before me? Where was he from? What was he here for? How long did he stay? What did he pray for?

And why did he leave these rosary beads?

On leaving church, Pat invites me to a going away party for Anthony, an inmate from Massachusetts. Anthony was a chef in the kitchen. He was quiet, talked to few, and trusted fewer. He weighed 280 when he arrived and trimmed to 225. No one ever saw him come or go, but there were nights when I would find on my pillow fresh fruit, like bananas, and I'd know they came from Anthony. I thought he didn't have many friends, but I was proved wrong.

The party on *D* range for Anthony is also a party to celebrate Pat's sixty-sixth birthday. The inmate running the show is the Bear, who's six feet four, 280 pounds. He wears cutoff shirts that expose powerful biceps and tattoos. What makes the Bear threatening is his demeanor, especially his walk. Everything about the Bear is awesome.

It's Saturday night at Schuykill, and what a party! There's a layout of Italian cold cuts, fresh Italian bread, cheeses, tuna fish, and a moist, freshly made cake inscribed with the names of Anthony and Pat.

It would be impossible to overstate the respect and affection these men have for one another.

Sunday, November 7, 1993

At 6:00 a.m., I check the latrine. There is a scene in the book and movie *No Time for Sergeants* in which the commanding officer comes into the latrine and, to his surprise, he is saluted by the rising of the toilet seats. I'd like to plan something like that for the brass here.

At 8:30 a.m., I call Elaine. If the weather is right, on Veterans Day, she and Bob are flying down. I find myself hoping it snows. That may be unfair and selfish, but my life here is in a pattern. Visitors set you back. It's a heart-wrenching experience that is difficult to explain. Only another inmate would understand.

The big topic today is the crime bill being debated in Congress. In the TV room, thirty to forty inmates are watching the CNN report on the bill. What appeals to inmates about this legislation are provisions for alternative sentencing, an increase in the rewards for good behavior, and, for first-time nonviolent offenders, home confinement instead of incarceration. Each inmate has a different version of what is said, what is intended, and what the legislation may or may not mean to each of us.

From the perspective of the BOP, any such report is helpful if it neutralizes inmates by creating a modicum of hope, however unrealistic. In the end, though, the BOP will do everything it can to prevent such legislation from passing, in part out of fear that there will be a decline in BOP jobs.

Congress, for its part, lacks the will to save taxpayer money. From the perspective here, it's mind-boggling to be aware of how misguided Congress is on this issue.

Today, we have new inmates, new problems. One new inmate is on the track, running, shadow boxing, and maintaining that he's a former prizefighter. A lot of guys, when they arrive, put on a Gene Wilder/ Richard Pryor *Stir Crazy* masquerade by practicing karate moves, kick-boxing, jumping rope, and shadow boxing to show they're tough and ought to be left alone. Most of the time, it doesn't work. What it does more than anything else is amuse the other inmates.

Polecat, expert in all disciplines, is asked to check out the new dude, who is suspect in part because he is Jewish. Not many younger inmates have ever heard of a Jewish prizefighter.

They don't know Boston's West End. Plenty of great Jewish boxers came out of the cities, but in order to win the support of fans, many of them abandoned their Jewish names and adopted Irish or Italian names.

The new guy is five feet seven, 160 pounds. He's forty-six years old and in good shape, wiry, with a full head of jet black, curly hair. With his horn-rimmed glasses, he could pass for a professor at Columbia.

"I saw you running," I say to him. "What's your mileage?"

"I'm going to do six," he says. "I do it all the time, for training."

"Training for what?"

"I'm the oldest professional fighter in New York. I fight under the name 'The Renegade Jew.'"

He says he also has a band, a rap group that he called The Renegade Jews.

I'm thinking this is a snow job, a guy who tried being himself, found it wasn't getting him anywhere, and so he recreated himself as the Renegade Jew.

After checking out the new guy, Polecat announces he's legitimate and confirms that his fighting name was indeed the Renegade Jew.

Turns out, he's also a Manhattan insurance executive who has a doctorate in literature from City University of New York, that he was a welterweight who fought Golden Gloves boxers young enough to be his son. Also, he really is a rapper, or as *Jewish Week* calls him, a hip-hop recording artist.

Instead of living his dream of winning the Nobel Prize in Literature, however, he's here serving two years for tax evasion. Sensing my disbelief, the Renegade Jew offers to show me a news article that proves he is a fighter and also to sing the lyrics to his rap music.

"The news article will do the trick," I say.

If the Renegade Jew sounds crazy, well, here at Schuykill, he proved to be one of the saner people. And give the Renegade Jew credit. He no longer arrives at the gym in a Rolls Royce driven by a chauffeur. He's no longer a millionaire, and they have taken the diamond studs he once wore in his ears. But, as he says, "I'm proud of myself because I'm a cool, tough Jew."

If the Renegade Jew is lucky, none of our African brothers here will hear his latest CD. It includes a cut called "Hymietown," a blistering attack on Minister Louis Farrakhan with such lyrics as, "Got an automatic for the anti-Semitics," and later, "Blacks, fuck you for hating the Jews." I ought to advise him against singing in the shower. These are lyrics that will contribute nothing to his health and longevity.

As it happens, however, today the Renegade Jew has a problem. In Manhattan, the Renegade Jew lives in what *Jewish Week* called a lavish Upper East Side apartment, a co-op, and he's fearful that snobby neighbors will discover that he's in jail and hold it against his wife and daughter. Letters that leave the prison bear a return address—Schuykill, P.O. Box 670, Minersville, PA,—leaving no doubt the sender is in prison.

Here's the problem, as the Renegade Jew described it to a group of us.

"At the co-op, the doorman sees all the mail. How can I send letters to my wife and daughter and prevent the gossipy doorman from spreading word that I'm in prison?"

There was a pause. Finally, one guy serving a long sentence and experienced in such matters spoke up.

"Why is this a problem? Have somebody shoot the fuckin' doorman."

My cellmate, who works in the kitchen, explains that if there are 300 inmates, they cook for 450. That is, they make 450 portions. That's enough for everyone, plus extras for the kitchen help.

Well, tonight, after 250 inmates had been fed, the kitchen ran out of corned beef, and there was hell to pay, including threats to call the administrator. I don't blame them, and you wouldn't, if you saw the substitute.

The inmates call it "mystery meat." The kitchen said it was Salisbury steak, although Danny T. was speaking for all of us when he said that Mr. Salisbury would deny responsibility for this.

"If I fed this to my dog," said Danny T., "he'd bite me."

Inmates come, inmates go. Word is out by now that a must-stop for new inmates is the latrine off the main lobby—my latrine! It's not unlike the impulse to visit the Empire State Building in New York or Plymouth Rock in Massachusetts.

Still, it's strange that people would think of the men's room as a tourist site.

Monday, November 8, 1993

Camel is on the job, waking me at 5:15 a.m. I ask if he ever got that second coffee roll Saturday morning. He swears seven times, five in Egyptian.

"I had tree, four rolls when I get back to *C* range," he says. "Fook the hacks."

Two friends leave today, on at 5:30 a.m., the other at 11:00 a.m. There is no shortage of replacements. In fact, there are hundreds waiting to take their places.

If the congressmen who talk so eloquently on the need for law and order ever knew how this money is wasted, Congress would disband the BOP. Prosecutors spend so much time inducing nonviolent offenders to plead guilty that the system is now clogged to the extent that habitual offenders are delayed in being brought to trial.

This morning, along the entire East Coast corridor, the forecast is for good flying weather. Elaine says she and Bob will leave Bedford,

Massachusetts, at dawn on Thursday. My reactions are conflicted. Elaine and I have never been apart for an extended period.

For me, the only positive experience since I arrived here has been the reminder of how much Elaine and the children mean to me. And how easy it is in life to take those things for granted.

So, I'm always glad to see her, but not here, not here. I mean, how do you act? Suppose she gets a bad time from one of the guards? If any hack did something abusive to Elaine, and if I lost my temper, I'd be here for the rest of my life, and then some. And what about the flight? The plane is small, a two-seater.

God, how I wish that this wasn't happening. But how can I explain that to Elaine?

At Catholic services this evening, I get a chance to try my new rosary beads from Fr. Dene. I still wonder who was the last person to use them. At Mass, there are usually twenty inmates. I wish I could make a video and take it home with me to show schoolchildren, especially the tough kids who think religion is for sissies. What they'd see in the video is this: some of the toughest guys they could ever imagine, kneeling in prayer, rosary beads in hand. It's a sight I shall never forget.

After the services, Fr. Dene brings in a video. I suspect that he doesn't screen them. This one's rated *R*.

Tuesday November 9, 1993

This morning, the Renegade Jew is having problems.

He had come to ask me for advice about a job here. I fixed him up with the electricians. The only thing he'd have to do is walk around with them all day, five days a week, and change light bulbs. We prepped him for his interview with the head hack.

"If anyone asks you what experience you have with electricity," the Renegade Jew was advised, "just say that you've done some wiring around the house."

How difficult is that?

So, the Renegade Jew met with a hack and the head electrician.

"What experience have you had with electricity?"

"I was a prizefighter."

The Renegade Jew was assigned to landscaping.

It's 1:30 p.m., and inmates are napping, reading, playing cards, or watching television, mostly soap operas and cartoons. I'm tired, and I'd sure like to take a nap, but once I give in, once that happens, they win.

I'm too tired to write. I can't keep my eyes open.

Do something, Joe!

Force yourself. Change clothes. Get on the rowing machine.

This is where discipline has to take over.

Some of my crazy friends are planning a parade for Veterans Day. Organizing the parade is Deke. He wants to line up three or four divisions and parade around the track in front of a reviewing stand. They want me to head one of the divisions.

"Any marine would be glad to do so," I say, and then, thinking quickly, "but I'm expecting an important visit that day."

The organizer, by the way, was in the army, naturally, and yes, he's nuts.

Wednesday, November 10, 1993

Breakfast. I can't help thinking that we eat better in prison than most Americans. Surely, better than most public school children. And you could feed the homeless in Philly with what we throw out.

A major decision has to be made today.

Let me roll back the camera. As I've indicated, I live in Unit Two. It consists of four ranges, *A*, *B*, *C*, and *D*. On *A*, where I live, the average age is twenty-eight. Most are white, extremely tough, and extremely loud in terms of both their music and the banter that extends into the wee hours of the morning.

B is mostly minorities, black and Spanish, whose taste in music runs to loud and to rap.

C and *D* are, by comparison, sedate, controlled by older members of the population. They are also cleaner and quieter. In fact, there are no loud noises permitted, and you cannot visit without an invitation.

A new inmate is usually sent to Unit One or Two, then assigned to one of the four ranges, usually the noisy ones, *A* or *B*. After a few weeks of scrutiny, he is quietly invited to join either *C* or *D*.

Upon my arrival, having been sent to Unit Two, I was assigned to a difficult range, *A*, where I was befriended by the toughest inmates. There was nothing I needed, nothing I couldn't ask for, and word went out among the general population that I was one of them, and that meant something.

Now, I have been invited to go to *C* or *D*. Given my age, my status as a white-collar criminal, most people here expect me to move.

But I have decided to remain on the tough range, *A*.

Why?

It's taken weeks, but I am now accustomed to the noise. I like the guys on *A* better, especially those from Boston. I like my cellmate, Billy. There is more food in *A* range because it houses more kitchen workers. And while there are no secrets here, because of the diversity (thirty-two residents, five black, three Hispanic) *A* range gets the news first.

That brings me to a story.

One night, recently, I overheard a conversation in which someone said that Ali, the orderly for *B* range, puts on a better fight than what is seen on TV, and that, a violent fight was, in fact, under way at that moment in the latrine of *B* range.

It had started as an argument between two black guys, who then needed a place to fight. So, something akin to a boxing ring was set up in the latrine of *B*. It was bare fists, and one guy was beaten pretty badly.

A few days later, I was cleaning the corridor in the administration building when I saw this black guy about twenty-five years old sitting there, a good guy. His face was swollen grotesquely, and it looked horribly painful.

I said, "Holy Toledo, what happened?"

"I'm on my way to the hospital," he said. "I got hurt on the basketball court,"

A few minutes later, he was approached by another inmate who is black, and a self-anointed spokesman for the black community. He sat down next to Swollen Jaw.

I heard the spokesman whisper.

"Don't change your story. Remember, you got hurt playing basketball." I put two and two together, and I realize, this is the guy who lost the fight in the latrine.

Prison is a place where the lines between truth and fiction and right and wrong are often black and blue. But the way to long life here is to mind your own business, and so I turn and head back to my cell.

At 6:00 p.m., I write for a while, then prepare for Elaine's visit tomorrow. I find a clean uniform, the one that fits me best, and hang it up overnight to take out the wrinkles. Got to try to look half decent. I had promised myself I wouldn't do this, but now it's out of my control. I know this: emotionally, it will take me a week to recover.

Thursday, November 11, 1993

It's 2:00 a.m., and the hacks are making their move. Without warning, four inmates are taken off *B* range and put in the hole, including Ali, the unit orderly and boxing promoter.

What started the argument that turned into a bloody fight in *B* range's latrine was a ten-cent phone call.

One phone, it seems, was out of order, and as a result, inmates for a period of time were able to make free calls. While one inmate was on the free phone, another was waiting. Words were exchanged about the length of the call. One inmate followed the other back to *B* range. It was then decided by Ali to let them finish it in the washroom, which resulted in the damage to Swollen Jaw.

Fighting is among the worst infractions. It can change your category from nonviolent to violent and evict you from a camp and move you to medium security.

Why did the hacks move in tonight?

Undoubtedly, Swollen Jaw changed his story to say that his injury was not incurred on the basketball court. He must have cut a deal with the administration, a reminder once again that in prison, there are no secrets, only rats.

This morning the hacks cancel the Veterans Day parade, saying they are afraid that anti-Vietnam War protestors will have a confrontation with the marchers.

Anti-Vietnam War demonstrations? This is 1993.

The real reason is that the administration wants the day off, and if there were a parade, a lot of them would have to work. If they only knew that it was a joke from the beginning, and nobody was going to show up anyway.

Or maybe they did know. Who knows?

At 11:00 a.m., my name is called over the intercom. "Timilty! Report to the office."

Hmmmm. That's not the usual visitor call. Something is up.

When I arrive at the administration building, I can see Elaine and Bob in the doorway, but they are being barred from entry. That is, Bob can enter, but Elaine can't.

His name, it seems, is on the list for admission. Hers is not. Thanks to my counselor, the problem is rectified, but the confrontation must have been uncomfortable for both of them.

After I empty my pockets and frisked by the hack, I am allowed into the visitor room. As I expected, this is difficult for me, as I know it was difficult for Elaine. It was hard for me and Elaine to be together and not make Bob uncomfortable.

They told me about the 750-mile flight. We laughed about the fiasco of allowing Bob to enter, but not Elaine. We talked politely about how everyone looked, but I didn't know what to say.

I was nervous. My throat was dry. My stomach was in a tight knot.

Elaine and I talked about the kids and then about our financial situation, which is not good, not good at all.

In one sense, it's wonderful to be so close to her, and in another sense, it's horrible to be so far away. Maybe that's why the BOP encourages visits. Of all the torments here, a visit from your wife is the worst punishment. How do inmates handle visits from family who fly from afar to spend the whole day?

We talked about everything from Boston politics to the fortunes of the Red Sox to real estate in Boston. I tried to keep it light, tried to tell only funny stories, but after sixty minutes, you run out of small talk and witty observations, and also the effort to pretend that this is anything but what it is; one of the most horrible moments of my life, is exhausting.

I admire Elaine so much. She's a trouper.

All of this is wrong. It's a travesty. But that is something for her and me to discuss at another time.

As we say good-bye, my stomach is churning. I can hardly swallow. I recommit myself to no more visits.

Still frustrated by Elaine's visit, I'm walking the track with friends.

From out of the blue sky comes the sound of a small plane that bends down toward the prison, circles, descends again, and then tips its wings—final salute. Bob's signature—class.

The inmates all wave. They don't know what the salute was for. I look up to the heavens and up toward Elaine in the plane, and I am waving the hardest.

At 10:30 p.m., it's lights out. What a depressing day, the worst since I arrived here. I fall asleep thinking of the people I love and then of the people who sent me here.

Friday, November 12, 1993

It's midday, and out near the administration building, I see an inmate named Jeff, who is about forty and handsome as a movie star. He's all dressed up, shoes shined, clothes clean and pressed by a real iron. This is odd, because it's not a visiting day, and so there's no apparent reason to dress up.

"Hi, Joe."

"Jeff, you look great, but why are you all, dressed up?"

"I'm getting married today, and we're waitin' for the justice of the peace. I'm a little nervous."

Jeff has four years to go on a nine-year sentence.

"Are you getting a furlough overnight?"

"No."

I can see the notice in the society pages. "The bride wore white, the groom hoped for parole. Instead of a wedding cake, guests munched on food from the vending machines."

Why does a man in prison marry? You know the answers. For attention. As a blanket against loneliness. To ensure there'll be regular mail and regular visits. For others, it may be no more than the need, when it comes time for parole, to have a home to go to, to have someone waiting at the gate to reach out her arms and smile and say, "Hi, honey!"

From a place like this, any sane man needs an escape. Some of us read books. Some of us eat too much food. Some of us work out with weights until or muscles become grotesque. Others get married.

A bit later, in the visitor room, I notice three people, two women and a man. One woman, a pretty blonde, is pacing. The other two are talking to her. They look nervous, too.

As it turns out, the blonde is the bride. The other two are the best man and maid of honor.

Why would a woman marry an inmate with four years to go? Ask the philosophers. All I know is that we do funny things in the name of love.

At 2:00 p.m., on my way to the track, I notice Jeff is still in the corridor. He still looks nervous.

At 2:30 p.m., Jeff's still in the corridor, still looking nervous. I wonder what's going on.

At 3:00 p.m., Jeff's in the same spot. Now, I'm getting nervous.

At 5:30 p.m., Jeff and I land at the same table in the cafeteria, and he's wearing a new wedding ring.

"What time did the justice of the peace arrive?"

"He never showed up!"

"The JP was mad. The last time the justice of the peace was scheduled to preside over a marriage here, he drove a great distance only to arrive and find that the inmate had been transferred, the wedding cancelled, and no one had told the JP. If there's no wedding, the JP doesn't get paid."

"So, did you get married today?"

"Yeah, they hunted up a Protestant minister, who performed the ceremony."

"Then what?"

"My new wife? They sent her home. Then a hack frisked me and sent me back to my unit for the four thirty count."

Some wedding.

As the Renegade Jew says, "Your future here is very much 'to be or not to be.'"

Saturday, November 13, 1993

I sleep till 5:30 a.m. so that my neighbor from the islands will have time to finish up in the laundry room. In order to make financial ends meet, he takes in laundry. He gets up at 2:00 a.m. on Saturday and works four hours before anyone else gets up.

I can get up early any morning. I don't need to interrupt him.

At 9:00 a.m., I make my weekly phone call home. Talking to my family could break my bank as well as my heart.

Tonight, instead of writing, I put down my pen and hop into my bunk to read, but it's tough concentrating tonight. There's too much going on. I put down my book, too, and listen and laugh. One of my favorite TV shows is *Sanford and Son*, the only program that makes me laugh out loud. The conversation here tonight is just as funny.

My neighbors and friends, Kiester and Mills, both African Americans, are at it again, each trying to one-up the other. First they argue about whose car is faster. Then, Kiester issues a challenge.

"I got a dog that's bigger than yours."

"No, you ain'," says Mills.

"Yes, I do. My dog weighs 750 pounds."

"That ain' your dog, man! That's your girlfriend. You always mixin' 'em up."

Sunday, November 14, 1993

Brunch. I sit with George, the Greek patriot, who reads me American Revolutionary War quotations. He's being released Tuesday, and there is talk that even though his time is up, before he walks out the door, he will be arrested by authorities from immigration and deported to Greece.

He has an American wife and a twelve-year-old son in Florida, and he has not seen them in three years. George has a lot of friends here, myself included, and we're rooting for him to walk out of here without shackles.

At noon, I'm walking with Pat, and the weather's in the midseventies. We're joined by Deke, who is busy checking the odds for today's pro football games. I knew there was betting on football games here but not that there was an office, a bookie, an oddsmaker, a bank, and a collector.

In the evening, Paul and I head for Catholic services. I sit with George, and we marvel that Fr. Dene has so many deceased relatives who need prayers.

Back on *A* range, big doings tonight. A going-away party for two inmates, George and Brutus. Again, I'm amazed at how much food is brought in—fancy dishes, salads, hors d'oeuvres, enough food to feed 100 inmates, and even better than what's served in the dining room.

The party begins about 7:15 p.m. It's like an open house. There are strong signs of affection. I have never been fond of hugging among men, but there is nothing physical about it. Here, it's a way of showing friendship. These guys have been through a lot together, and there is a mutual respect for one another.

At 10:00 p.m., the party is still going on. Five inmates from *B* range are called to the administration office, where they are shackled and taken to the hole. Their offense: drinking alcohol. I don't know whether it was brought in or whether they made it. The ringleader is an inmate who comes from Massachusetts. I know his father, a lawyer from the North Shore. Most of the inmates work in the kitchen, and so the suspicion is they were making it.

It's not that they were caught drinking. Someone ratted on them, and they were raided.

Everybody believes that an inmate sold them out in exchange for a better deal for himself, and the likely suspect is Ali, who was involved in the fight.

Monday, November 15, 1993

In my little neighborhood, there are five new inmates. Our friend, Pat the gay, has been lying low since he was caught in bed in the middle of the night with another inmate.

Most people call Pat "she," then catch themselves, because in a way that seems to condone the behavior.

Now, Pat has a new friend, who has arrived from another jail, and they're as close as two coats of paint. His name is Shannon, and he makes no pretense about his preference for men.

As Pat says, now that Shannon's arrived, he's in love once again, and he has started wearing makeup and carrying a pocketbook. To see him skipping around, it's obvious that he's happy. Also, now that Pat and Shannon have found one another, they're both shaving their legs.

This is a strange place.

At 9:00 a.m., over the intercom, we hear the name of George, the Greek patriot, and we all know what that means. Walking by the latrine, he opens the door.

"Joe, good-bye, and good luck."

I say good-bye. A few minutes later, I see them take George out the front door. He's shackled hand and foot.

At midday, I'm walking the track with my friend Jim, who has been helpful since I arrived. He's leaving the day *after* Thanksgiving. That says a lot about the BOP: they couldn't let him go one day early so he could celebrate Thanksgiving with his family.

The turnout is light for tonight's Catholic services, rosary, and benediction. Maybe it's the movie that's scheduled afterward—*Ghost*, with Demi Moore and Whoopi Goldberg.

I liked it. And Fr. Dene didn't have to squirm.

Back in the cell at 9:00 p.m., I decide not to answer my mail tonight but to read instead. Tonight's snack, pirated from the cafeteria, is a fresh apple pie, and it's delicious.

Tuesday, November 16, 1993

This morning, the latrine looks good. Everything shines so that I feel obligated to remind patrons that they may need sunglasses.

At 8:00 a.m., working in the hall outside the latrine is a Spanish painting crew. After a few days of conversation and then showing them how to use the rowing machine, I persuade them that they should paint the latrine. I figure that's the easiest way to get rid of what the soap commercials call stubborn stains.

One of their crew is Jose, who is always in trouble. He says it's because he doesn't understand English, but I've watched him, and the only English he doesn't understand is the word "work." He walks around all day, shrugging his shoulders and saying, "No comprende." Unless you mention food. Then he understands.

He begins to refer to me as Jose Sr. and himself as Jose Jr. Well, that was quick!

By 8:30 a.m., the administration has approved the suggestion by the Spanish paint crew, submitted as a favor to me, that their next assignment be my latrine.

In discussing a schedule with them, I'm told there are seven in their paint crew, although I hav e never seen all seven of them together at one time except in the chow hall. If all seven worked at painting the latrine, it would take five hours. They insist the job will take two to three weeks. Also, they cannot start for several days; they need to rest after their last job.

This morning, an inmate from the warehouse slips me a note that describes the tremendous waste.

Take buffers, for example. Floor buffers. There are thirty-four floor buffers in stock, and Schuykill uses two a year. Long-sleeve shirts? There are 8,762 in stock, a seven-year supply. And yet there are no belts, no buckles, no shoelaces, no large or extra-large T-shirts in stock. And no liquid soap for dispensers in the latrines.

As I write, I am looking through a library window where a work crew is hauling out the three exercise machines that were assembled wrong and are now being thrown away so they won't be seen by an inspection team and embarrass the administration.

By midday, the word comes down that George is going to get a hearing from the Immigration Department. That means he'll be able to post bond and get out of the shackles and leg irons.

His wife called. It seems he had some help from a congressman from Massachusetts. I must remember to thank my daughter Kelly for her intercession on behalf of George.

By 9:30 p.m., I've written seven letters, plus notes for my journal. This is among my favorite times of the day, the hour to read.

Wednesday, November 17, 1993

On latrine duty this morning, I expected to see my paint crew, but none of them showed up.

At 8:30 a.m., George, the head painter, arrives. His six assistants are watching television. We discuss colors. One temptation is to be fancy, to pick something bright, but my survival instincts kick in and remind me that the way to endure here is to maintain a low profile and so I agree that, yes, the best color for my latrine is a shade favored throughout Schuykill, battleship gray.

"There's no rush here," I say, tongue in cheek. "No reason you guys have to jump right into this."

"OK," says George.

He thinks I'm serious.

Thursday, November 18, 1993

At 7:00 a.m., it's work call at the latrine, although the painters are not due till 7:30 a.m.

At 7:30 a.m., no painters.

At 8:00 a.m., still no painters.

At 9:00 a.m., the painters arrive. That is, two of the seven show up. They have their equipment, brushes, tape, large paint cans, and several drop cloths.

"Where's the rest of the crew?" I ask.

"Watching television."

They post several "Wet Paint" signs, then the two who showed up depart. They head across the hall to the recreation room to shoot a game of pool.

Painting the latrine may take longer than my sentence.

At 10:30 a.m., the painters return.

At 10:45 a.m., the painters break for lunch.

At 1:00 p.m., work call. The gear is here, the painters are not.

Tonight, word passes quickly that the evening meal is no good. But inmates stack on their trays great volumes of food they have no intention of eating.

I was trained in Marine Corps boot camp that if you take food on your tray, you eat it before you leave the dining hall, or the drill instructor will see that you wear the food out of the dining hall.

The reason inmates are taking lots of food they won't eat is that whatever is not consumed today will be served again tomorrow in another form, and if it doesn't taste good today, it will taste even worse tomorrow. For example, in the Reuben sandwiches we had last night, the corned beef was horrible. It appeared this morning disguised as corned beef hash, and it was still horrible.

I just read an article in the *Boston Globe* of November 16, 1993, that refers to 4.9 million elderly people who worry about their next meal. They're afflicted with what the story describes as food insecurity. At the same time, here at Schuykill, we take as much on our tray as we can so that we can throw it away.

Friday, November 19, 1993

Winter has arrived in the mountains of Pennsylvania, where the wind is howling, and the temperature has dropped below twenty degrees.

At breakfast, I am sitting with Danny T.

"So, I see the 'Wet Paint' signs," Danny T. says. "Does that mean the latrine is closed?"

"No, as difficult as it will be on me and the painters, we're going to keep it open during renovation. I got to tell you, though, the way this paint crew operates, this could be a long, long project."

"It's like what we got in New York," says Danny T.

"What do you mean?"

"Highways to the airport are always crowded, and you know why? Because of the NYC Transportation Authority. They got plenty of workers putting up yellow cones for five or six miles, backing up traffic, but you never see anybody working. All you see are cones, and no one ever seems to check on why nobody's working. It's just like here."

The inmates miss my strategy. I don't care if they ever finish painting the latrine. With painters and ladders and drop cloths and "Wet Paint" signs all over the place, fewer people will use the latrine, and inspectors will be less inclined to be around with their check sheets.

Saturday, November 20, 1993

I didn't get up until 6:30 a.m. Now that I've been here six weeks—Wow! Has it been that long? Maybe I'm sleeping better.

At breakfast, to everyone's amazement, there's fresh orange juice.

"No kidding," says Danny T. "Did they shut down the still?"

Another inmate left yesterday, the Hand Washer. He brought it on himself, but he did hard time, as hard as it gets. Everything he touched, he'd put on gloves. The Hand Washer was a college professor. He did not have a single friend. He was alone, and by choice. He walked alone, sat alone, ate alone.

Late one night, an inmate came in and was assigned to the bunk over the Hand Washer. The next morning, the new inmate climbed down, saw the Hand Washer and stuck out his hand.

"Hi," he said.

The Hand Washer glared at him and said, "You talk too much."

Ironically, I saved his behind. There's a tradition that when a guy's getting out, there's a party with cold cuts, ice cream, tonic—stuff that's not on the menu but somehow shows up in the cellblock at night.

For Hand Washer's last day, they planned the opposite. They were going to short-sheet his bunk, empty cigarette ashes onto his sheets, cut one leg off his pants, hide his clothes, and throw cold water on him as he slept.

I went around to the principals and said, "I hear there's a plan for this, and I don't think it makes any sense." Enough of them agreed that it was cancelled.

Hand Washer lived twenty yards from me for a month and a half, and I bet I didn't hear him say seven words. On his final trip to the latrine, he walked by me.

"Good luck," I said.

Without looking at me, he replied, "I hope I never see you again."

Lunch is Texas hash. Does anybody know what Texas hash is?

At Mass, Fr. Dene's presiding seems to be getting better, although he has yelled at us lately about poor response during the Mass and poor performance during collection.

Usually, everybody sits in the same seats. I always sit with George, because I love his wry humor and his conjectures about which dead relative Fr. Dene will conjure up to pray for today.

There's been a subtle change, though. Pat, the tough guy, usually sits with me, along with his companion, the Bear, but lately, he comes in, looks over, waves, and heads to the other side. This bothered me, and a few days ago, while Pat and I were walking around the track, I asked him about it.

The explanation was simple.

Sitting in front of me in church was a rat who had testified against his codefendants. Pat didn't want to sit with me because he didn't want to be near the rat when the priest said, "Peace be with you."

Pat didn't want to disrupt Mass, but he had no intention of shaking hands with the rat and certainly not of wishing him peace.

It's Saturday night, as Frank Sinatra used to sing, the loneliest night of the week. It's even lonelier at Schuykill. Nearby, Mills, the most feared black man here, is drawing cute cartoon animals to send home to his kids.

Sunday, November 21, 1993

At coffee hour, the big topic is the crime bill. Rumors are rampant. It seems every inmate has a relative who knows somebody in Washington who has the inside scoop on what is going to happen.

If Americans knew what goes on here, how well we are kept, there would be a revolution.

In America, some of the elderly do not have enough good food to eat, and yet inmates here throw food away. In America, some kids in ghettos and in rural areas don't have enough heat in winter, and yet, there's so much heat that sometimes we have to open the windows, even when the temperature outside is zero. And the same Congress that appropriates more than $20 billion for new prisons is also cutting housing subsidies for the working poor.

At 8:00 a.m., I check the latrine, the maintenance of which has become a matter of pride to me. Now that my name is associated with it, I find myself stopping in more often to make sure there is nothing awry, that there are plenty of supplies for the weekend. I hate to think what might happen here if the place ran out of paper.

But there's a problem. Someone's sneaking in at odd hours and stuffing the urinals with paper. It's obviously personal, obviously someone who has a problem with me. I just hope I don't catch him, although I think I have narrowed it to three inmates.

In the cafeteria at dinner, I leave my table to grab utensils, and when I return, I am surprised to see that the two empty seats have been taken by Pat and Shannon, the gay inmates, who are waiting to see my reaction.

I have two choices. One is to pick up my tray and find another table. There are inmates here who would do that. Or, I could sit down and have dinner with two inmates who have as much right to the table as me.

So, I sit down. They say hello.

Pat is an accident waiting to happen, but Shannon is bright, college educated. Both are in their middle twenties. Pat has short hair and wears a lot of jewelry, earrings, sometimes a necklace. Somebody said that on the outside, Shannon worked in computers or in finance. In here, Shannon is assumed to be intelligent simply because he types a lot. Anybody who needs a legal brief typed will seek out Shannon.

Around straights, Shannon acts straight. Around gays, he acts gay. He doesn't flaunt his homosexuality, and he doesn't hide it, although it's clear by his clothes, not to mention the lipstick and the purse he carries over his shoulder. Shannon affects a high-pitched voice, and instead of walking, he sways. On weekends, when there are fewer guards around, Pat and Shannon dress in more feminine clothes, that is, slacks that are tighter and shirts that set off their jewelry. The weekend guards seem indifferent.

Wherever these guys got together for their romance, to this day I don't know, and neither did any of the other straight guys, although we assumed it was in alcoves, in the latrine, or outdoors.

Gays have a tough time on the outside, but it's tougher on the inside. Most of the straights are plainly uncomfortable around gays. If I hadn't acted as a bridge between straights and gays, my group never would have spoken to Shannon. It would have been as though he didn't exist. There were other gays who were quiet and withdrawn and deep in the closet, and while they were suspected of patronizing gays like June Bug or Shannon, no one was really sure.

Sometimes, the straight guys taunt them: "Here comes everybody's girlfriend." One night when Shannon walked by, sashaying, he was the object of catcalls.

"Hey, Shannon," yelled Kiester. "I got a hard-on for you."

Everybody laughed.

"Thank you for that crude remark, honey," said Shannon, "but I got to tell you, from what I seen, you ain' got much to brag about."

It's fairly well known that many of the loudmouths who are so vocal in condemning homosexuals are probably struggling with uncertainties about their own sexuality.

It's 6:30 p.m., and back on *A* range, Kiester and Mills are at it again, the "can you top this" competition.

Tonight, Kiester is talking about how many different women come to visit him, although I have never seen him head for the visitor room. He tells us about the time one of his women wanted so badly to visit him that the person she manipulated into driving her down from New York City was, of all people, her ex-husband.

At 10:30 p.m., lights out. Another night on the mountain.

Monday, November 22, 1993

It's 5:15 a.m., but no wake-up call from Camel. He must have seen me last night at dinner, talking with the gays, Shannon and Pat, and now he's showing me that he's angry. Camel is not one of America's leading liberals. I'll have a talk with him.

It's common knowledge that if you want a few laughs, stop by to monitor progress on the painting of my latrine. The painters, by the way, have not returned. And regarding the "Wet Paint" signs, nobody heeds them anymore.

Well, glory be! It's 9:30 a.m., and who should arrive but the painters, with a great welcoming fanfare from me, the head gringo, Jose Sr. What makes the arrival of the painters different today is that they have paint, not to mention additional drop cloths. To the inexperienced observer, they appear rarin' to go. Once they have thanked me for welcoming them so enthusiastically, however, they head across the hall to play pool.

Later, on the track, I'm walking with Jim, who'll be out in a few days. It's an oddity about prison to be thrown in with people you have never met before and to share so many hours under difficult circumstances and often come to like and respect them, only to separate and, in most cases, never see them again.

Sometimes, Jim and I walk for miles without saying a word. On other occasions, we've chatted about Massachusetts politics, about families, mutual friends, movies, sports. Today, we vow not to let our friendship fade.

At 1:00 p.m. work call, we have no painters, only cans of paint. At 2:30 p.m., I check the latrine. The painters are not here, and now even the paint is gone.

Not many attend rosary and benediction tonight. The movie is *Yankee Doodle Dandy*, with Jimmy Cagney—a great movie. For Fr. Dene, this is a record, two terrific movies in a row. As it turns out, it's a small crowd for the service, a large crowd for the movie. This is one of the best nights of the week. I enjoy the religious service and then the opportunity to relax during the movie.

Tuesday, November 23, 1993

At breakfast, I bump into George, the head painter.

"We'll be by today, for sure," he says.

At 7:30 a.m. work call, there are no painters. At 8:00 a.m. no painters. At 9:00 a.m. the painters arrive, all seven of them, and with plenty of equipment, extra cans of paint, more drop cloths, and even a ladder. Two of them head to the library. They're going to research their cases. The others drift over to the recreation room to play pool and watch television.

At the 1:00 p.m. work call, there are no painters. Summing up, thus far, after one week, not a drop of paint has been applied, not a can has been opened. At 3:00 p.m., the painters arrive, and in their most friendly manner, they exchange greetings and salutations as if everything is normal. They are very friendly as they pack up their brushes and some of their unopened paint buckets and head back to the paint shop.

At mail call today, I receive more mail than all of *A* range combined. That means I have more to answer. This is Thanksgiving week, but it's as if there's no such thing here as a holiday. It's never mentioned, except when people talk about food.

I am sitting with Rock Bottom, my neighbor, and Ray, all 280 pounds of him, and Danny T. There is ice cream on the menu and ice cream in the conversation.

Ray says that in Philly, he used an ice cream truck as a cover for the numbers racket that he ran. It was tough work. Along the ice cream route, he was obliged to stay focused on the details of the illegal gambling operation and to monitor his pickups of large sums of money. The sale, therefore, of popsicles for fifty cents tended to distract Ray, and so, rather than be diverted, he simply gave away the ice cream.

Danny T. recalled his brief tenure in the ice cream business. Having always wanted to be a legitimate businessman, when someone said there was a lot of money to be made in ice cream, Danny T. rented an expensive freezer, stocked it with ice cream, asked where the nearest crowd might be, and, when advised there was a state college down the road, he embarked on his adventure into legitimate business. Seeing the brick buildings alongside the highway, Danny T. pulled his ice cream truck to a central point, turned up the rock music, and, to his surprise, was besieged by a crowd that overwhelmed him and his truck and cleaned him out without paying.

Instead of setting up shop at a state college, Danny T. had driven onto the grounds of a mental hospital that was populated by folks who loved ice cream but had no money to pay for it.

"That's what happens when you go straight," said Danny T., ruefully, "and I, for one, will never try it again."

At 10:30 p.m., Mills and Kiester are at it again. This time, it's the crime bill. Their analysis of the legislation may not measure up to what Ted Koppel will provide on "Nightline," but it's not far off the mark, either.

"Hey, Kiester, what's the crime bill gonna mean to you? Nuthin', that's what. You ain' gonna get out any sooner."

"Like the monkey said, when he got his tail cut off, won't be long now."

Wednesday November 24, 1993

Lunch today is hot dogs. But wait, not just any hot dogs. These are turkey hot dogs, the worst taste you can imagine. I try one, but even with onion, mustard, ketchup, and relish, they still taste like turkey hot dogs.

This morning I get a visit from Jeff, the inmate who was married here the other day. He needs a favor. He's run out of money in his telephone account, and he needs to call his new wife to tell her about the visiting schedule over the Thanksgiving holidays.

I agree to help. Who can resist the appeal of young love? I tell him that if his new wife is at a number where she can be reached, I'll put a call through on my bill at 9:15 a.m.

It's 8:30 a.m., and don't quote me, but we may be making progress in our campaign to get the latrine painted. The painters arrive, all seven of them. Today, it turns out, they're to be inspected by a hack who is in charge of their work detail.

"I have to tell you this," I say. "The facilities have to be hosed down before you can go in, and that will take about fifteen minutes."

"OK, gringo," says George.

I get a hose and sanitize the place. Fifteen minutes later, when I have finished, the painters have disappeared again, and so has the hack. All that remains is their equipment.

At 9:15 a.m., it's time for the telephone call from Jeff to his new wife. It's complicated. Because none of Jeff's numbers are on my list, I have to telephone one of my numbers, then have that person dial Jeff's wife, and then I put Jeff on. The downside is that the connection has to stay on the line with the newlyweds, an awkward circumstance. And from my financial point of view, what was promised to be a thirty-second call stretches into ten minutes before I can get them off the phone.

It's an expensive investment in young love.

Upon arriving at the latrine at 9:35 a.m., I am surprised to see drop cloths on the floor. I am not surprised that there are no painters in sight.

Fr. Dene celebrates Thanksgiving by throwing in an extra Mass, and the inmates appreciate this. Forty show up, a great turnout. This is my first holiday here, and I'm shocked at the reaction of the inmates. There is a tremendous amount of laughter, people telling jokes, and no evident sadness. At Mass, people seem almost joyous, shaking hands, wishing each other a happy Thanksgiving, and making plans for tomorrow.

You have to admire the human spirit. There are times when I don't think I'm good enough to be in the same room with some of these guys. How can they keep coming back time and again after the beating they've taken in life? I'm doing only four months or 120 days. Some of these guys are doing ten years.

Thanksgiving Day

I wake up at 5:15 a.m., and my first thought is, what a strange place to be spending Thanksgiving. Camel wakes up a few people and wishes them happy holiday. It's still dark here and cold and quiet, because most of the inmates are sleeping.

I'm alone in the washroom, and I can't help thinking about Thanksgiving Mass. Of all holidays, I've always liked Thanksgiving best, a real family day in the Timilty house, and when you have a wife and seven kids, family days are important.

On Thanksgiving, Kelly would be home from Washington. The family would head to Chestnut Hill to watch Greg play defensive end for Boston College High School against Catholic Memorial High School and then head home for a day of family fun with relatives and friends who would start arriving at three o'clock and stay to midnight.

On this day, I miss my family most. This is my first Thanksgiving away from my family, but a lot of these guys have been through this experience time and again

Coffee conversation does not change, however. The same people at the same tables, carrying on the same conversations about the same topics. The only difference is that they greet one another by saying Happy Thanksgiving. I expected a more somber overtone. Most inmates seem to be in a surprisingly good mood. I had been warned that inmates would be depressed on a holiday. If so, they're hiding it well.

At 8:00 a.m., I check the latrine. As Permanent Latrine Orderly, my work is never done. Today, the latrine looks pretty good.

One clue that it's Thanksgiving is the length of the lines waiting to use the telephones. Ordinarily, on a Saturday or Sunday, no one would be using these phones. Today, each telephone has about six inmates in line.

After waiting in line for dinner for more than two hours, I finally arrive inside the dining hall at 4:30 p.m. Because it's a holiday, the tables have tablecloths, and the hacks seem to be paying more attention to providing good food, although the line is so long that at this point, not all the food is hot.

As Danny T. said, the only thing warm here is the ice cream.

Tonight is Jim's last night. I head to *C* range to say good-bye. There is a small get-together for Jim, who's well liked. Camel lives directly across from Jim, but he is not invited. Camel is not liked by the Jewish group.

On my way back to *A* range, I stopped by Camel's cell. As usual, he looked like a nervous bird. He is homely as hell, five foot three, 130 pounds, olive complexion, and try as he may, he cannot swear with the boldness of the Irish and the African Americans. In the morning, when he wakes me at 5:15 a.m., he says, "C'mon, you Irish kook sucker, git yo' fookin' Irish ass up." I don't wake up fearful. I wake up laughing.

On stopping by his cell after Jim's party with the Jewish contingent, I said to Camel, "Why weren't you at the party?"

"Dey din' invite me."

"Why not?"

"Because..."

He made the motion of holding a machine gun and spray firing.

"Because this is what we do at Jewish parties, mow 'em down."

He was not smiling.

I am back on *A* range and turn to see that Camel has followed me. He is even louder than usual, calling everyone stupid and yelling, "Fook you, fook you, you kook sucker." When inmates respond in the same language, he makes an obscene gesture.

Camel is pushing his luck. After Camel has insulted three or four of the toughest guys on *A* range, as he is about to leave, Camel is called by Rock Bottom, who is stretched out in the top bunk.

Camel arrives at Rock Bottom's cell, and Rock Bottom gestures for Camel to move closer, as if Rock Bottom is about to whisper something, and Camel steps into the cell. That is a mistake, because Rock Bottom lands on him. Rock Bottom weighs 280 pounds, Camel 130.

Two other inmates emerge with duct tape, and, around the range, everyone can hear the muffled sounds from Camel, whose mouth is quickly covered with tape. By the time they finish wrapping Camel in what seems like yards and yards of duct tape, he looks like a rolled-up rug, taped from head to toe, unable to move a muscle, unable to make a sound.

"That's the idea," says one of the inmates with tape.

Camel is tossed over Rock Bottom's shoulder and carried to the second floor, to the TV room, where the inmates are watching Thanksgiving football games. The room is packed, standing room only. As Rock Bottom strides into the room, he sees an empty corner, walks over, and dumps Camel onto the floor.

Word passes around the camp, and everyone agrees Camel had it coming. He had uttered "Fook you" one too many times.

As uncomfortable as it has been for Camel, it will be worse when he peels the tape from his bare skin. There is no way he can free himself, and some of us are worried whether he can breathe. Amid howls of laughter, after twenty minutes he is freed. But his skin will hurt for a long time and his pride for a longer time.

Maybe this will quiet Camel. Maybe not.

Friday, November 26, 1993

At coffee hour, I sit with Jim and cannot believe he is leaving, that he is soon to walk out the front door and, in all likelihood, never be seen by most of us. I'll always remember him as the fifty-year-old Israeli who was willing, even eager, to take on the thirty-year-old skinhead who was making anti-Semitic remarks—a profile in courage.

At 8:00 a.m., I check my latrine and discover that last night, someone kickboxed the plumbing over a urinal. Must have been one of my fellow inmates disappointed over the warm ice cream. It needs to be fixed, but not by me. I'll report it later.

At night, this place is a favorite hangout, and in the morning, it shows. The place looks well used; more than a hundred cigarette butts litter the floor. Smoking is not permitted in the prison, but the rule is not enforced.

Here's some poetic justice. Having insisted that my friend Jim not be discharged early, and, therefore, that he spend Thanksgiving here and be released on Friday, the hacks are now angry because, in order to process Jim's discharge, they have to come to work on what otherwise might have been a day off.

I head to the office to report the damage to the latrine. The duty hack calls the plumber, then hangs up the phone and turns to me.

"Let it go till Monday."

At 9:45 p.m., two hacks arrive with Breathalyzer equipment. They look at me and then move down the hallway until they see the Renegade Jew. They tell him that he is to be tested. Why they chose him, no one can say, except that maybe he was just standing around looking stupid. They tell the Renegade Jew he can refuse to be tested, but he'll be sent to solitary.

"Go ahead," he says, "I don't care."

They finish the test and leave. Later, I ask him, "How did the test come out?"

"They didn't find any evidence of alcohol," he said, "but they did say that I have bad breath."

Saturday, November 27, 1993

The longer I'm here, the dumber this system seems. But until the public finds out about the abuses, about the nepotism, and waste of money, they'll never pressure Congress to make changes.

This morning, the latrine is worse than ever. Not being able to flush one urinal has made it worse. The administration seems content to let it fester.

At brunch, I'm in line with the Renegade Jew and his sidekick, Mad Dog, who is five feet three, 140 pounds, and always in trouble, always picking fights with inmates twice his size.

The second week the Renegade Jew was here, he was waiting for a visit from his wife. He hired an inmate to press his shirt. Unfortunately, his wife overslept and never arrived.

The Renegade Jew is the product of an Ivy League education. He became a millionaire through his father's business and ended up in jail on tax evasion. He works on the landscaping crew with Tom from Baltimore, a drug dealer so smart at street life that he picked up the name Mad Dog.

At Catholic services tonight, Fr. Dene offers Mass for his deceased grandparents.

On my way back, out of curiosity, I step into the TV room. They're getting ready to watch the movie that comes on in five minutes, and there's plenty of jostling. It's a movie about vampires in the Los Angeles Police Department. The maneuvering for position goes on for more than ten minutes, almost erupting three times into fistfights because someone tripped over someone's feet or sat in front of someone or bumped someone with a chair.

There's more action on the floor than on the screen. No wonder sensible people stay out of here.

Sunday, November 28, 1993

At 10:00 a.m., I'm reading the paper in the TV room when two inmates, both in their sixties, start an argument over which station to watch. It gets loud and very personal. What an odd world that two men in their sixties would think so little of themselves and their lives that they would spend Sunday morning arguing over a television program.

Overheard at brunch: "I made only two mistakes in life. One was getting caught, the second was landing here."

At 3:00 p.m., my son Joe Jr. comes to visit, unannounced, which is vintage Joe. Visiting hours are over at 3:30 p.m., which is all right, because he didn't need much time. We have always been able to communicate well. I wonder what it's like for a twenty-seven-year-old to visit his father in prison. But I don't ask.

An hour after Joe leaves, I realize it will take me a day to recover from his visit.

Tonight, everybody's excited. It's the highlight of the week, bingo! Seventy-five percent of inmates show up to play.

Monday, November 29, 1993

This morning, the latrine looks like it has been hit by a hand grenade.

Now, I've been here eight weeks. How much information have I compiled and what do I do with it? There is no question that what I have seen as a "ward of the federal government" warrants a look by some congressional committee, whether it's Phil Kagan's death, the nepotism, the waste, or the pilferage.

Whether I'm capturing the flavor on paper is a different story.

There are organizations involved in penal reform, and I'm going to start writing them now.

At 8:30 a.m., I'm at the latrine. It's Monday morning. Do you know where your painters are? Privately, the painters assure me they're going to start work here tomorrow.

At 2:00 p.m., I head down to do a wash. My blankets haven't been washed since I arrived. Someone visited me the other night. I was seated at my desk, writing, and he sat down on the lower bunk, my bed. I was embarrassed because, when he sat down, a cloud of dust rose. I don't think he noticed, but I did. As I throw the blankets into the wash, I can't believe that in such a short time, they have gotten so dirty.

After Catholic services tonight, the movie is *Little Caesar*, with Edward G. Robinson, a classic, but I cannot stay. After all the mail I received today, I have work to do.

Tuesday, November 30, 1993

It's been several weeks now since I took over as Permanent Latrine Orderly. Few believed that a politician from Massachusetts could do this job without complaining.

At 8:00 a.m., the painters arrive. They set down their paint cans.

"We'll be back in a few minutes," said one, and they all head for coffee.

At 10:00 a.m., I return to the latrine and discover a hopeful sign. For the first time, the paint cans are open, and someone has put masking tape on the fixtures, although there's no sign of the painters.

Wednesday, December 1, 1993

At breakfast, I notice an oddity, There are two brother teams here and one father-son team. I find that strange. The difference in how one brother team adjusts is remarkable.

They're from the East Coast, were arrested, tried, convicted, and jailed because of the same infraction. One is well liked by inmates and staff, the other despised. The disliked one has been demoted to kitchen duty, where he was unable to survive as a server because of his arrogance, and now he has been demoted to sweeping the kitchen.

At 8:00 a.m., my friends the painters arrive. They say they need coffee before they can start. But the kitchen is out of coffee.

Boy, there is a crisis a minute here!

This is a historic moment. Mark down the time, 9:30 a.m. I can't believe it, but I am watching the painters actually apply paint to the walls. They're talking in Spanish, so I don't know what they're saying, but I can guess.

Meanwhile, the prison underground is roaring mad. The inmate committee appointed by the administration to vote on what movies we watch and what items will be sold in the commissary has decided not to put up Christmas decorations in the visitor room. The reason is that for certain non-Christians, the decorations are offensive.

Thursday, December 2, 1993

At breakfast, I am witnessing the scene the rest of the world should see when arguing about the need to jail first-time, nonviolent offenders.

If people expect to see inmates in gray and black striped jumpsuits, wearing balls and chains and seated at tables eating bowls of cold mush with mean-looking guards standing over them with nightsticks, they are mistaken.

It is a leisurely stroll of 150 yards to the dining hall. Once in the front door, you pick up a tray, order what you want, take it to one of forty four-seat tables, set down the tray, go back for your choice of coffee, tea, milk, juice. Can someone in the Justice Department explain how this makes sense, in light of the hunger and poor nutrition in America?

One thing is clear: every effort to integrate the population here in the mountains of Pennsylvania seems to fail. Here's an example.

Take Herb, an African American from Orlando. I am his mentor in long-distance running, and this irritates some of the brothers on his range. They have expressed to him strongly that to have a white coach is to be an Uncle Tom. Someone told him I had run the Boston Marathon a number of times, and he asked me for a training schedule. The training schedule for him was easy to draw up but difficult for him to execute.

He had to start by running thirty-five miles per week for the first few weeks, then graduate to fifty miles per week. I told him I was not interested in his speed per mile, only distance. I also told him I wanted him to run a distance of double-digit miles one day per week.

Herb ran in all kinds of weather, rain or shine, pounding out the miles. He senses that I am writing something, and occasionally, he will leave on my desk a copy of his writings, which are difficult to follow and very angry.

This morning, the latrine looks good. The administration thought I'd be screaming for help in a few days, but instead, I've stayed right through, and the latrine has never looked better.

At 1:00 p.m., however, there is a major crisis. Next to the latrine is the laundry. During lunch, one washing machine explodes, flooding the area. Inmates are working feverishly to clean up what (on closer inspection) is a flood with particles of food.

Where did it come from?

Big Boy, an inmate in the laundry who loves to eat (and it looks it) has a deal with the chef. He washes the chef's clothing in return for the chef's providing extra food. Usually, Big Boy stashes the contraband food between his bed and his locker.

Today, while Big Boy was in the kitchen picking up the chef's laundry, the chef gave him a huge turkey roll. Big Boy hid it under a cloth in the laundry basket, then wheeled the basket past the hack and out of the kitchen to the laundry.

Unfortunately, another worker emptied the entire laundry basket into the washing machine, including the twenty-pound turkey roll.

Friday, December 3, 1993

Regarding Camel's behavior, it would be excessive to say that he has become a gentleman, but he has been acting much more civilized since he was taped ankle to pate.

When I arrived, the inmate health code was explained to me, and it boils down to this: don't get sick.

There are several strategies. One is to get as much fresh air as possible, which gets you away from the constant coughing and sneezing. Second, eat lots of fresh, uncooked vegetables, and make sure you wash them off. Third, ingest lots of garlic; get fresh cloves from friends in the kitchen and put them in and on everything. Fourth, consume daily doses of at least 1,000 milligrams of vitamin C, which is sold in tablet form at the commissary. Fifth, every morning while brushing your teeth, brush your tongue, including the back part, and move the toothbrush back until you vomit. This cleans poisons from your system.

Personally, I have adopted the first four. I'm holding off on the fifth.

At breakfast this morning, Danny T. says he is in an odd mood, both philosophical and theological. He's wondering what happened to all those guys who are burning in hell for having eaten meat on Friday, only to have the church announce that Catholics henceforth are permitted to eat meat on Friday.

As it happens, Fr. Dene is sitting with us. Fr. Dene tightens his brow and formulates a thoughtful answer, but before he can articulate it, Danny T. asks, "So, what happens to these guys, Father? Are they all up for resentencing?"

At the latrine at 8:00 a.m., guess who's here? The painters, and with their boss coming by this morning, they're slapping paint everywhere. Nothing is spared their brush, including the chrome. Everything that's not moving is painted. I advise arriving patrons not to stand in one place too long.

Tonight, it becomes clear a schism has developed among our black brothers. Ron has heard through the prison pipeline that someone sent a love letter to a gay inmate and signed Ron's name. He is furious.

Within the black community, there are a lot of leaders, but Ron is the most effective, the most articulate. He's a talented artist who has lived in prison for eight years and yet, he's quiet, almost shy.

But now, he is the target of considerable ribbing.

His response: "I didn't send any motherfucking note to any mother-fucking motherfucker, and besides, there are so many misspellings in this note, you can tell that the motherfucker who wrote it is just plain stupid."

That is why he suspects his cellmate, Kiester.

The note reads as follows: "To my preshus rose, I would love to have you for a snack, and this lovely flower shows you how much I would love to be yours. Love, Ron."

Saturday December 4, 1993

I wake up at 5:30 a.m. It was a long night. Someone was singing a Latin serenade at 1:00 a.m., after which three Latin inmates decided to have a sing-along.

Today, my friend Nolan, the Philadelphia lawyer who drove me here from Harrisburg that first day, is visiting. This gives me an opportunity to study the visitor room and to evaluate the policies at work there.

At 1:00 p.m., Nolan arrives. They let me into the room, which gives me a chance to politic with visitors. It's been a while since I've worked a room politically, but I'm happy to realize that I still know how to do it.

Some visitors may find reassurance in this visiting room. There are no bars, no handcuffs, no Jimmy Cagney talking through the glass. At the same time, the experience is demeaning. For one thing, the guards go out of their way to make people uncomfortable. The crude treatment is supposed to remind everyone how bad we are, and it works. The guards search everything—adults, babies, carriages, baby clothes—and they do it in a way that emphasizes their authority.

Also, there is always the chance a guest will be chosen at random for a strip search, and it doesn't matter whether a visitor is black, white, old or young, male or female, adult or child. It's one reason why some inmates forbid their families to visit.

Nolan and I are close, but there's little to talk about.

"The next time I see you," I say with pleasure, "will be February 2 at eight o'clock in the morning, the day I get out."

Later, I get some bad news. The crumb cake being served today in the cafeteria has mold on it. I found out about that because I was alerted by the kitchen crew, who thought that as Latrine Orderly, I should be notified of the potential for an outbreak of intestinal flu.

I should have known something was strange. Usually, the cake goes quickly. Tonight, after word was passed about the mold, there was plenty left over. Unfortunately, before I got the word, I had four slices.

At Catholic services, Fr. Dene offers Mass for an elderly couple from Minersville that nobody ever heard of.

Sunday, December 5, 1993

Today, it's the oranges. Three hacks are there to ensure that no inmate takes more than one orange, and they are not much bigger than golf balls.

Remember the scene in *The Pink Panther*, when Peter Sellers, as a patrolman on a street in Paris, harangues a poor organ grinder for not having a license for his monkey, while, in the background, three thugs are beating up a nun?

It's being replayed here. The guard in the kitchen is counting each tiny orange, while through the window, I can look out and see inmates in white kitchen clothes lugging crates of oranges back to their unit.

Tonight, Mills and Kiester are involved in a titanic card game, and the loser has to pay with push-ups. But something new is added to the mix—Muff, a black inmate from Unit One who is notable for his slurry speech, which is attributable at least in part to the fact that he has no teeth. At five feet two and 110 pounds, Muff is easy to miss.

As we tune into the card game, Mills is screaming at Muff.

"You take those teeth out yo mouf. They not yo teeth. They belong to some liar. They is liar's teeth. They not yours."

Kiester: "Why should he?"

Mills: "Because they belong to some lying motherfucker."

Muff is laughing too hard, and that irritates Kiester.

Kiester: "What are you laughing at, Muff, you dumb motherfucker? You're the only con here who brushes his teeth with a glove and flosses with a sock."

Old Muff is laughing so hard his gums are showing.

At 10:30 p.m., the lights go out. At 12:20 a.m., the smoke alarm goes off.

Everybody is rousted out of bed. What a racket! Ear-shattering.

It lasts for fifteen minutes, until the duty officer arrives with a key to shut it off. Everybody is furious. When the hacks ask what's going on, everybody yells that it was a malfunction.

But seated under the smoke detector were Rock Bottom and three other inmates, playing Monopoly by flashlight and smoking cigarettes.

Monday, December 6, 1993

The painters arrive at the latrine at 8:30 a.m., which surprises me. I thought they were finished. Maybe they are, because they just set out their tools and disappear.

I kid the painters, but I have become their godfather. I write their letters in English. I help translate stories in newspapers and magazines. They tell me I am the only gringo who treats them with respect. Maybe what they're expressing is gratitude for the fact that, every morning, I provide them with a perfect cover, in that the hacks think the latrine is being painted.

Now the Latinos are negotiating with the kitchen workers to paint the kitchen next. Given their performance in my latrine, the kitchen will be finished about the time the Red Sox win a World Series. For the kitchen job, they are negotiating with Danny T., and the sticking point is how much food they can take while working.

Jose Jr., my favorite, tells me in broken English that he'll be getting out of here in 1996, just in time for the new president. The Latinos don't like Bill Clinton.

If you wonder why some inmates are cynical and consumed by bitterness, consider what happened today to Jeff, the inmate recently married.

Jeff was summoned to the administration office and handed a piece of paper mater-of-factly and without comment. On the handwritten note, obviously a telephone message, were the words:

"Jeff's father had a serious heart attack in Florida. Please have him call home immediately."

The message had been taken seven days earlier.

Tuesday, December 7, 1993

My friends the painters are back at the latrine this morning, but not to work. They're discussing their schedule, and the question they're debating among themselves is whether they should take off the rest of the week.

Here's the good news: the prison underground is going to get me Christmas cards to send out. Here's the bad news: I get every rotten job in *A* range.

This time, it's a sad inmate from Baltimore with a peculiar problem. He stinks. He doesn't take showers, doesn't wash his clothes, and, in fact, doesn't even change his clothes. Ironically, in order to keep himself in cigarettes, soda, and candy, he washes the clothes of other inmates, but never his own. Although he's young, he has bad teeth.

Other inmates have had it with the stench. The options are to give him a GI shower, that is, to strip him and scrub him clean with a brush, or to wrap him in blankets with his clothes on and throw him into the shower. The message is left for me to deliver to him. At my insistence, he's going to get one more chance to clean up his act and himself.

I tell him this without pulling any punches. He gets the message. He now showers regularly and washes his clothes. But he no longer speaks to me.

Wednesday, December 8, 1993

At breakfast, Herb and I discuss his progress on the track. He's kept at it through rain and snow, every day, doing six miles. We are now increasing the daily run and incorporating a longer run on Saturday, eighteen miles. If he completes that run for six weeks, I tell him, then he's ready for a marathon.

Today, he wants to talk about his friend Winslow, the six-foot-five-inch, 400-pound inmate whom I found cuddled up in my toilet stall sleeping.

As Herb explains it, "Winslow would like you to be his coach. He's going to be here another eight months, and he'd like to shed about 200 pounds." That, it occurs to me, is a lot of coaching.

"If Winslow wants my help," I tell Herb, "Winslow ought to talk to me himself."

I've seen Winslow making his way around the track. You cannot call it walking, actually. What he does is waddle around. Everything moves, more or less, like a waterbed.

After a few days, for some reason, Winslow quit walking. I have a feeling there is more to the story than Herb is telling me, and sure enough, when pressed, Herb says there is peer pressure within the African American community, especially from a brother named Famous, who is a major drug dealer from New York and a self-proclaimed leader. Famous has been ridiculing both Herb for jogging and Winslow for walking, claiming both endeavors were "whitey" sports. Rather than risk rejection by his black brothers, Winslow simply quit walking.

As it turned out, Winslow never approached me, which is too bad. He was the loser.

As we are finishing our French toast, the Renegade Jew arrives to hear Herb defend Famous.

"I don't blame Famous," says Herb. "It ain' his fault. The white establishment sent him here."

The Renegade Jew looks puzzled.

"So what? The white establishment sent me here, too."

In a place like this, there is heartbreak every minute. At two this afternoon, an inmate calls his home, which is occupied by his girlfriend. A man answered. When the girlfriend finally came to the telephone, she notified the inmate that he doesn't live there anymore.

Thursday, December 9, 1993

Our ranks have been depleted by transfers and discharges, but veterans say the facility will fill again, right after January, with an influx of what are called "self-surrenders."

There are two ways you report to a facility like this. One way is, after you are sentenced by the court, you are given a date on which to surrender. That, presumably, allows you time to set things in order. The other way is to be brought in shackled and handcuffed.

Oddly, the more seasoned prisoners do not like self-surrenders. Their dislike of them was exacerbated a few months ago when two brothers from Brooklyn arrived by limousine. The "self-surrenders" were accompanied by two attractive women, and all four of them were swizzling champagne. The two "self-surrenders" climbed out of the limousine carrying clothing bags and tennis rackets.

I sometimes hear older inmates say, "What do you think I am, a self-surrender?"

After dinner, I meet with a few inmates to talk about the theft of merchandise from the warehouse. On many days, foods and juices are listed on the prison menu but never served in the prison cafeteria, and inmates who work in the warehouse say that it is because a great deal of food is loaded into automobiles owned by BOP staff. Major items are sugar, fish, and orange juice.

Those who work at the warehouse say the BOP is probably paying a high price for goods of poor quality, that there is a lack of qualified bidders competing for contracts, and there is a lack of accountability. For example, it is standard procedure for food companies to measure the weight of all goods that arrive, but not at Schuykill. My contact at the warehouse says that since his arrival here, he has never seen the scale used.

Friday, December 10, 1993

Herb is psyched. Although he talked himself out if it last weekend, today he's committed to running one half of a marathon, which is 13.1 miles. I hope he's as ready mentally as he is physically.

My next-door-neighbor, Rock Bottom, does not have a high school diploma and, therefore, is in the GED program. Classes are held in the library. On occasion, I stop by to see friends in the class, like Rock Bottom, Kiester, the Hasidic Jew, and others.

It's so chaotic that it's like *Blackboard Jungle*, with Glenn Ford. The classes are run by inmates, who, of course, have no authority, no carrot as a reward, no stick to wave as a threat.

Here's an advisory to Hollywood: come to Schuykill with a video camera and tape these classes. Erase all references to "motherfucker"—this will cut the dialog in half—and what you have left is the material for a sitcom that cannot miss ranking among the top ten.

At today's class, the topic is Michael Jackson and his affection for little boys. Rock Bottom opens the discussion.

"How much would it take for anybody here to sleep with Michael Jackson?"

Kiester does not hesitate.

"For $50 million, ol' Michael could have whatever he wanted."

"If the motherfucker touched me," said Rock Bottom, "I'd kill him."

Kiester laughs.

"Nah, ol' Rock Bottom would sell out for a lot less than $50 million."

Rock Bottom is so fearsome that the teachers are reluctant to break the news to him that his reading skills are virtually nonexistent. One teacher approaches me to suggest that I tutor Rock Bottom.

"Can you get him to read at night, instead of watching TV or playing cards?" the teacher asks.

I come to Rock Bottom's defense.

"He reads, but it's mostly comic books and *Playboy*, *Penthouse*, and *Hustler*." I did get him to read *Cathedral*, by Nelson DeMille, but after three days, he quit, and now he's trying to read *Mobbed Up*, by James Nuff, the sordid life of teamster boss Jackie Presser.

The next time I see Rock Bottom, I bring up the subject.

"How come you quit reading the DeMille book?"

"It sucks. I like books with more action. There was too much time between shootings."

"You're always napping. When you're sleeping, you could be reading."

"OK, OK."

"As long as you read three chapters a day, I'm satisfied," I said. "And if you do my exercise regime, in three years, you'll look like me."

He snorts.

"If I looked as skinny as you, my wife would leave me."

I arrive at the latrine at 7:45 p.m. If it weren't for the smell, this job would be one of the best here. Inmates have renamed this the Lysol Room, and some joke that I am the Permanent Lysol Orderly. At least the place is germ-free.

I spend only ninety minutes a day here, and a lot of that is talking to inmates inside and outside the door of the latrine. In the time I have been here, inspectors have stopped by only once, and that was for equipment repair.

Here's how you know you're running a successful latrine. Some inmates leave their own living area and walk all the way over here to the administration building to use my latrine.

George, the head painter, stops by to see if his supervisor has been around. He hasn't. I walk along with George to the kitchen to see Danny T. They're still trying to figure out a tasteful color for the kitchen.

After lunch, the temptation is to lie down on my bunk. I've had a cold for several days, and I need to beat it. Rest is the key, but I've been here sixty days and haven't had a nap yet. I'd like to watch television, but I don't feel like fighting the politics in the TV room. A few minutes ago, while thirty inmates were watching a program on television, someone walked in and changed the station, and all hell broke loose.

Another problem is that it's becoming increasingly difficult to write notes for this journal. More and more people are becoming suspicious and looking over my shoulder. Some of the problems I have created myself, but a number of inmates are convinced that I am writing a book.

At dinner in the cafeteria, Pat, the tough guy, motions to me, then whispers that he wants to talk to me outside. This is unusual. Something is up. After the meal, Pat and I rendezvous at the track.

He tells me that he wants to talk to me over the weekend about a growing problem between Catholics and Jews, not in the Sinai Peninsula, but right here at Schuykill.

It's something that was ignited right where these things usually start here, in the TV room. One inmate made some anti-Semitic remarks that were overheard by a Jewish inmate and then disseminated around the facility with the speed of a Scud missile.

"If this thing isn't nipped in the bud," says Pat, "it could turn into a holy war."

The reason Pat has come to me is that the gentile in this equation, the guy who made the anti-Jewish remarks, is a neighbor with whom I used to work in the library.

"Shut him up," says Pat, "until we can come up with a solution."

Tonight, two great movies are scheduled: *Scent of a Woman*, with Al Pacino, and *Body of Evidence*, with Madonna. The TV room is packed. You couldn't add an inmate with a shoehorn.

Since early afternoon, guys have been staking out their turf by draping a blanket over the chairs they want to reserve for the night. Any interference with these territorial declarations is an invitation to war.

With everyone at the movie, I seek out my neighbor, the gentile who made the anti-Semitic remarks, and I make it crystal clear to him that he is expected to cool it until he hears from me.

He agrees to tone it down.

Saturday, December 11, 1993

Arriving at the latrine at 7:45 a.m., I realize that I have been here ten weeks. I try not to count. I have too much time to go. The strange part is that I cannot remember being anywhere else, can't remember getting up and going into any other setting. That's how much a place like this takes over your mind. Right now, I know only here, nothing else.

It's late morning and icy cold as Pat and I walk the track, talking about the dangers of a holy war in here. For more experienced inmates, this is a delicate issue, as it should be. The last thing needed in these close quarters is a revolt along racial, ethnic, or religious lines.

What started as a nonreligious dispute between two older guys who simply didn't like one another has now mushroomed into a debate as to whether Christmas decorations are appropriate. It's a controversy fueled by people whose self-esteem is so fragile they somehow feel more important when they are engaged in confrontation.

At Catholic services tonight, Fr. Dene announces that Mass is being offered for Mr. and Mrs. Richard McDonough of Minersville, Pennsylvania. The inmates look at one another and shrug. None of us ever heard of Mr. and Mrs. Richard McDonough.

Sunday, December 12, 1993

Ooohh, the mornings are cold here in the mountains of Pennsylvania. It's between five degrees and zero, and that's only a warning nip of what's coming in the next few weeks. At night, it's so cold inside that some of the inmates go to bed wearing a stocking cap. Others go to bed fully clothed. I sleep in my undershorts wearing my heavy winter coat over my legs. In the middle of the night, a trip to the latrine is not for the faint of heart.

At 9:00 a.m., and while I'm picking up supplies for the latrine, I am near the administration offices when I hear an argument in the room where the visitors are processed. I also hear an infant crying. A young woman has arrived with her baby daughter, six to eight months old. She is here to see her husband, who is the father of her child.

It was a seven-hour drive for her to get here. Among the items she packed was enough baby formula to get through the entire day. But the hack, a woman, will not allow the formula into the visitor room without first opening each bottle to check its contents.

The mother explains that each bottle is sealed, and that when the seal is broken, the milk has to be used immediately or thrown out. Her pleadings, however logical, fall on deaf ears. All the bottles are opened. Much of the formula has to be thrown out. The infant cries much of the day, making many inmates and their visitors uneasy.

There is no indication that the hack is in the least troubled by the discomfort she has caused the visitor and the baby.

It's 6:00 p.m., and I'm trying to write Christmas cards, but it's difficult to get into the spirit of the season here. I must force myself to remember that there are other people out there celebrating Christmas, people I love.

Monday December 13, 1993

It's 6:00 a.m., and the hacks are on edge. Word is that inmates at the medium security facility down in the valley are restless. Yesterday, there was a food strike.

As bad as we are here in this part of the prison, we're easy to deal with compared to those in medium security. Most of them are in for at least fifteen years, some as long as forty-five years, and so, when things do not go smoothly for them, they are quick to explode, for they have little to lose. After the food strike, the administration confined all inmates to cells except seven who were transferred to another prison.

Tensions are further exacerbated by congressional inaction of legislation to reform prisons. Of greatest importance to inmates here were provisions for alternative sentencing, which Attorney General Janet Reno had said was a priority. Good behavior now can mean as much as fifty-four days a year off an inmate's sentence. The attorney general wanted to double that to 100 days a year. Once again, nothing has happened.

Many inmates here watched a CNN broadcast of the debate in the House and Senate. Inmate morale was not improved by the repetition of such phrases as "keep 'em locked up" and "throw away the key" and "let's do away with the good-time gimmick."

As inmates watched the debate and recognized the politically obsequious bow to the conservative Republican movement, they just sat there, silent but seething.

This morning, there is another example of why this system is nuts. A new inmate has arrived. He's sixty-five years old. He's suffering from advanced cancer, and he's on chemotherapy. He's a first-time offender, nonviolent.

And so, you wonder, what is the purpose of keeping this guy in prison? What is the advantage? What danger would he pose to society if he were in an alternative program, like home confinement or a halfway house?

At 8:30 a.m., the painters arrive at the latrine, but only to drop off supplies, and then they are off again. I'd love to interview their boss. I wonder what he does all day.

After lunch, on the way back to my cell, I pass my neighbor in A-10, a new inmate, Neil, twenty-six, an Orthodox Jew from New Jersey.

This guy's in the wrong range. It's too tough here for him. I make an effort to get him all the things he needs until he can get to the commissary. He's taking the place of Mike, who was gone for three days before anyone realized he had been transferred to one of the less-threatening ranges.

I hope Neil fits in better. I'll watch out for him. I should just take care of myself, but that's not the way I was treated when I arrived. Neil will have it extra tough, though. Because he's Orthodox, he requires a special diet, time for prayer, etc. I hope he makes it.

After rosary and benediction service, the film is *Scent of a Woman*, a poignant movie. The theme is particularly relevant here and especially embarrassing to rats who have testified against someone. You can feel their discomfort. The movie ought to be mandatory viewing for inmates.

It's 10:30 p.m., lights out. Another day. What a great movie.

Tuesday, December 14, 1993

At breakfast, Danny T. is reminiscing about Brooklyn, the Little Italy of New York, and about the neighborhood he ran with an iron hand, about his gambling enterprises, about the guys who worked for him, and how tough it was collecting the money owed to him.

"The bad debts were a killer. If they couldn't come up with the cash, I'd have to take something of value, and so I ended up owning all kinds of different businesses—restaurants, taverns, cars, luncheonettes, boats, beauty parlors.

"The weirdest one was this Italian funeral home I inherited from a guy who couldn't pay up. Every once in a while, I'd stop by and check the place out, and it seemed OK, 'cause it was the busiest funeral home in Little Italy. Everybody who was anybody got laid out there, all the Italian wiseguys.

"One night, we're holding a wake there, this wiseguy they made Swiss cheese outta. So, I stop by to pay my respects. While I'm talkin' to my manager, I notice that, as people approach the casket, they're reaching in. So, I says to the manager, 'Why they reachin' into the casket?' The manager whispers to me. He says it's customary to leave a few dollars in the casket for the trip to heaven so that the deceased does not arrive empty-handed. Now, being the nice guy that I am, I didn't want a lot of cash rolling around the casket, so I tells my manager, "Empty the casket. Give me the money, and I'll replace it with one of my checks."

After breakfast, I'm back in range *A*, helping Neil clean up and make his bed. I give him a brief tour, pointing out key sites, the administration building, the laundry room, etc.

At 8:30 a.m., the painters arrive at the latrine. They put down their gear and leave, some for the pool room, others for the TV room.

Now, painting is one of the easiest jobs here.

If there are a million stories in the naked city, there are two million in this prison. Take George, the night orderly in the administration building. All he has to do is empty baskets, and there is no one to check to see that he does that much, because, by the time the hacks arrive the next morning, the day crew is already on the job.

George is the senior half of a father and son team here, both serving time for the same crime.

From time to time, George stops at my latrine to say hello, and when he does, I cannot keep my eyes off his hair, because he has what they call a weave, and boy does it look painful.

When George arrived, he walked around for two weeks without shower shoes. No one does that. In terms of health, it's just too risky. Finally, George was persuaded to buy shower shoes, but he didn't seem to understand the purpose. That night, he walked around the cell in his shower shoes, showing them off. Later, he headed to the washroom, but when he arrived at the shower, he took off his shower shoes and left them outside, then walked into the shower barefoot.

Wednesday, December 15, 1993

I wake up at 5:15 a.m., as usual. I'm scheduled to attend a meeting I've been waiting for. It's called a prerelease meeting, and it runs from 8:15 a.m. to 3:15 p.m.

It turns out that the meeting is for all inmates with less than a year to serve, and by 8:45 a.m., the room is packed. The purpose is to prepare us for the street.

According to the schedule, one person we are to hear from is an employment counselor who will advise us about job availability. But he doesn't show up.

We are also to hear from a counselor who will educate us about life in the halfway houses we're destined for. But he doesn't show up either.

In their place are substitute speakers, hacks from the BOP, who don't know what they're talking about. Next is a representative of the probation department to warn us that even one violation of probation will land us right back here.

The final speaker is a shrink who talks about the transition from prison to civilian life.

"Among the things you'll have to be prepared for," he says, "is the possibility that your wives or girlfriends could be living with another man."

The whole exercise is another waste of time, and when the long meeting is abbreviated, nobody complains.

At mail call, watching the response of inmates can be heart wrenching. Almost all inmates look forward to mail call, even those that rarely get any mail. There's always hope, I suppose.

But when the final letter is given out, among those who received nothing the disappointment is obvious.

Some creative practical joker caused a stir tonight. He put up a bogus sign that invited everyone to bingo, and about 100 inmates showed up. When they discovered it was a joke, they were not happy.

First in line was Kiester, who expressed the sentiments of many: "If I find out who did this, his ass will be licking the earth."

Thursday, December 16, 1993

In the latrine, there are no painters this morning, although their supplies are still here.

At 9:30 a.m., after the latrine is in order, I head for the library to read. The topic on everybody's mind is an article in *Business Week* about prisons.

One conclusion I'd have a difficult time disputing is the claim that more police are needed on the streets. But the major premise everyone agrees on—and it doesn't matter whether you are liberal or conservative, young or old, black or white, rich or poor, Republican or Democrat—is that the criminal justice system in America is not working.

The article tries to assess the cost of crime for each of us, particularly the hidden costs. Among the proposed remedies is a job corps that might be more effective in rehabilitating inmates and also be cheaper than prison.

But if you are running for Congress, you do not win votes by proposing a job corps in place of prisons, even for white-collar criminals. What plays better at home in the congressional district is rhetoric about locking 'em up and throwin' away the key.

The article outlines the high cost of building and maintaining prisons, and yet Congress is debating the construction of even more prisons that will cost the taxpayers another $2 billion.

The answer, it seems to me, lies somewhere in between. In some cases, perhaps we need longer sentences. In others, however, we need a sentencing policy with the flexibility to acknowledge the difference between violent and nonviolent criminals. We also need the imagination and the courage to take advantage of the potential for a job corps and also saving taxpayer dollars in more sophisticated home detention systems and in halfway houses.

After eighty days here, I am convinced that there are people at Schuykill who are a menace to society. They belong here. On the other hand, I'm also convinced of the potential for a great savings of taxpayer dollars. Most of the inmates here are no more danger to society than fans leaving Yankee Stadium after a ballgame and no more of a threat than yuppies emerging from bars on Newbury Street in Boston late on a Saturday night.

There are doctors here who could be working at health centers in New York or with AIDS patients or on a reservation with Native Americans. There are tradesmen here whose skills could be utilized to rebuild areas of the nation that have been devastated by natural disasters. There are teachers, lawyers, and cooks who have more to contribute to the country than sitting around this place, eating too much food, and yawning away the afternoons watching Bugs Bunny cartoons.

Late in the afternoon, we get word from inmates who went to early chow, warning us not to eat tonight's veal. It's gone bad. At dinner, as I go through the food line, servers tell me the veal is vile, and everybody should take double helpings so we can throw it out. Otherwise, they'll serve the bad veal for lunch tomorrow.

Friday, December 17, 1993

Up at 5:15 a.m., thanks to Camel. This is the best time to clean up, shower, and do laundry. On cold days like this, the hot water often runs out.

The rumor this morning is that there'll be budget cuts across the board that will affect every aspect of prison life, and specifically that they're going to cut back on the amount of food that is served, and also that inmates' wages will be cut from eleven cents an hour to eight. I do not help morale by joking that we're out of toilet paper in the latrine and that I doubt there'll be any more available until after the first of the year.

At 9:45 a.m., I'm in the library when an inmate whispers to me that the camp administrator is in the hallway with a clipboard and that he is headed toward my latrine.

So, that's how they inspect my latrine—they wait until I leave, then come in and snoop around. Best way to deal with this is head-on. When I arrive, the camp administrator is surveying the latrine. I identify myself as the inmate responsible for the latrine.

"This is a tough one," he says, by which I assume he means a tough assignment for me.

"We've had trouble with this place since the camp opened."

"This job," I say lightly, "is like cleaning the men's room at Boston Garden between periods of a Bruins game."

He doesn't smile.

"It looks real good, today," he says as he heads out the door.

Time elapsed: two minutes.

At lunch, as I go through the line, one of the servers nods toward the salad bar, and sure enough, there it is, the rancid veal from last night's supper. Talk about slow poison.

The Renegade Jew sits at my table. I like him. But now, he's having marital problems, which is not uncommon here. Nothing worse for an inmate than an argument with his wife over the telephone. It festers for weeks.

Walking the track after lunch, I marvel at the beauty of the day, and I wonder what the rest of the world is doing.

Tonight, the Jewish community has a movie, *Silence of the Lambs.* The Jewish group has made arrangements to have seven of the latest movies sent to their rabbi, who places them in the locker reserved for Jewish religious items. One inmate has access to the locker.

It's a great idea, and Pat and I meet on the track to set up a similar procedure for our group after Catholic services. First, we need seven or eight Catholics to pick a movie and pay for it. After we have the list of movies and the money, I will order the movies, pay for them, and have them sent to Fr. Dene.

Before we can get the idea off the ground, Fr. Dene vetoes it. His reasoning: for him to accept movies from inmates might be interpreted as bribery. End of discussion.

Saturday, December 18, 1993

As the weather gets colder, outdoor activity becomes less appealing, and many inmates find it difficult to fill the weekend days. Many of them simply increase the amount of food they eat and then sleep longer.

It's snowing this morning, and inmates from the South revel in it. Some of them are out walking the track for the mere pleasure of being in the snow, and that mystifies those of us from the North who have shoveled it all our lives.

Tonight, while I'm writing, an argument erupts nearby. A neighbor whom I dislike immensely, the Whiner, is playing his radio so loud it's disturbing people around him. Another neighbor, Jerry, an older guy who rarely speaks, addresses the Whiner.

"Turn that fuckin' radio down!"

The Whiner, apparently, had already turned down the radio once, and this time he took the heat and began to complain that the only reason he was being told to turn down his radio is that he's white.

"If I were black," he whined, "no one would dare say anything."

It was an odd thing to say. Jerry, as it happens, is white, so it obviously has nothing to do with race. I've never liked the Whiner. I've been waiting for a chance to confront him, and this is it. I tell him in no uncertain terms what I think of him, his whining, and his stupidity about race. An argument ensues, and it gets heated until three inmates step between us.

Rock Bottom and Paul take me aside.

"It's time for a break," says Paul. "Let's go over to church."

He's right. I'd love a chance to engage the Whiner. He's a lousy dope dealer from Philadelphia, who turned in his uncle and his friends. Still, Paul and Rock Bottom are right; it's not worth it. On the way to church, though, I'm still seething. I hate whiners.

At Mass tonight, Fr. Dene is on a roll, plenty of hymns, loud singing, and a fiery sermon. In a gesture that induces a snicker from some in the congregation, Fr. Dene offers Mass for his deceased grandparents.

Back on *A* range, some inmates are complaining that there's nothing to do. That's just more whining. There's plenty to do. Write a letter, read a book, watch television, work out, wash clothes. There are always things to do.

It's 9 p.m., and I can hear conversation by my neighbors, the oddest couple I know—Neil, the Orthodox Jew, and Louis, the Puerto Rican cocaine dealer. Neil eats a kosher diet. Louis eats junk food. Neil uses the cell for daily prayers. Louis uses it to store his dirty books.

Tonight, Neil is worried about an interview for a job.

"When I report to the work pool Monday," he says to Louis, "what should I say when they ask me what I'm qualified to do?"

"Tell them what I told them, that you're qualified to sell illegal drugs."

It's 10:30 p.m., there's five inches of snow on the ground, and it's coming down heavy.

Oh, great! It's almost midnight, and some jerk turned on the fire alarm. The hacks on duty don't have a key to shut it off. They have to send down to medium security for a key. It clangs for an hour, driving everybody crazy, until finally, a little after 1:00 a.m., it's shut off. At last, silence. My ears will be ringing for days.

Sunday, December 19, 1993

Well, now it's 2:30 a.m., and the same crew that works in summer on landscaping is assigned in the winter to snow removal, and a few minutes ago, the hacks came round to roust them out of bed.

It's quite a transition. One guy who just arrived here and was happy to be assigned to landscaping now finds himself shoveling snow. He doesn't know what hit him. A few minutes ago, when the hack shook him to wake him to shovel snow, the inmate thought he was having a nightmare.

"Up and at 'em," said the guard. "C'mon, let's move some snow. Get up and grab a shovel."

The new inmate was stunned.

"I don't have any boots," he mumbled.

"I don't care if you have to go out in bare feet. Get up, and shovel the fucking snow or your ass is going to the hole."

Hours later, on my way to the dining hall for breakfast, I see the same poor guy, still shoveling snow in his running shoes.

Sunday morning meals are getting better, thanks to my neighbor, Neil the Orthodox Jew. He gets three or four pieces of whole wheat bread with every kosher meal, and he saves me a few slices to go with my can of tuna fish.

Oh-oh. As I approach my locker this morning, I notice that someone has attached to the door a quotation from *Reader's Digest* for everyone to see. The quotation reads: "Politicians are just like diapers. They need to be changed often and for the same reason." Sounds to me like this guy probably favors term limits.

It's almost noon, and although the only radios allowed are those with earphones, today you can hear the muffled sounds of Christmas carols. Among inmates, I don't see the sadness I'd been warned to expect. On the contrary, many inmates hum along with the carols or even sing aloud. The mood is not what you would find at Boston's Symphony Hall on those December nights when the perform *The Messiah*, but nevertheless, the Christmas spirit prevails.

After a workout, I'm back on *A* range for a shower and a "Timilty Special," which is a sandwich of peanut butter and banana, washed down with ice water. This tastes better than it sounds.

It's quiet here today, few hacks. Inmates are watching pro football, reading, listening to Christmas carols. Outdoors, there is a game of football. Inmates are tackling one another in the snow. Another group is making a gigantic snowman, although, on closer examination, I guess it's a snowwoman.

I've finished my Christmas cards and also a few letters to friends back home. *A* range is loud tonight, but tonight the atmosphere is different. There's a sense of anticipation, rather like kids awaiting Santa Claus.

In retaliation for the ringing of the fire alarm last night, a commando raid is being planned tonight against Unit One. The weapons: snowballs. Now, that may sound like a game played by Rebecca of Sunnybrook Farm, but it's not. These snowballs were made this morning. They've been left outside all day. They're frozen solid and hard as rocks.

One thing that surprises me is the genuine laughter here among guys who, if they thought about it, don't have that much in their lives that's amusing, given that in some cases they're here for as long as ten years.

The commando group assembles at my end of the range. They will leave and return by the back door. To disguise their identities, they're wearing gas masks. Now, where on earth would they come up with gas masks? Nobody seems to know.

The mission has been planned down to the finest detail. It will take no more than five minutes. By 9:05 p.m., they're back. They undress, hide their clothes, hop into their racks with books, and pretend to be reading,

The raid could not have been organized more effectively by the command staff of Desert Storm.

Monday, December 20, 1993

I wake up at 5:15 a.m.

Welcome to Christmas week at Schuykill.

Actually, the only signs of Christmas thus far are the radios that play Christmas carols without interruption.

Today, however, we have another crisis, and it involves Miss Personality, my coordinator, who recently married the Protestant minister and who, because of her arrogance, is not popular among the inmates.

Yesterday, when she arrived at the barracks, she was stunned by what she saw on the front lawn. It was an eight-foot snowman, or, more precisely, snowwoman. The face had a carrot for a nose and prunes for eyes. The snowwoman was grotesquely wide of beam and, depending on your outlook, was either blessed or cursed with massive breasts that were set off by two prunes for nipples.

And worse, the snowwoman wasn't wearing any clothes.

There was no question in the minds of anyone who saw the snowwoman that what the sculptor had in mind was not Cindy Crawford but our own Miss Personality. Most inmates applauded the work as creative, inspirational, and worthy of an award. As it happened, however, neither the administration nor Miss Personality was amused, and, at the instruction of the hacks, Miss Personality—the snowwoman, that is—was demolished.

At breakfast, the major topic of discussion is last night's report on *60 Minutes* about prisoners escaping from halfway houses in Washington, D.C., 2,500 of them, some very dangerous.

The *60 Minutes* report attempted (and failed) to make the case for no more halfway houses, no more home confinement, a truly absurd idea.

What *60 Minutes* appears to have done is what the press is guilty of doing from time to time. That is, to focus on one obvious failure, in this case the mismanagement of halfway houses in Washington that enabled violent men to escape, and then to use that frightening fact to argue that the failing of one halfway house automatically applies to all of them.

The question *60 Minutes* ought to address is this: who is the mental giant in Washington who is responsible for discharging violent criminals to halfway houses that are so badly managed they become drug centers?

There's a situation here are Schuykill that demonstrates my point. An inmate who had been incarcerated for a long time was looking forward to his freedom and to a new start in life. He was discharged to a halfway house where he would live for ninety days to ease his transition back to civilian life.

He left Schuykill with fanfare, a big party. Eight days later, he was back, and why? As he explained it, there were so many drugs all over the halfway house that he assumed it was only a matter of time before he was entrapped in some way and eventually incriminated and sent back to prison for an extended period.

And so he appealed to the Bureau of Prisons to cancel his probation and return him from the halfway house to Schuykill so that he would not run the risk of being ensnared in the drug culture at the halfway house.

It's 7:30 a.m., work call, some inmates hate the words, but not me.

Without work, the weekends drag by. Once I hear "Work Call," I know the day is half over.

My routine is this: I get to the latrine, work ninety minutes, and I'm through for the day. Others move around here like the walking dead, checking in at work, then looking for a place to hide so they can fall asleep, a routine they repeat after breakfast and then after lunch.

What a way to exist! Or not exist!

At 7:45 a.m., after a light cleanup, the latrine is A-OK.

The Permanent Latrine Orderly is like the town crier. He has an opinion on every subject. On the other hand, if he wants to, he can clear the latrine in an instant. All he has to do is bring out the Lysol.

Tuesday, December 21, 1993

Camel wakes me, as usual, at 5:15 a.m.

"Git oop," he says. "You goot only four shopping days to Chreestmas."

Then he laughs and disappears into the darkness, like some alien character.

Outside, a blizzard is raging, and guards have pressed into service the entire landscaping crew for snow clearance, plus all new inmates not yet assigned a permanent job. All of them are awakened at 2:00 a.m. and herded outdoors to sand walks and shovel snow. It is the third night in a row they have been shanghaied from their beds, and each time, their moans grow louder.

At breakfast, Danny T. predicts the food here is going to ruin him as a normal person.

"When I get out of here and go to fancy restaurants, which I do a lot, I'll order French toast, and if it comes out hot, I'll send it back and say that I can't enjoy it, that it's just not cold enough."

At 9:00 a.m., I'm on my way to the dentist; I had given up trying to make an appointment. It's common knowledge that you have to wait months. Then an inmate told me how the process works. Or doesn't work. The way to get an appointment with the dentist quickly is to complain that you cannot work because of an infection in your mouth. Then, right away, they set up an appointment for you.

While my teeth are being cleaned, I sit in awe, listening to the small talk between the dentist and his assistant.

It isn't what they were saying, but how. They're not cursing, whining, or threatening one another. They're civilized people. They're bantering, joking, laughing. I had forgotten that there were people in the world who still act normally, who still converse in reasonable tones about interesting topics.

I could have listened to them all day. How different from my initial encounter trying to give an appointment to a prisoner in pain.

Wednesday, December 22, 1993

I look for signs of Christmas but see none. The only reference to the holiday concerns the menu and who will eat first, the inmates from Unit One or Unit Two.

Around their cubes, inmates display Christmas cards. The greater the number of cards, the greater the status and the greater the esteem in which an inmate is presumed to be held. More important, Christmas cards serve to remind an inmate that he is cared for by someone.

At this time of year, photographs are passed around more frequently, and the response is almost always the same: "What a good-looking woman!" or "What a handsome kid!" It's painful.

Regarding my latrine, this ought to tell you something. The inmates responsible for cleaning other latrines in Units One and Two both come here to the administration building to use mine.

After dinner, back to *A* range, where a new batch of dirty books has arrived. It's a mystery to me where they come from. There is no way a guard who opens the mail would let these publications pass. These are not your run-of-the-mill *Playboy, Penthouse,* or even *Hustler.* These books could not possibly be more graphic. Many of the hardest criminals here dismiss the books as demeaning. They neither read them nor look at them. In fact, the toughest guys, those spending the longest time here, prefer there be no discussion of sex whatsoever.

In any institution like this, masturbation is a fact of life. Occasionally, you hear a veiled reference to it. An inmate might say that he has a date tonight with a book. Otherwise, it is not addressed. At the same time, consorting with gay inmates is frowned upon.

A few minutes ago, I walked by Caro's bunk, and he was reading one of the graphic pornographic books.

"Does your mother know you read that stuff?" I ask.

He never looked up.

"My mother sent it to me."

Thursday, December 23, 1993

When I wake at 5:15 a.m., there are three feet of snow on the ground, and the ground crews are still at it. They must be hurting.

At breakfast, Danny T. is philosophical about his future. He realizes that he cannot go back to New York City, that he is too well known to the cops, and so he's moving his operation out to North Dakota, to Bismarck.

"The Feds will never find me there," he says.

"I never heard of the place," I say.

He looks at me as if I just arrived from Mars.

"Didn't you ever watch Jackie Gleason?" he says. "Did you ever see *The Honeymooners* on television? Ralph Cramden and Norton belonged to a lodge, the International Order of Friendly Raccoons, and every Raccoon and his spouse get to be buried for free in the Raccoon National Cemetery in Bismarck, North Dakota."

"You're right," I said. "The Feds will never find you there."

Arriving at the latrine at 7:45 a.m., I'm pleased. The place looks good. Keep at it, Joe.

By the way, if one more inmate in here calls me "Pop," I'm going to pop him.

I talked to the Bear this morning. We have become friends. He'll be leaving in mid-January, and we have a standard joke.

"I'll be real glad to see you leave," I tell him, "because when you go, I know I'll be right behind you."

Every prison should have someone like Bear.

The Bear settles arguments, conciliates disagreements, and has done more than anyone else to keep the peace in here. He's one of the toughest guys here, and everyone pretty much agrees that it's just not a good idea to challenge the Bear.

For the past year and a half, the Bear has been told by the administration that he'll spend his final four months in a halfway house. Now, two days before Christmas, they break the news to the Bear that instead of leaving in January, he must wait until March.

So, from the Schuykill administration, Merry Christmas, Bear, and thanks for all your help in keeping the peace here.

The Bear must be coming apart inside. I know I would be.

Word passes this morning that a friend, Jim, a source of information for me, has had another argument with the boss hack at the warehouse, where he works. Another Merry Christmas from the administration.

It occurs to me this morning that there a lot of hacks patrolling the corridors today. I haven't seen this much force since the days before Thanksgiving. This must be BOP policy. Holidays, they say, are the most explosive times in any prison, and the additional show of force is intended to stop trouble before it starts.

At 1:00 p.m., we are ordered back to our cells for a count. This is an odd hour for a recall. There's no storm, no fog, no escapes—or at least none that I've heard of in the latrine, where I have developed one of the better communications systems here. Sometimes we know things in the latrine before they do in the front office.

Inmates who've been around for a while suggest that we have been locked up so the hacks can enjoy their Christmas party. A hack walks through and gives each inmate a package. It's our Christmas present. The package contains one box of crackers, four ounces of hot cheese, five ounces of salami, five ounces of sausage. The date on the package is 1985.

That night, Pat and I decide that we need to liven things up, and so we hatch a plot to provide entertainment on Christmas Eve. The Jewish group has seven new movies. All we need is a VCR, a television, and a room where everyone can watch a movie. Pulling this off will be my Christmas present to the inmates.

The key is Mr. Heater, head of the education department, who sided with Ponytail and against me a few weeks ago. He has found out since who was right in that argument because in the interim, he has had to chastise Ponytail several times because of his slovenly work habits.

As it turns out, they both did me a favor. In any case, Mr. Heater has been friendly to me since. We speak regularly, as a courtesy. Now, I have a political agenda, because he has the TV, he has a VCR. It's supposed to be used for educational purposes with one exception: it also can be used by the rabbi and the Catholic chaplain in order to show movies after religious services.

I meet Mr. Heater in the corridor and mention that Christmas Eve Mass will be at 7:15 p.m. instead of the customary 6:30 p.m.

"Can we borrow the TV and VCR for that time?"

"Yes, of course, Timilty," he says, eager to agree to so easy a request.

Great. Everything will work out here on one condition: that he makes no mention of this to Fr. Dene.

"Wait a minute, says Mr. Heater. "I just remembered. Friday is Christmas Eve, and all administration personnel will be leaving at midnight for the weekend, so there'll be nobody to put away the TV and VCR."

"I can take care of that."

"No, that's not a good idea."

"As you know, I have access to the administration offices."

"Well, OK, as long as they're both put away on Christmas Eve. Don't keep them all weekend to watch football games."

"Oh, absolutely not."

Friday, December 24, 1993

I wake up at 6:00 a.m., without Camel. Just as well. If Camel woke me this morning and said "Git oop. You got only one shopping day to Chreestmas," I'd have whacked him with a Christmas card.

At coffee hour, it occurs to me that Dunkin' Donuts has no competition from the doughnuts here. They taste like cobblestones. You can always tell when Doc oversleeps. From the second-string bakers, we get these jawbreakers. There are plenty of doughnuts left over, and I smuggle some of them back to *A* range. Must be the Christmas spirit within me.

As I distribute the doughnuts, I approach Coach's cell. To keep out the light while he sleeps, Coach wears blinders, which he calls his "Head Bra." I've never seen anyone sleep in that gear before. As I near his cot I see that, sure enough, the Coach is wearing his "Head Bra" over his eyes, and without touching it, he says, "Hi Joe." He identifies me by my footsteps.

At 9:15 a.m., over the intercom, I am summoned to the office.

Turns out to be a telephone call from friends from Boston who are visiting in Allentown, Connie and Ed, who want to stop by on Christmas Day. But that's when the focus here is on visits by children; Rock Bottom is playing Santa Claus, and all other visits are discouraged. I tell Ed and Connie that I'll catch them at home.

Meanwhile, my neighbors, the Odd Couple, Neil and Louis, the Orthodox Jew and the Puerto Rican drug dealer, have decided that because it is so cold, they will prepare lunch here in *A* range.

Neil contributes tuna fish and whole wheat bread. Louis adds fresh tomato, onion, garlic, and pepper. I provide two bananas. It's a great lunch, and as I leave, the Puerto Rican and the Orthodox Jew are debating the nutritional merits of Spanish versus kosher foods.

In terms of the movie, it's decision time. I still don't have the video-tape in hand. That was Pat's job, to get the movie from the leader of the Jewish group. I don't want to be strolling around Schuykill with a TV and VCR and no videotape.

I've got to see Pat at dinner.

After dinner, I pick up the TV and the VCR, get it to the visitor room, and set it up before Mass.

What should I choose for the Christmas Eve movie at Schuykill?

It's a Wonderful Life with Jimmy Stewart? No. Tonight's Mass and weeks of Christmas carols will have satisfied those needs.

Good Morning, Vietnam with Robin Williams? No, too militaristic.

Aliens, the science-fiction movie? No, too inane.

Ah, here it is, *Bugsy*, with Warren Beatty, the story of Bugsy Siegel, the crackpot gangster who helped establish the monstrosity we now call Las Vegas. Whether you liked the movie or not, you have to admit, it's perfect for our constituency.

It's 6:30 p.m., Christmas Eve, and Mass is packed, including people I have never seen at Mass, which is great, because everyone is welcome at a Catholic service. Before Mass, a longtime inmate, now attending his third Christmas Eve Mass here, takes a moment to express his thanks publicly to Fr. Dene for showing up every week. The good father gets a standing ovation.

His sermon tonight is about sacrifice. I guess that means we all need to sacrifice more.

After Mass, we watch *Bugsy*, and it hits the spot.

Merry Christmas to all from Schuykill, and by the way, I didn't like the movie.

It's midnight, and there's an emergency. An officer comes around with a book and with pictures of inmates that he uses to check off every inmate. This is done when someone has escaped. But no one is missing. They're guessing that Christmas is a night when an inmate might go over the hill.

Just before lights out, I mention loud enough for most inmates to hear, especially my friends Kiester and Mills, who are black, that the only black in the movie was a waiter.

Bingo!

That does it. The whole range erupts in laughter and camaraderie.

"Waiter?" yells Kiester. "Waiter? I'll show you a waiter, he was just waiting to rob your white ass."

It lasts till long after lights out.

Somebody yells, "Timilty started this, and then he went to sleep!"

Later, I felt good that on Christmas Eve, when most of the guys fell asleep, they did so with laughter in their hearts.

Christmas Day

I wake at 5:15 a.m.

It's Christmas Day.

Outside, it's fifteen degrees. Inside, it feels like twenty.

Chow hall doesn't open until seven. This is a great time to do a wash. I'll probably have the room to myself. With seven children, I know from experience that families rise early on Christmas Day, especially the children. One year ago today, I never dreamed that I would spend Christmas morning, 1993, doing a wash at a prison in central Pennsylvania.

To breakfast, I bring some great baked ham with me. It was cooked last night for today's Christmas dinner, and last night, my cellmate brought some of it back from the kitchen. I made a thick sandwich, using Neil's whole wheat bread, and it was great. In honor of Christmas, there are tablecloths today. They're trying, I guess, but for all their efforts, the coffee doesn't taste any better.

After breakfast, I head to the administration building to check the latrine and, sure enough, it took a beating last night. There are so many activities going on here at night, it's better that I stay out of here.

By 8:30 a.m., you can here children coming in the prison. Can you think of a crueler way for a youngster to spend Christmas morning than here in prison, visiting Daddy?

Santa Claus heads for the visitor room. This is as sad as I've seen it. The 90 percent of inmates who do not have visitors today have little to remind them it's Christmas.

It's too cold to walk outside. TV is a sad reminder of what they are missing at home so they head to their ranges to read, play cards, or sleep. What else are they going to do?

You cannot get to a telephone. The conversations are long, and the lines are three, four, five, and six deep.

At 11:15 a.m., I head for the workout room and my trusty rowing machine, and lo and behold, I find the warden's present to the prison, a cycle—one lone cycle for some 300 inmates.

Merry Christmas, boys!

There's no question there will be fights over the Lifecycle, and the probability is that it won't work for long. It was assembled by inmates without proper tools. Already, because the wrong batteries were used, the timing mechanism does not function.

At 2:00 p.m. on Christmas Day, at an hour when most families around the world are celebrating the joy of family, here at Schuykill a few inmates are playing football in the snow, others are watching the movie *Cliffhanger*. Lines at the telephone are longer than ever. Most inmates, as usual, are sleeping.

Several times during the year, the administration goes to great lengths to make a great meal, and Christmas is one of those days. They serve pot roast, baked ham, mashed potatoes, apple pie, and ice cream. My compliments to all the inmates who prepared, cooked, and served this meal.

Because I was one of the last inmates to go through the line, after telling the chefs what a great job they did, I was given enough pot roast and baked ham not only for today but for tomorrow's breakfast and lunch.

What's odd about today is that I'm feeling comfortable here, and that disturbs me. It's as if I've always lived here. I'm getting to know this place. Maybe too well.

At 7:30 p.m., Catholic services are held in the visitor room. Fr. Dene offers Mass for Joseph Coleman. None of us has any idea who Joseph Coleman is.

The evening is a time to reflect on Christmas at Schuykill. Tonight, I make a promise to myself. I shall never attend a Christmas Mass without thinking not only of the inmates here at Schuykill but also of all those people, wherever they may be, who are locked up on Christmas. Old pros say that when you leave prison, you leave something of yourself there. I know that among the things I'll carry with me forever are the images of Christmas at Schuykill.

At 10:30 p.m., I am lying in my bunk. I am thinking about my day here and, with longing, about my family at home and then, suddenly, they just turn out the lights on Christmas at Schuykill.

Sunday, December 26, 1993

I wake up at 7:00 a.m., an hour late, but what a great night's sleep! What is it they say about a clear conscience?

The outside temperature is zero.

At coffee hour, yesterday's bagels are cooked just right, and the leftover pot roast with cream cheese makes a great breakfast sandwich.

At brunch, the line is long for scrambled eggs, but I'm better off avoiding the cafeteria and working out instead. While on the rowing machine, I can hear noise from the visitor room. It must be the families who visited yesterday, who came from a long distance and are making a weekend of it, visiting their husband, father, son, whatever. I wonder if it gets easier for them on the second, third, and fourth visit? Or does it get harder?

The afternoon provides an opportunity to write. Although I am always playing catch-up, the writing serves to occupy my time. Other inmates waste their time by doing nothing more constructive than wandering around. Psychologically, they're better off on workdays, occupied.

At least they have someplace to go, something to do, some reason for existing.

At dinner, we're back to the usual bill of fare, processed turkey with lumpy mashed potatoes. Well, good food was fine while it lasted.

Knowing that I have access, at least for the weekend, to a TV and VCR, inmates are pressing me for a movie tonight. The Jewish group suggests *Dr. Zhivago*, the sprawling story that stars Omar Sharif as the Russian orphan who becomes a poet and marries an aristocrat. It's a classic, all right, but it's a classic that was released originally at three hours and seventeen minutes.

At 6:00 p.m., *Dr. Zhivago* starts.

At 8:40 p.m., we break for count, and everybody seems to like the movie.

At 9:20 p.m., it's back to *Dr. Zhivago*.

At long last, at 10:00 p.m. the movie ends, and I return the VCR and TV to the education room.

Monday, December 27, 1993

Camel is back on the job, waking me at 5:15 a.m. and slamming Christmas, which he refers to as "Holy Rip-off."

With a wind chill of thirty below zero, the walk to the dining hall is painful.

After breakfast, I report to the latrine. Looks like it took a direct hit. The condition of this place says volumes about inmates. Can it be that they live at home in the same kind of filth? Still, this job is better than the library, simply because I make my own hours. But it takes longer than usual to get the place clean. I use a gallon of Lysol.

The painters (remember them?) have disappeared. I see them every day in the dining hall, where they eat, but never in the latrine, where, for the present at least, they're supposed to be working.

After Catholic services, the movie is *The Untouchables*, with Kevin Costner as Eliot Ness in David Mamet's update of the TV series about the earnest but naïve federal agent trying to wipe out crime in Chicago in the days of Prohibition. The Bear attends because he's been told there's a lot of gunfire, but he leaves midway through, complaining that the movie has the wrong good guys.

Tonight, we hold a surprise birthday for Rock Bottom. Here's a challenge for a host or hostess. On short notice, you are obliged to prepare a party for twenty people. Here, on *A* block, however, to my amazement, we are having a spur-of-the-moment party for twenty inmates, and the food, the cakes, the rolls, and the meats are all superb. The kitchen staff has done it again.

Tuesday, December 28, 1993

Boy, it is cold!

In five days, the temperature has not climbed above five degrees. In some ranges, inmates sleep fully clothed, wearing stocking hats, trousers, shirts, jackets, even gloves.

Even for me, a New England boy, this is cold. I can't imagine what it's like for guys from the South. When I take my shower at 5:30 a.m. every day, it's easy to step into the hot water, but it takes courage to step back out into the cold air.

This morning, for a change, the latrine is looking good. In any facility like this, with 250 to 300 men, you're going to find bullies who harass those they perceive to be vulnerable inmates, those who are weaker because of age, ethnic origin, disability, or whatever. I've always had a special loathing for bullies, and so, in the latrine, I'm on the watch for them.

I give them a great big hello, which never goes over well, because they know from experience that I don't mean it. They know I see through them. They don't like me for various reasons—where I come from, my ethnic background, my allegiance to the Democratic Party, and my disdain for them. And so, when they come in, they often find themselves herded by me into a stall without toilet paper, or worse, one with toilet paper that's wet.

My new neighbor, Neil, took verbal abuse from one of the worst of these guys for no reason that I could see except that Neil is Jewish. The bully will pay, though, I'll see to that.

In recent days, several inmates mention to me that I'm getting close to the end of my stretch. It's a matter of degree. To someone still facing five years, my five weeks seem like the snap of a finger. To me, that much time without seeing Elaine and my children is an eternity.

At 4:00 p.m., at mail call, I get a surprise. They must have been holding back my mail, because I get forty cards and letters. I'll never be able to answer them all.

Tonight, over in the cell where Kiester and Mills live, there is a black social gathering. Among those attending is our friend, Pat, the transvestite. When offered an opportunity by Kiester to speak, Pat announces that he's making a New Year's resolution, that he's going to become a man again and that he's going to have no more homosexual relationships. Pat's vow is met by howls of laughter. Privately, the prediction is that Pat's resolution won't last the night.

Wednesday, December 29, 1993

The walk to the dining hall this morning is tough. The wind chill makes it thirty degrees below zero, and when the wind whips across the open fields, it cuts to the bone.

My latrine has become a place for political conversation about everything from the crime bill to Clinton's health plan. At 7:45 a.m., guess who shows up? The painters. They say they want to come back on January 3 to finish painting the latrine. What they don't know is that I couldn't care less.

A fringe benefit of running the latrine is that it's next to the kitchen. Because the chefs all think I need to put on weight, they often bring fresh samples of the day's menu. In exchange, I tell them to take any commode that's vacant.

Today, the chef came by with hot food, but I stepped out to the administration office, and the painters ate it in my absence.

Thursday, December 30, 1993

It's hard to believe, but today is colder than yesterday. Those of us who sleep in lower bunks can feel the cold penetrating through the cement beneath our beds. In the middle of the night, making your way to the la-trine, even in stocking feet is like walking on ice. Outside, the wind howls as if Schuykill were the backdrop for a Stephen King movie.

But the real challenge is getting from Unit Two to the administration building for breakfast. As I shower, I look out a window and see inmates hunkered down against the bitter cold and bent over into the wind that whips the snow and sleet against whatever skin is exposed.

However cold it gets, I shower every morning. I wish everybody else did the same. As the days get colder, fewer inmates venture out of bed and out of doors through the snow and the blistering wind to breakfast.

In one sense, the politics here have changed. Back in the balmy days of Indian summer, the landscaping crew would walk by the latrine, and as they headed outdoors for an afternoon in the sun, they'd snicker and make smart-aleck remarks about how clever they were to have finagled a better job assignment for themselves outdoors than I had for myself in the latrine.

Now, with the hacks hauling them out of bed in the middle of the night, with temperatures well below zero, and with snow drifting to three feet and more, the landscaping crew is too busy to make wisecracks, too tired to smile. That is to say, from the warmth of my latrine, I don't think they're smiling. To be honest, I can't tell because their faces are covered by mufflers to prevent frostbite.

They can renew acquaintances with each other in the spring. I'll be home in Boston.

This afternoon, the inmate who distributes mail has a question for me. "How come you get so much mail?"

Someday, maybe, he'll figure it out. It's because I write a lot of letters and answer my mail.

Friday, December 31, 1993

After checking the latrine this morning, I head for the library to write.

Louis, my Puerto Rican neighbor, expects visitors today, his ex-wife and girlfriend, who are driving down together from Spanish Harlem.

On the telephone, Louis's mother demanded to know: "How can you have your ex-wife and your girlfriend visiting you together?"

Louis answered, "I don't know. Maybe they are going to do a hit on me."

At Catholic services, Fr. Dene dedicates mass to his deceased parents.

Tonight, I am just about to hop into my bunk when the fire alarm goes off again, and the hacks are furious, The pizza they ordered has just arrived, and now it's getting cold while they deal with the fire alarm, which is driving everyone crazy. No one can find a key to shut it off. Finally, the hacks send over to medium security for the duty officer, who orders all of us out of the building.

It's zero degrees outside. We are not happy. I hope their pizza congeals.

It's ten minutes to midnight. We are back in the unit, the lights are on, and everyone is awake, awaiting the witching hour. There's not a man here who doesn't hope that the new year is better than the old.

Midnight! Salutations all around. Happy New Year, everybody!

My first New Year in prison.

Pat, the gay inmate, comes in and again announces his New Year's resolution. "I'm going back to being a man," he shouts. "No more men for me, only women from now on!"

It's hard to take his resolution seriously, though, because he's still wearing lipstick and eye makeup, and his resolve is met with catcalls that drive Pat out of the room.

Oh-oh. 12:15 a.m., and the alarm is going off. We are herded outdoors once again to stand around in zero degrees for another fifteen minutes.

This procedure is losing its charm.

Saturday, January 1, 1994

It's 5:30 a.m., and something is wrong. I can sense it. Then I hear commotion outside. I see lights. I hear trucks and voices, and then, they're carrying out a stretcher. There's a body on it, but who? I can't see. The head is covered.

An ambulance backs up to the door. It's dark outside. They load the body into an ambulance, attach tubes, then slam the door shut and drive across the lawn, speeding like hell over the snow. Who is it?

Nobody knows. Then, the word passes. It's Pat, the gay, He tried to commit suicide. One report said he took sixty pills. I hope Pat makes it. I wish now that I had been more friendly toward him. I wonder if it was his New Year's resolution that took him down. I hope not. To be honest, though, even as he announced his resolve to avoid sex with men, he looked like he was dressed for a date with a guy.

Schuykill was tough on Pat. He was always trying to get along, but it was not easy, not with so many tough guys riding him. Here's the irony. Some of the guys who rode Pat the hardest were secretly hitting on him, having sex with him, then afterward hating him for it. One night, Kiester was kidding Pat about his sexual preference, and another inmate came along whose own sexual preference was suspect. He began to needle Pat until, finally, Pat looked him right in the eye.

"Look, honey, you don't want to bang pocketbooks with me."

Before I fall asleep, I say a prayer for Pat. Someone heard: Pat survived.

Today, the hacks use the four o'clock count to pass out dinner tickets. On the menu is steak, and the BOP wants to make sure no inmates get seconds. The inmates find this hilarious, because at the ranges where the chefs live, inmates have been enjoying this steak for two days already.

Sunday, January 2, 1994

At coffee hour, the topic is an article in the *New York Daily News* by a Philadelphia lawyer who writes about the money wasted by the government for pretrial incarceration at fifty-one dollars a day for jail as opposed to electronic surveillance at six dollars a day for an ankle bracelet.

After lunch, I hear my name over the intercom.

"Timilty, report to the visitor room."

What a surprise! It's my sons, Joe Jr. and Greg. They have driven down from Boston. I tried to discourage this, but Elaine said the boys wanted to make the trip and that I should not fight it.

When I walk in, the visitor room is wall-to-wall people. I see my room-mate, Billy, with his wife, a beautiful blond woman. Billy is in his midthir-ties, and his wife is in her early twenties. Billy plays with his little son, who jumps around and insists on meeting everybody, boldly offering to shake hands. It's the only time I've ever seen Billy's human side, the only time I've ever seen him happy.

Tom Thumb is there, too, sitting with his girlfriend, their hands out of sight.

I introduce Joe and Gregory to Billy, and after we are seated by our-selves, I say to my sons, "So, how'd you guys get here?"

Joe Jr. answers.

"We thought we'd take a ride."

"Thought you'd take a ride? It's a seven-hour trip!"

Seeing these two guys take time from their vacation to make the long drive to Pennsylvania to visit their father in prison is heart wrenching. It will take me days to get over the sight of the two of them.

At 10:00 p.m., lights out, and before I fall asleep, I wonder about the latest rumor, that someone set my latrine on fire. I'll deal with it tomorrow.

Monday, January 3, 1994

At breakfast, everybody's talking about the fire. I'm told by inmates who have seen the damage that the hacks were in there last night, taking photographs.

There are two major investigations. The first is by the hacks, who want to know who the hell set the fire. The second is by the inmates, who want to know who the hell put it out.

Today, there is a subtle but tangible change in the personality of the entire institution. Everybody's on edge, the administration as well as the inmates. We're all suffering from cabin fever. There are not enough ac-tivities to work off the frustrations of being cooped up. I've noticed it in myself. I've had several arguments about things that, normally, I would have let pass.

Visiting the latrine, I discover that the damage is not as bad as I had feared. As it turns out, the fire was confined to a small trash receptacle. There is some staining from smoke and some water damage. The worst problem is something that will linger for a while, the charcoal stench.

At 9:30 a.m., I'm wondering where the Latino paint crew is, now that I need them because of the fire. Then it occurs to me. They're staying away *because* of the fire.

I'm told that the Latinos who use the TV room next to the room where I work out on the rowing machine have agreed upon a nickname for me: Rawhide. That, at least, is the English translation. I was told of the nickname by a painter who said it came from someone on the Spanish council who referred to my constant working out on the rowing machine. He said the council knew I had assisted a number of Latinos, especially in terms of helping them write letters. Rawhide, he said, is a name of respect because I work out so much.

Having asked to see the eye doctor in October for new glasses, I am called to his office three months later. Following the examination, it takes six weeks to get eyeglasses, and I feel obliged to tell the doctor of my status.

"I know it takes six weeks to get glasses, and I'll be discharged to Boston in four weeks."

"That's OK," he says. "No problem. I'll send them to you in Boston."

It's another ball game to bilk the government.

There are young people in every state going to school who are unable to see the blackboard clearly or to read comfortably because they don't have eyeglasses, and if they do, sometimes it's the wrong prescription. There are elderly people wearing glasses that are taped and pinned together because they don't have the money to repair them. And here's the federal government not only giving me a new pair but also mailing them to my home in Boston. Where does it end?

Tuesday, January 4, 1994

At 9:30 a.m., I hear my name over the loudspeaker, and I don't like it. As the Irish say, no good can come of it.

I'm supposed to see my coordinator, Miss Personality, the woman whose form was frozen into a snowwoman and, sure enough, she baits me by referring to me sarcastically, over and over, as "Senator."

My guess is she's disappointed to have to inform me that the paperwork for my transfer to a halfway house has arrived. The halfway house is in Boston; it's at the Coolidge House, across from the YMCA where I work out.

I have to sign a paper that lists the rules. I insist on reading every one of them. After all, that's how I got here, signing papers I didn't read.

Wednesday, January 5, 1994

Thanks again to Camel for waking me at 5:15 a.m. When I get home, maybe this is something I can develop for my kids. Just rap them once at 5:15 a.m. and assume they'll get right out of bed. Sure.

It's snowing again and drifting. Five degrees outside, a little warmer inside.

After the surge at Christmas, the food is going downhill. Yesterday, hacks informed kitchen workers that because of the continuing theft off eggs and milk, both items would be cut by 50 percent.

This is a typical strategy: in order to catch thieves, the hacks cut the supply until other inmates rat them out. Peer pressure, a vintage BOP tactic. What the hacks don't understand is a fundamental lesson in supply-side economics. When the hacks cut back the supply of eggs and milk, the impact is to make both items worth more on the inmate black market.

My money's on the inmates in this struggle. There's always plenty of extra food on *A* range, and the weight lifters always have about thirty eggs a day. Something about needing protein.

At breakfast this morning, other inmates are talking about my replacement. Keep talking, I like the sound of it! I take pleasure in merely uttering the words, "my replacement."

At the latrine, there's no sign of the painters. I'm told they're still negotiating with the kitchen staff about colors, hours, and how much food they'll get.

The volume of snow here, by the way, is impressive, even to a New England boy. We usually measure snow in inches. Here, they measure it in feet.

The mail today brought a copy of the *60 Minutes* report on prisons that supports my contention that the medical component of the BOP is an utter waste of money, often criminal, and in some cases a violation of the human rights of inmates. But where is the Justice Department? Where is Congress? Does anybody care?

At 10:30 p.m., lights out, one more day in the mountains, and I'm tired.

Thursday, January 6, 1994

At 1:30 a.m., I wake with a start. An inmate from Philly in a nearby cube, apparently fell asleep with the radio on. It's blaring, and my cellmate, Billy, is yelling for someone to shut it off. The radio continues to blare.

Frustrated, Billy gets out of his rack and heads over to the cell where the radio is blasting and, in the process, Billy wakes several other inmates. I'm half awake, half asleep, and unsure of what's happening except that it involves a lot of shouting.

The conversation is not particularly intellectual.

"What the fuck are you doing?"

"Go fuck yourself. Turn off the fucking radio. If you don't turn that off, I'll throw you *and* the fucking radio out of the fucking window."

Suddenly, the blaring of the radio stops, and I drift back to sleep.

As usual, thanks to Camel, who's more reliable than any alarm clock, I wake at 5:15 a.m.

At breakfast this morning, I feel good. I've got a smooth operation. The latrine is operating efficiently. My workouts are easier. I have plenty of friends here. The days are passing quickly, and I have only four weeks to go.

By 7:45 a.m., I'm on duty at the latrine. It's crowded here this morning. The snow workers are hiding out here, and there's plenty of noise from guys who are smoking, drinking coffee, ribbing one another, laughing.

Into the latrine comes a guy who lives near me in *A* range. He's a big guy, and he looks mean and menacing. He is cellmate to the character who fell asleep last night with the radio at full blast.

I have left the door to the latrine open for fresh air and to let out the smoke and odors. Also, with the door open, I can maintain a lookout on the main corridor of the administration building to see who's coming, who's going. So, with the doors wide open, this guy glares at me and then shouts at me in a voice you would not call friendly.

"Your fucking cellmate woke me up last night."

Having said it so loudly and in such a threatening way, he now has the attention of several inmates using the urinals.

"My name is Joe," I tell him in a normal voice. "My cellmate's name is Bill. If you have a problem with Joe, you take it up with Joe. If you have a problem with Bill, you take it up with Bill."

He screams at me: "I'm taking it up with you!"

"If you have something to say to him, say it to him. I'm not your messenger."

Other inmates don't like what's brewing here, and they slip out of the latrine one by one. I don't look at them. I don't want to lose eye contact with the screaming meathead in front of me. As they taught us in the Marine Corps, the eyes tell the intent before any other part of the body, and if he's about to make a move, I want to be ready.

He keeps it up, screaming about my cellmate and warning me that if Bill comes into his cell again, he'll be thrown out on his ass.

"I told you before, and I'm telling you again," I repeat in a normal voice, "if you have anything to say to my cellmate, then have the courage to tell him yourself. I'm not carrying your illiterate messages to anyone."

I can tell by his eyes that my remark has personalized the argument and redirected it so that it is no longer a dispute between him and Billy. Now, it's between him and me. A voice within me says, be careful, Joe! If this goes much further, you could come out of this with a stretch in solitary confinement, loss of the latrine job, transfer to another prison, or an extension of your sentence. You've got only four weeks left, Joe, twenty-eight days. It would be asinine to be caught fighting.

At the same time, although I'm spotting this guy eighty pounds and twenty-five years, I can't stop. Then, I hear myself say, "And now that you've brought up the subject, my cellmate was right, and further, he should have pulled both of you guys out of your bunks and thrown both of you out the window into a snowbank, along with your radio!"

That gets to him. He goes bonkers.

"I'm going to crush you!" he screams, moving toward me.

With the door of the latrine open, the screaming is loud enough so that it draws the attention of a hack. Unfortunately, as the hack arrives, I am the one yelling, pointing, and pushing. The hack looks at me. Everyone else has slipped out, even my adversary.

"What's going on?" the hack says.

I shrug.

"Nothing."

A few inmates gather at the door to watch, including the painters.

"It doesn't sound like nothing," says the hack. "I can hear screaming all the way down the corridor. What's it all about?"

"It's nothing," I repeat.

"Why all the noise?"

"Sometimes you have to get loud to get this place clean."

He's not satisfied with my answers, of course, but seeing no blood, no bruises, and no physical evidence, he leaves.

It will take a while for my blood pressure to come down. On the other hand, I'm lucky the hack came along. That was a close call. One of the painters walks in, pats me on the shoulder, smiles, and says, "OK, Rawhide!"

I think they lingered in the door in case I needed help.

Two hours later, it occurs to me that time in prison is elusive, and the encounter in the latrine 120 minutes ago now seems like it never happened.

At lunch, an inmate refers to our "Desert Storm Food," and then I discover that a number of boxes that have arrived at the warehouse were earmarked for our military forces during the Gulf War.

It was predictable, I suppose, but somebody squealed to the administration that I had a beef in the latrine this morning. In the evening, I am in bed reading when I hear over the intercom: "The following inmates report for pill line."

Pill line is the opportunity for inmates to pick up medication that was prescribed for them that morning by the doctor. Oddly, they call my name. But I haven't ordered any pills, didn't want any. So, I don't go. After all, it's snowing, the wind is howling, and the temperature is below zero.

"You'd better go," says Bill, my cellmate. "Why take a chance of pissing them off?"

OK, so I wait in line with inmates getting pills, with the sick, the lame, the halt, and all of the phonies and fakers. These guys look like something out of an old war movie. I arrive at last at the window. This physician's assistant in charge is a round, black man with a pleasant face and an easy demeanor.

"My name's Timilty, I think you got something wrong."

He looks up.

"Have a seat."

Now I know something's up. When all the medications are distributed and everyone else has gone, he gestures for me to enter the inner office.

"In there," he says, motioning me to a small room.

Inside, there are three hacks watching, the inmate turns to me.

"I've been ordered to examine you."

I take the heat.

"For what? Who ordered it?"

It's clear that someone heard the argument this morning and then reported it to the hacks as a fight, some rat with an axe to grind. I press the issue.

"Who ordered this? What is this for?"

"The order comes from a lieutenant at MCI [Medium Correctional Institute]."

Obviously, however, I'm confronting the wrong guy. The inmate I'm challenging is only doing his job. The hacks are impatient.

"Strip," says one of them.

I take off my clothes.

"Let me see your knuckles."

He's looking for abrasions. He checks my body for marks.

"You had a fight," he says. "Who with?"

"I didn't have a fight."

"We know you had a fight. We have a report on it."

"Well, there are no marks on my body. How could I have been in a fight?"

"We know you had a fight, and we know who with."

If I had admitted to having a fight, I would have gone to the hole. They check all over my body, especially my hands to see if I have punched somebody and my feet to see if I've kicked somebody and also my knees and elbows. They find no marks, nothing to lead them to believe that I was involved in a fight. So, they send me back to my quarters.

Back on A range, I'm furious. Paul suggests we take a walk, outside, into the hall. He tells me that the individual I argued with is the leader of a group from Philly and that the Philly group had approached him.

"They told me they're bullshit with you," he says to me, "and there's going to be trouble. They say they're going to finish what was started, that they're going to get you. I said to them, that's allowable, if that's what you want to do, but I have to tell you, that you won't be getting just Timilty. You'll be getting me and Coach and Bill and a lot of other guys who'll stand with him."

That was not the answer they wanted to hear, and so they agreed to put it away, if I would. I agree, of course, and Paul says he will mediate with the Philly group.

The lights go out at 10:30 p.m., and I decide to spend as much as possible of my remaining time with Paul and my Latino friends as a way of staying out of trouble. Still, I'm seething about that medical exam. It takes me a long time to fall asleep.

Friday, January 7, 1994

At 5:15 a.m., the wake-up by Camel.

He's great but odd. One second, he's not there. Then he appears at precisely 5:15 a.m., bangs me on the leg, mutters, "Git oop," and a moment later he's gone. He shakes my leg because he no longer dares get too far inside anybody else's cell, not after the night he was wrapped in tape and deposited in the TV room.

As I dress, it occurs to me that this building is amazing. The contractor who built it ought to be in prison himself because of faulty construction work, along with the inspector and along with anyone else in BOP who had anything to do with it. Here's one reason—it's minus five degrees outside, but it's so hot in here, I have to leave the windows open. The heat comes on at 6:00 a.m., and it goes off at 10:00 p.m.

As I report to the latrine at 7:45 a.m., I make a New Year's resolution. I know I'm starting late, but I vow to be quiet, courteous, and gentlemanly in the latrine. I'm going to be known as the Permanent Latrine Orderly who barely speaks. No arguments, no giving bullies wet toilet paper anymore, no splashing dirty mop water on inmates who linger too long at the mirrors. And I'm determined to ignore any wisecrack that might lead to a dispute.

At the same time, however, at the latrine, I have instituted a "No Reading" policy. When I took over this job, it was like an adjunct to the library, a hideaway. Inmates would stop in at the library, pick up a newspaper or magazine, then head to my latrine and not emerge for forty-five minutes. Two new policies will cure that. I keep plenty of water on the floor in the back room, and splash it around regularly. Also, inmates are no longer permitted to take newspapers and magazines out of the library. This makes my job a lot easier.

Around 9:30 a.m., the painters drop by to say hello to Rawhide and to talk about what happened yesterday. From my perspective, however, the less conversation about it the better. The Philly group is made enough as it is. These groups, as they are referred to, in reality, are gangs. They're a serious threat to safety in prison, and inmates are almost forced to ally with one or another for survival, whether it's a black, Latino, or white gang.

At 10:00 a.m., somebody in the kitchen crew stops by with fresh, hot peperoni pizza, which is on the menu for lunch, and it tastes great.

What a difference an hour makes, though. At 11:00 a.m., I'm in the dining room, and the pizza being served is burned, cold, tasteless. Also, I'm told later the box this pizza came in was dated 1990.

To my surprise, I hear my name over the intercom.

"Timilty, report to the administration office."

Friends point out that I have been summoned, but I decide to finish lunch first. Suddenly, at my shoulder is an inmate who is a good friend, an administrative orderly.

"Joe, it's the camp administrator who wants to see you."

Great. Now that I've been notified in person, I cannot claim that I didn't hear the announcement. On the way to the office, I ask him, "Do you know what this is about?"

"No, I don't."

But I know what it's about. It's about yesterday's argument. When I arrive, the administrator is on the phone. I wait.

Called into his office, I see him sitting behind a desk, motioning me to sit down, but before my rear end hits the seat, he says, "I understand you were involved in a fight yesterday."

His directness surprises me.

"That's not true."

"Well, the *Boston Herald* called the Justice Department in Washington, and they have a report that you were involved in a fight, that you have been moved to a different facility, that you are under quarantine, that you face additional charges, and that your sentence will be extended."

He's as cold as ice. He says the strip search was as a result of the call from the *Herald*. He asks me to sign a release saying there has been no assault.

"No, I'm not signing anything. That's how I got here, signing documents."

"Let me ask you this, since you have been in this facility, have you been assaulted?"

"Only by the food."

He doesn't crack a smile.

At noon, I call Elaine in Boston.

"Diane Kottmyer [my lawyer] is looking for you. She's got a nasty report from the *Herald*. They want confirmation of a story that says you've been involved in a fight, taken away in cuffs, placed in solitary, and that you're awaiting transfer to a higher security facility, after which there will be additional charges that will add to your sentence."

"Elaine, we have to put that report to bed right now, and for one reason: because it's just not true."

I call Diane.

"I got a story to tell you," she says, "that you were involved in an assault, and you're in isolation and going to be brought up on charges."

"Diane, if I'm calling you, then I'm not in isolation. I need you to call the *Herald* and put that to rest. There's no basis to it, it's just not true."

It's clear some inmate is spying for the *Herald*. I'd love to find out who.

It's 2:00 p.m., and I need to go for a workout. Paul is going to join me. He's decided to spend more time with me. His intention is to send a message to the Philly group that he is serious about supporting me.

When we get to the workout room, we find that the cycle, the administration's present to the camp, has been dismantled. Word is, that last night, just before count, two inmates were arguing about who was next on the bike. After count, parts of the cycle were missing, and the two-week-old cycle, therefore, is no longer usable.

The hacks are furious. They have parts to repair it, but they have no intention of using them. The theory is that if the cycle remains broken, it will draw the wrath of other inmates, and peer pressure will build to the point that someone will expose the perpetrators or, at least, force them to return the parts.

"That's stupid," says Paul. "Who would save the parts and risk discovery? If the hacks were smart, they'd realize that whoever stole the parts would naturally dispose of them right away."

As usual, Paul is right. Given the limited logic of the hacks, however, the chances of them solving this mystery are two—slim and none.

It's Friday night, and there's plenty of activity—cards, movies, conversation, stories, jokes, laughing.

Saturday, January 8, 1994

It's snowing again, and the landscaping crew was pressed into service in the middle of the night to shovel snow. Those guys need rest. I guess the administration figures they rested last summer.

At 11:30 a.m., I'm in the workout room when the Latino group shows up to weigh themselves. At their request, I show them how to do stomach exercises without using the sit-up board. They say I'm the only gringo who respects them. They don't like many inmates, and they hate the hacks especially.

Mass tonight is celebrated by Fr. Dene for his deceased grandparents. Since I've been here, this is the fifth Mass dedicated to his grandparents. Wherever they are, I hope it's helping them.

The movie tonight is *Mr. Baseball*, with Tom Selleck, a fun film, and the inmates laugh throughout.

Sunday, January 9, 1994

This morning, Schuykill looks like a postcard, the sunlight so bright it sparkles off the smooth snow that is broken only by the footprints near the woods, of deer, rabbit, and wildcat.

At 8:00 a.m., I check out the latrine. There are no words to describe the abuse this place endures over a weekend, and the question persists, how do these people live at home? It's one thing, I suppose, to trash the latrine at Fenway Park, where you visit once or twice a season. But for the time, at least, this is where these guys live, and they use this place every day.

I refuse to clean it seven days a week. The most I do on weekends or holidays is to make sure there are paper towels. After all, this is the latrine used by the kitchen help, and I don't want to give them any excuse not to wash their hands.

Once again, by 8:30 a.m., you can hear the voices of children arriving for visiting hours. Of all the sounds at Schuykill, this is the one I cannot steel myself to. In this setting that is cold, dark, impersonal, sometimes hateful and violent, the laughter of children is horribly out of place.

Monday, January 10, 1994

I check the calendar, and it's hard to believe, but I've been here fourteen weeks. Pretty soon, I'll have to deal with being on the street. On the one hand, I can't wait. On the other, I know that things will never be the same again.

As my time here gets shorter, there is a discomforting change in attitude toward me by a number of other inmates. I had been warned this would happen, but I did not expect it so soon. Or has it been happening gradually, and I didn't notice?

Some inmates seem less friendly than they have been. Maybe they resent my departure, and in a way, I cannot blame them. Compared to their sentences of 120 months, my 120 days must seem like a moment in their time.

At Catholic services tonight, there are new faces, and it occurs to me, in the past three weeks, there must be at least twenty new Catholic inmates. I wonder if they know Fr. Dene's grandparents.

Tonight's movie after Mass is *Under Siege*, with Steven Segal. Fr. Dene watches with us. There are violent scenes and, for this movie, my prediction is there'll be no Oscar nominations.

Tuesday, January 11, 1994

My replacement (I love the phrase!) is not due until Wednesday or Thursday, but that's OK. I'm in no hurry. I'm here for three more weeks, and my obligations in the latrine will occupy my time.

During lunch, a new hack whispers that there'll be a surprise inspection of living quarters after lunch. The word is passed quickly, and the next two hours are hectic, with inmates cleaning, polishing, buffing. My cellmate and I get a perfect score for the tenth week in a row. A perfect score doesn't mean anything. A less than perfect score does. It draws attention, causes trouble, and can cost privileges.

Wednesday January 12, 1994

Wakeup at 5:15 a.m. Camel would have made a great marine. He never misses.

Today's the day I've been waiting for. I'm expecting a visit from one of my lawyers, George McMahon, but as I look out the window, it's snowing. The forecast is for three inches, and here in the mountains, that's a dusting. For my lawyer driving from Boston, even a dusting can be onerous.

Today, they're taking seven inmates out of here to Fort Dix, New Jersey. Those inmates are lucky. Any means by which you can get out of this place (other than feet first, the way they took Phil Kagan) is a blessing, because Schuykill is thought of as among the worst facilities in the system. Back in the unit after breakfast, watching other inmates pack to leave is troublesome for the rest of us who are left here, particularly those with long sentences.

One issue I have a tough time dealing with is the number of inmates who stay in their bunks right up until the last minute, when work call is sounded. Then they jump out of their racks, put on their clothes, and head to work without showering or even brushing their teeth. I'm glad I don't work with them.

At 7:45 a.m., there is no sign of the painters.

All morning, it snows, and inch by inch, it piles up outside. Good thing George canceled his drive here.

Thursday, January 13, 1994

It's a glorious morning.

I am grateful to Camel for waking me every day. And although this is a small point, my day would begin on a happier note if he would merely tap my leg rather than shake the hell out of me. But you have to take the bitter with the sweet.

At this time of year, there's an abnormal amount of sickness here, coughing, wheezing, flu on every range. The living quarters are so close that when flu starts, it spreads like gossip. The printed menu promises fresh fruit, and juice is far from what is actually served. That's part of the problem. I came down with a bad cold that it took a week of rest to cure. Now I consume plenty of fresh garlic, maybe too much, and daily doses of vitamin C tablets.

My replacement in the latrine is due this morning, but I'm told he's on the list for a doctor's appointment. Around here, that probably means he'll take off the entire day. Now, if that were me, I'd have shown up here before the doctor's appointment, and then I'd have rushed to the appointment, after which I'd have returned to the latrine to help out. This guy is made differently.

Among the characters here is a long-term inmate called Little Caesar, because he's five feet two but walks and talks like a hack. Little Caesar, as it turns out, doesn't like the way I'm running the latrine.

I use one stall at the rear of the latrine to store supplies and equipment, towels, large jugs of Lysol, mops, brushes, and gloves. Obviously, that stall is closed permanently. Today, Little Caesar comes by and, because all the other stalls are being used, he is obliged to stand there with his legs crossed. Big deal! Couldn't happen to a nicer person.

In his Napoleonic voice, he suggests to me that the other stall should be open. I forget the rule that I imposed on myself not to answer inanities like that, and I cannot resist responding.

"Who died and left you in charge?"

"I'm speaking for my boss," he says.

I wasn't sure what he was talking about, and so I didn't say anything. Later, one of the Latinos tells me Little Caesar has taken the equipment from the stall where I have been keeping it and placed it in a closet. I take it from the closet and put it back in the stall.

Now, Little Caesar lives in Unit One, where the Bear calls the shots. I mention the situation to the Bear, who hates Little Caesar, too.

"Don't worry about it," says the Bear. "I'll take care of it."

And he does. Not only does Little Caesar no longer bother me, he is forbidden by the Bear from ever speaking to me or even using my latrine.

Late word is that a cold wave is due to hit the mountains in the next few days and that temperatures may fall to thirty below zero. Inmates in charge of the prison's heating units warn that they system can compensate only for temperatures as low as minus ten, and if the thermometer drops below that, inmates need to make their own preparations to keep warm, which means sleeping in coats, scarves, gloves, and anything else that will maintain body temperature.

Friday, January 14, 1994

At 5:15 a.m., I look out the window, and it's snowing again. In these cement-block buildings, once the blocks get cold, they stay that way until spring, which is why the floor here, day after day, is like ice.

Even before the coming drop in temperatures, inmates sleep in their underwear, full long johns, white socks, sweat suits with hoods over the head. Some sleep in work clothes, which discourages them from taking a shower in the morning when it's dank and ice cold.

I sleep in shorts and a T-shirt, although last night, it was so cold, I must have awakened ten times, just to turn in the rack and get the bed warm. I still shower in the morning before the sun comes up. It's warmer in the bathroom than it is in the cell. It's just that when you come out of the shower, it's like being taken from the equator and dropped at the South Pole. The cold is painful.

At 7:30 a.m., I arrive at work in the latrine, and I am looking forward to meeting my replacement.

At 8:00 a.m., I realize that he's late.

At 8:30 a.m., he drifts in to introduce himself and say that his clothes are in the washing machine, and he'll see me later.

At 9:00a.m., he arrives and expects me to show him how I keep this place clean, but it's too late. The work's complete, and so I suggest that he come back after lunch.

The snow continues to fall through the day, hour after hour, until the countryside is covered, and everything is whitened by the snowy, narcotic powder that stimulates by its beauty but then sedates and smothers and depresses all of us until we are squabbling and snapping at one another, imprisoned twice, once by the state and again by nature.

By midafternoon, if forty-four inmates on *A* range, ten are sleeping. I read once that if your body gets used to a nap in the middle of the day, then it will need it regularly. I guess you could get your body used to sleeping eighteen hours a day, and these guys in bed right now seem to be on their way.

At 7:00 p.m., I am happy to be back on *A* range, for the only place to be warm tonight is in your bunk.

Lights out at 10:30 p.m., and boy, it's cold!

Saturday, January 15, 1994

It's 5:15 a.m., and as inmates wake, one by one, they can talk of nothing else but the cold. Many inmates are imaginative in the layers of clothing they wear. For me, it's tough getting out of the hot shower this morning. Unfortunately, it's an experience many of my fellow inmates will not choose to endure.

When I arrive at the latrine at 8:00 a.m., my replacement is there, sweeping the floor. I had mentioned to him on Friday that I checked the latrine weekend mornings at 8:00 a.m. to replenish stock. I'm amazed that he showed up and that he did not have to be handed a broom. Maybe this guy is all right after all.

At Catholic services, Fr. Dene announces that tonight's Mass is celebrated for Ann Baxter, whoever that is.

For tonight's movie, the Jewish group has brought in a video called *A Stranger Among Us*, with Melanie Griffith. I've never heard of it, but I'm told the story line is set in the Hassidic community in New York. I've been fascinated with Hassidic culture since my days in politics in Boston. I identify with their strong discipline, although the behavior of my fellow inmates during the movie indicates that they do not share my enthusiasm.

In fact, their reaction was embarrassing. They snickered and poked fun at the customs and the appearances of the Hassidics. It was anti-Semitic behavior, and the Jewish inmates were keenly aware of it but said nothing. It must be like this in all prisons. No wonder the Jews stay together. I thoroughly enjoyed the movie, though, good plot, good acting.

After the movie, there is a discussion about a new problem we have. One inmate went to the administration to claim that showing the movies is illegal because we are not paying royalties. This guy is a hater, and some of his hatred is directed at me. One day, I caught him cutting in chow line ahead of other inmates, and I yelled loud enough for everybody to hear, "Any inmate that cuts in line is destined to go back to jail." He stood there amid the catcalls and jeers directed at him, and he glared at me. He'll never forget the moment. Nor will I.

Sunday, January, 16, 1994

At breakfast, at long last, we have an explanation as to why the pastry tastes like a hockey puck. Someone in the kitchen whispers to me that after the hacks leave, the bakers are frenetically busy. Although they are bakers, they have been cooking chicken, and why? Because chicken has more value in the black market back in the cells.

My friend Jim tells me that yesterday, at the warehouse, they were transporting hamburger patties to the kitchen for Sunday night's meal. Jim was asked by a hack to run a fictitious errand. When he returned, there were 200 hamburger patties missing. When you're feeding 300 inmates, that's a big dent in the menu. The hacks steal a lot, and the kitchen crew feels entitled to steal its share. By the time John Q. Inmate arrives in the cafeteria and holds up his tray, there's not much left of the main entrée.

The weather continues to dominate everyone's attention. It is bitter cold beyond anything experienced in New England. This weekend, the wind chill was fifty-eight degrees below zero. I thought that temperatures went that low only at the North and South Poles.

On *A* range, I can't help noticing that food is being brought into the range through both the front and back doors at the same time—hamburgers, fruit, cookies. There's food coming from all directions. Yet at dinner, there'll be a hack posted to ensure that no one takes an extra chocolate chip cookie.

Monday, January 17, 1994

Shortly after midnight, I am awakened by the howling of the wind whistling through the mountain darkness, a frightening sound. I wake at 6:00 a.m. to a blizzard. Nobody is moving, outdoors or indoors. These are the days when this place makes the least sense. People sleep throughout the night and throughout the day, waking only to eat a meal, watch a movie, eat some more, then sleep some more.

Tonight, on *A* range, we have extra chicken, but for the first time, I am not offered any. That's a sign that the inmates have changed their attitude toward me, and the reason is that I am a short timer.

At 7:00 p.m., it's still snowing as I climb into my rack to write letters.

It's time I started thinking about how I'm going to alter my life when I leave here. Today, I sent a letter to the sentencing commission, asking to testify in Washington in March. I intend to spend time working to correct the wrongs I've seen here. I also sent a letter to the Washington office of

Vietnam veterans, hoping to address the more than 20,000 inmates who served in Vietnam and who are now incarcerated in American prisons.

Tuesday, January 18, 1994

Wake up at 5:15 a.m., thanks to Camel, who is more reliable than the US Postal Service. It's hard to describe how cold this building is at night, but those in the construction business would understand just by looking at it: cement blocks set on a slab foundation. That's great construction for southern Florida, but not the mountains of Pennsylvania.

Last night's rosary service was canceled. We could have held our own service, but the recreation department had taken over the visitor room for bingo.

When my replacement arrives in the latrine and sees what happened to this place on a weekend, he looks despondent. The floor is littered with cigarette stubs, and why? Inmates flick cigarette butts to the floor. On the other hand, he says he understands this, that he's seen it all before.

"How's that?" I ask.

"I spent two years as a master sergeant in the air force."

That was not the best recommendation to give me, not with my background in the Marine Corps. The marines have never held the air force in high regard.

Although my time is getting short, I am not going to begin my countdown until I have only one week left.

Because of the blizzard, Fr. Dene cannot make it here today.

I've arranged for the TV and the VCR, but in order to have our movie tonight, we have to have a religious service, and guess what? In the absence of Fr. Dene, the Catholic group expects me to lead the rosary service.

A few minutes before service, it's whispered to me that one of the inmates has just been notified that his mother died. The inmate is not one of my favorites. He has an eating problem. He eats all the food he can get his hands on. He was fat when he arrived, and he's put on another thirty pounds.

The problem, however, is that he's suspected of being a rat for the front office. On the other hand, his mother just died, and that should mean something to every inmate. And so, contrary to Schuykill policy, I offer the rosary tonight in memory of his mother, and I start the service this way.

"Tonight, we will say the rosary with the Five Sorrowful Mysteries."

At my high school, St. John's Prep in Danvers, Massachusetts, Brother Bosco taught me a device for memorizing the sorrowful mysteries.

"Remember this one phrase," he said. "A soldier can carry his cross."

Taking the first letter for each word: *A* is for agony in the garden; *S* is for scourging at the pillar; *C* is for crown of thorns; *C* is for carrying the cross; and *C* is for crucifixion.

Thanks, Brother Bosco! Four decades later, and it still works.

There are twenty Catholics attending. I didn't know how they would accept me. After all, by comparison to others who have been attending Catholic services here for years, I am a rookie. But then it becomes clear to me, once the rosary begins, that the only concern the inmates have is not the person leading the prayer but the God to whom the prayer is addressed.

A few inmates leave after the rosary, skipping the movie, but they are the exception. After the service, about ninety inmates are in the room for the movie, *Misery*, with James Caan, a great white-knuckle Stephen King flick so suspenseful that it has everybody guessing throughout.

I fall asleep hearing myself lead the rosary in prison.

Wednesday, January 19, 1994

It is now eighteen below zero outdoors. The Commonwealth of Pennsylvania is in an emergency situation. There is not enough energy left in Pennsylvania to heat homes and businesses. We have our own generator here, although in this weather, it's not sufficient. Maybe they'll close this place and send us home.

At 7:45 a.m., I arrive at the latrine to find my replacement at work. Unfortunately, he's done it so poorly that I have to follow him and do it all over again. But at least he's trying. An hour later, the painters show up. Not to work, of course, but to let me know that the head Latino painter is sick. He has the flu, so the rest of the crew will not be around to work for the rest of the week.

The party is almost over. It's hard to believe, but two weeks from tonight, I'll be at a halfway house in Boston. That's when the real challenge starts. It's been easy here, I guess, in comparison to what life will be like when Joe Timilty goes home as an ex-con.

Thursday, January 20, 1994

Today, there is a meeting to talk about my transition to a halfway house, which has becoming a reality.

Time here is odd. A few months ago, the halfway house seemed a long way off. Now, in a few days, I'll be there. There is a suggestion that I skip the halfway house and go straight to a leg bracelet. No, I tell them. I'd rather stay at the halfway house.

I love to watch the action takers here, the bookies, the individuals who back the action on the sports pages or run poker games. You get the same odds here you would if you bet on the outside, and by telephone, bookies have access to last-minute changes in the odds.

How, you might ask, do they move an operation like this in a prison, where nobody has any money? Each prisoner has a commissary account with money on deposit but with a spending limit of $150 per week, a substantial amount here.

The topic came up at breakfast, because somebody missed a payment. One inmate lost eighty-four dollars on a Sunday afternoon, betting on pro football. The usual currency at the commissary is soda, cigarettes, or stamps, which are easy to get rid of. The inmate has let a week of commissary go by without paying his debt, and he has been sent warning signs. He gets the message quickly. This is not the place to welsh on a debt.

At 10:30 p.m., the lights go out, and although I'm exhausted, I can't sleep. You can tell my time is getting close.

Friday, January 21, 1994

At breakfast, the big news is the arrest of a new inmate, a workout junkie and an oddball here in that he has a long ponytail, a common fashion statement on the outside, but not within these walls. I have heard him on more than one occasion on the telephone, yelling at his wife, and so I don't like him. He lives on *C,* that gentlemanly range that has a reputation for getting perfect scores on inspection day. They use this as a selling point in recruiting inmates to leave other ranges, and to be sure, it's a lure, because, as I have said, inspection is the only stressful time of the week.

Here's how they do it. They hire an orderly who does everything to keep the range clean except make beds, and in return, he is paid five dollars a week by each inmate.

This violates every rule here in prison, and therein lies the problem. Our friend, Odd Ball, had subscribed to the service but had neglected to pay up. On the telephone, he tells his wife to send money, or he's going to be hurt by other inmates. He was overheard, either by a rat or by a tap, and within thirty minutes, he was arrested, and now he's segregated.

The rule is that any transaction of cash or goods for services is illegal. In other words, all those elite characters on *C* have been scoring high at inspection, but they've been violating the law.

At the latrine, my replacement is at work, but once again, I have to follow him and point out all the dirt and grime he misses.

Today, I saw Steve who has monitored theft by hacks at the warehouse.

"So," I said to him, "you'll be getting out of here next week. I'm getting out of here a week later, and we're both going to be in Boston. We ought to get together and go over the documents."

"Great idea," he said. "As soon as I get back, I'll get in touch with you. It'll take me a couple of days to get acclimated to the halfway house."

The day Steve got out of prison, however, he got cold feet. He said that to feed me further information would implicate him. He said that the Feds were going to get me and that he didn't want to get dragged into it. It didn't take Steve long to panic.

On the menu for lunch is pizza, everybody's favorite. About thirty minutes before the door to the dining room opens, I'm sitting in the hallway, talking to the Bear and his associates, when someone walks over to give us hot pizza that is as good as what the kitchen serves to the front office and which bears no resemblance, by the way, to what it about to be served to inmates in the cafeteria.

The Bear hands me a slice.

"Here," he says. "This will prepare you for what you'll be eating soon on the outside."

On my way to the latrine to work, I pass the administration office, and there, standing out front and looking none too happy, is Jimmy, the orderly on *C* range who has been cleaning for the elite characters who live there. While the administration previously had congratulated Jimmy for his efforts in keeping all of *C* clean, they have now decided that Jimmy is guilty of extortion.

"Good luck, Jimmy," I say to him.

He winks. The next time I see him, he's in handcuffs, being taken to the hole. If Jimmy's counting on his fellow inmates to stand by him, then he's in trouble.

At 4:00 p.m., we learn that mail call is canceled. The administration did not sort the mail. The one daily event most inmates wait for is canceled at the last minute. Cruelty at its best.

Tonight, the natives are restless and decide to do some cooking, which arouses my interest. How do they do this? They don't have a hot plate or a microwave. The answer is prison ingenuity.

The cooking device is not an expensive pan. It's a conventional iron that's used to press clothes. What they do is, they heat the iron, then turn it over and set a makeshift pan on it and—presto!—indoor cooking.

On the menu tonight in the cell block are omelets, all kinds, made to order, because, from the cafeteria, we have plenty of eggs, and from the salad bar, lots of peppers and onions, and from the Christmas gift the administration gave us, we have plenty of pepperoni. Julia Child would be proud of us.

Saturday, January 22, 1994

As I look out the shower window, I see several inmates trying to get from Unit Two to the administration building, and they are struggling against the wind that howls across the field, swirling the snow and making the temperature seem even lower than the twenty below zero registered on the thermometer.

But the sun is coming up, and perhaps it will warm up.

At 8:00 a.m., I arrive in the latrine for work, but my replacement is not yet here. I saw him at breakfast, and he left the cafeteria before I did, although he was not headed here. As I do every Saturday, I give the latrine the once-over, sweeping the floor, replacing paper products, and flushing the toilets for those who grew up without running water.

I also need to replenish supplies, which gives me a chance to float around the offices on Saturday and Sunday when there's no one around. That is not the case today. The brass is here in full force, all over the place, including officers from the medium security facility, in full uniform and ready for action. I notice two lieutenants. This is highly unusual.

As I pass through the office, one hack from medium security says to his colleague, "Who's that guy?"—meaning me.

"He's here to pick up supplies."

I hear one of them say, "Let's get the guys from *C* range down here."

Obviously, they are pressing the investigation. From what I pick up, apparently after they sent Jimmy to the hole, they went through his gear and found, of all things, a ledger that he kept, detailing his cleaning service. Can you imagine keeping a ledger of your illegal activities? It contained all his dealings, names, locations, amounts, who paid on time, who was late.

The administration now has all of them, cold. What's unfair about this is that the administration knew full well that Jimmy was cleaning the entire *C* range in return for some kind of payment. That's why they would congratulate him week after week for its cleanliness. Indeed, on only one occasion did *C* range score less than perfect on an inspection, and that was because the Doc was cited for having too many cookbooks on his desk.

The names of everyone on *C* range are called over the intercom to report to the administration building. As they pass along the corridor in front of my latrine, I am standing in the doorway to the latrine, wishing them, one by one, "Top of the morning."

At 2:00 p.m., my name is called over the intercom to report to the visitor room. Obviously, I have a visitor, but who? I'm just glad I took a shower. I head out into the cold to the administration building, and as I walk into the visitor room, there he is, my son Joe Jr., who has driven down from Boston. He has marine buddies in Washington, DC, and Philadelphia whom he can visit while he's in the area.

Even though I'll be released soon, I find a visit like this tough, the toughest aspect of the whole experience. I wonder what Joe Jr. thinks, visiting his father in prison. But Joe Jr. wouldn't tell you if your coat were on fire. I'll say this for him, though, he looks real good.

Tonight, Mass is offered by Fr. Dene for his deceased grandparents. I wonder what Fr. Dene's relatives did here on earth that they now require so much praying. When Mass ends, the movie starts. Tonight, it's *Driving Miss Daisy*, and everyone says it's great. I stay for the beginning and then leave.

The movie had just started when a hack walked in and turned on the lights.

"Recall," he said. "Everyone back to your units."

Something is up. This is highly unusual. This happens only when fog rolls in or someone goes over the hill. At 10:00 p.m., we learn that my speculation is right. Someone is missing. Two Latino inmates have vanished. I hope they didn't take the paint with them.

One hack tells us they have found their footprints in the snow and are closing in on them.

"Bullsheet," says a Latino, privately. "They're too smart to run in the snow. Besides, they don't like snow."

Every inmate is rooting for them to make it, especially me. Heck, I can always find other painters.

The hacks have been conducting this count for more than two hours, and the tally hasn't changed. There are still two inmates missing. Gone. Over the hill. Still, the hacks keep open the count. As long as they do, they can keep us locked in our ranges, which means no movie, no telephone calls, no washing machines, no nothing.

The hacks, meanwhile, are angry, and they're taking it out on us. The count continues for another hour as if, at some point, our number will increase by two and, miraculously, the two Latinos will be there, standing next to their rack.

At midnight, the lights are still on, and they've brought up the first team from medium security, the mean group, who are even more furious to be disturbed than the guards at the camp. These hacks are looking for trouble. They're waiting for one of us to laugh or to talk or even to smile, just looking for the opportunity to send one of us to the hole.

Sunday, January 23, 1994

This morning, the hacks say they've caught one Latino, that he's in local jail, and describing for the BOP precisely where the other Latino is heading.

The Latinos here say they're lying. They say the two men were friends, that they never would have separated, and that if the hacks caught either, they'd have caught both.

The plan was obvious: leave after the 4:00 p.m. count, which would give them five and a half hours before the next count. But someone tipped off the hacks, because they called for a special count at 7:30 p.m., and they knew precisely who was missing, where to go, which building, which range. Further confirmation that 90 percent of the population here are rats.

At 8:00 p.m., my Latino friends stop by the latrine. In here, they can talk. Asked about their two comrades who fled, they laugh, and one says, "They are presently having a piña colada in honor of their good hombres, us, who are still cooped up on this mountain."

Both escapees are from the Dominican Republic and both are headed home. They would have been deported there at the end of their sentence, anyway.

Hacks are still boasting they've been caught, that the two men surrendered after a night in the woods. That makes the Latinos laugh.

"They didn't spend the night in the woods at all," said a Latino. "What do the hacks think, they're crazy? In this weather, they were picked up by a van at five o'clock last night."

Monday, January 24, 1994

When I wake at 5:15 a.m., I realize that I'm still tired. I'm not sleeping well, and I know why. Do you know what I can't get out of my mind? The Boston skyline.

The issues I'll be dealing with at home become more and more of a concern. My vacation here will soon be over. This is wrap-up week. All the papers from Schuykill have to be finalized this week, and I need a sign-off from the medical staff.

The only one in the administration I might have a problem with is the prison doctor. He was instructed by Dr. Feingold from New England Medical Center that I have developed skin problems that need to be monitored each month, and that I need to use a certain moisturizing cream daily. I arrived with enough medicine to carry me through the 120 days, but they took it away and sent it home. I have not had an examination since I arrived here. The doctor and I have been feuding over the facial cream.

Breakfast this morning is the worst since I have been here, creamed beef on toast. Without the toast.

At the latrine, my successor is on the job. This morning, he seems intent on making peace with the bullies who are always hanging around the latrine.

Before I came on the scene, the back room (where the stalls are) was nothing more than an extension of the library. Reading and sleeping were the order of the day. I put in an unpopular curfew, and the entire latrine was closed for forty-five minutes every morning. That gave me a chance to Lysol the facilities and mop down the floor, then let it dry. Now, my replacement is telling them that when he takes over, he will not close the latrine at all. Wait till he has his first inspection. He'll have lots of friends and a dirty latrine.

At the medical office, the doctor signs my check-off sheet, but will not give me any medication.

When I am discharged, my cellmate, Bill, wants to move from the upper to my lower bunk. The Renegade Jew will move into the cell and take the top bunk. Bill and the Renegade Jew get along well. They work out together. I wonder if they'll miss me.

Tuesday, January 25, 1994

At breakfast, the new chef sits at our table.

"How did you like the French toast?"

"It was OK," said one inmate, "but it had an egg taste to it."

The temperature this morning has climbed to twenty degrees.

At 9:30 a.m., I'm in a new meeting room off the visitor room, with other inmates standing watch over me. I'm meeting with several inmates to go over my testimony before the United States Sentencing Commission.

I spend the evening in my cell. Since my problem with the Philly crowd, I spend a lot of nights here. As one inmate advised me, "Joe, you're too short to get in trouble now."

At 9:30 p.m., there's a major disruption in the TV room. The issue is whether to watch President Clinton's speech to Congress or the movie *A Leap of Faith*. Clinton wins out. He's expected to address prison reform, according to an inmate who has a friend in Washington, but this turns out to be untrue.

Wednesday, January 26, 1994

This morning, I meet with more inmates who want to contribute ideas to my testimony before the United States Sentencing Commission. The inmates see this as a one-time opportunity, and I'm the designated hitter. I'm scheduled to be at the halfway house then, and I'll need approval by the Probation Department to make the trip.

One phenomenon here is the abrupt end to relationships and how the person who departs, oddly, is rarely mentioned again. Across the hall was a black inmate named Joe. He was very popular among African Americans. He's been gone ten days now, and I have not heard one person mention his name. Nobody has said, "Say, I wonder how Joe is doing?"

Lights out at 10:30 p.m. One week from tonight, I'll be sleeping somewhere else. Let the countdown begin.

Thursday, January 27, 1994

At 7:45 a.m., Permanent Latrine Orderly Number One (that's me, at least for another couple of days) hears from Permanent Latrine Orderly Number Two (my replacement), who says he has a dental appointment at 8:50 a.m. That probably means we won't see him for the rest of the day.

When I have an appointment outside, I work around it. I wonder what he'll do after I leave. I wonder who'll do the work. On other work details, it's easy to find a replacement to pick up the slack, but not at the latrine. That's the beauty of working alone but also the liability.

The sun has set, and it's snowing again. It's minus eleven degrees, and the wind is raging at sixty miles an hour, creating a wind chill of forty-one below zero. The news media are pleading with people to remain indoors. Here, the snow detail is summoned to work outside.

Friday, January 28, 1994

Camel shakes me awake at 5:15 a.m. and reminds me this is my last Friday here.

From the shower, I look out the window, and the path from Unit Two to the administration building is a sheet of ice. The chef and his assistant are stuck midway between the two buildings. They're stranded, at least momentarily. The chef tries to stand up again and falls again, and now he's crawling back to Unit Two.

Dinner tonight is Mexican food. In the kitchen, food supplies are at an all-time low. In the cell blocks, supplies have never been better. Last night, at Unit Two, we had a terrific fresh fruit salad.

Saturday, January 29, 1994

At breakfast, the apple roll should be classified as an illegal weapon. Put it inside a sock, and you could do a lot of damage.

After breakfast, it occurs to me that the administration has been watching me carefully of late; I don't think I've given them reason.

Another example this morning of the racial tension that simmers beneath the surface. Herb, the black inmate from Orlando whom I've been training to run a marathon, was spreading salt on the path he intended to use. Suddenly, he heard a hack yell at him.

"Hey, Buck, what are you doing with the salt?"

Now the name Buck is short for Buckwheat, a word that is insulting to an African American, just short of calling him Sambo or Nigger. Herb replied in a loud, crisp voice.

"I don't answer to Buck."

The hack, knowing he'd made a mistake, backed off. Later, Herb was called to the office. The hack told him that whatever Herb thought he'd been called, the hack had witnesses who would testify otherwise.

Tonight is my last Catholic service with Fr. Dene, who offers Mass today for Mr. and Mrs. Richard McLaughlin, who are later identified as his dead aunt and uncle.

Lights out. The quicker I get to sleep, the quicker the day is over. I'm that close.

Sunday, January 30, 1994

At 5:30 a.m., it's dark and still outside, with a three-quarter moon and a sky full of stars.

My friend the Doc is on duty in the cafeteria today, and he has a special treat for me. Knowing this is my last coffee hour, he's made raisin and cinnamon toast with butter, and it's great.

This is Super Bowl Sunday, and inmates are making plans as to where they'll watch the game, with whom, and what to serve for food. The game doesn't begin for another eleven hours.

It's 8:00 a.m., latrine time. I'm not on duty and don't have to be here today, but I don't know where else to go or how to do it any other way than show up to work. My successor is nowhere to be found. I'll stock up, give him plenty of material to work with. Maybe I should be more like him.

Back in the cell block, Neil, my Orthodox neighbor, wants to talk about a problem. Items of value are missing from his locker. We have an idea who is stealing them. The question is, should Neil confront the thief?

My answer is no, that Neil does not have proof. Neil may be right, but without proof, he has nothing. I suggest he move to another range, and I offer to make arrangements for him before I leave. Just as it was important for me to remain on *A* range, it seems important for Neil to leave. He's just not going to survive here.

At 9:30 a.m., a new inmate who resembles Brian Dennehy complains of a bad toenail. He can't walk. It's an ingrown nail. He goes to the infirmary, but the doctor refuses to treat it. He says the inmate will have to wait till it becomes infected.

Later, I'm working out with Butch. He does his 500 push-ups and 1,000 sit-ups, counting quietly. The Latinos come in.

"Hi, Rawhide."

But Butch discourages any conversation.

"We're here to work out," he says, "not shoot the breeze."

The TV room is a madhouse as inmates gather to watch the Super Bowl. As the third quarter ends, Buffalo is losing to Dallas, and so, having seen the best part of the game, I head back to *A* range to read my DeMille book.

Monday, January 31, 1994

My first thought when I wake is that as of today, I've been here seventeen weeks. I wish I could say it flew by. It hasn't. It seems as if I've been here forever.

I have a lot of last-minute loose ends to attend to, papers from other inmates, letters, addresses. I have to mail home my notes, letters, publications, and I have to make arrangements with the administration for my transfer to the halfway house.

My friend Steve leaves today. He's headed to a halfway house in Lawrence. His only means of transportation is a bus. He tells the administration he has no money. The administration gives him ten dollars for the eighteen-hour trip.

Not long after I arrive for latrine duty today, it's obvious that there's an organized effort involving my friends here to stop by for a final good-bye. I didn't pick up on that until what seemed like the fiftieth inmate came in and said that he just wanted to come in one more time to use my latrine before I leave. Well, at least I've left my stamp on this place. And their aim has improved. Now, occasionally, they hit the water.

I'm reminded by the administration that while I'm on probation, it will be illegal to communicate with other felons. Fine. Then, why is everybody giving me his address?

At 2:00 p.m., I hear, "Timilty, report to the administration office."

That's usually a problem, and it is this time, too.

The mental giants who run this place believe they've uncovered my plot to escape from here. Hacks from the mail room have discovered that a letter to me contains an airline ticket, and they confront me with the evidence. I explain that I'm leaving Wednesday, and the ticket is for my return to Boston.

"How will you get from here to the airport in Harrisburg?" they ask.

"I'm being driven by an attorney from Philadelphia, Nolan Atkinson."

"How long will it take you to get from the airport in Boston to the halfway house in Boston?"

"Oh, four or five days."

Nobody laughs.

At mail call, I get twenty-five letters. I wonder what happens after I leave. The mail they give me today has been around here for days.

At dinner, lots of inmates wish me good luck. I've looked around this dining room hundreds of times, and now it occurs to me that I haven't seen the faces of these men, not really. What I see now is a mixture of pain and hope, mostly pain. The lines in their faces that come from spending so much time in prison are permanent.

Most of these guys who are here were punished for their crimes before they arrived. In most cases, they were punished the day they were indicted and then again on the day they were convicted, and the larger reason they are kept here at great expense instead of at a community halfway house is to keep the BOP staff working.

From time to time, people with a social intelligence make an effort to send the nonviolent, first-time offenders from here to home confinement, to reunite them with families, to have them perform community service and donate their salaries to the government. But the BOP wants these camps full. It's their reason for being, and neither the Justice Department nor Janet Reno has the wisdom, the desire, or the political strength to force the issue.

In my case, there should be no question of the role religion has played in helping me through this, especially the rosary and benediction service.

I have been critical, and probably unfairly, of Fr. Dene. He introduced me to the Monday night services, and on November 6, he gave me the rosary beads I hope to carry with me always. Every Monday at 6:00 p.m., I'll think of Schuykill, the Catholic services, the rosary and benediction. The scene I'll always remember is the inmates, great, big, tough men on their knees in prayer, their gnarled, scarred fingers holding the small beads of their rosary, appealing for something better.

One more crisis: my cellmate, Bill, learns tonight that he has been fired from his job in the kitchen. Someone reported to the administration that he was bringing food back to the unit. In spite of the difficulty he now faces in adjusting to a new job here, do you know what his biggest regret seems to be? That my going-away party will be dampened because he longer will be able to provide food from the kitchen. Here's a guy who's got to spend another ten years in this place, who's just lost his prized job, and this is what he is worried about?

Throughout the evening, there was plenty of traffic here, with inmates dropping by to say good-bye and good luck. When the lights go out, I'm so excited, I can't fall asleep. It won't be long now. I'm thinking of you, Elaine.

Tuesday, February 1, 1994

For the last time, Camel wakes me. He has not been talking much to me in recent days. It's almost as if I'm deserting him.

At breakfast, with my friend George behind the counter, my eggs are made to order. Back on *A* range, I make my bed. Boy, will I be glad to see the last of this bunk.

At 7:45 a.m., I head for the laundry room. When Schuykill gave me these clothes, they were clean. When I give them back, they'll be clean.

My biggest problem today is getting my papers out of Schuykill, 120 days of information, memos I have been able to hide away, official documents and other papers that I intend to use if I ever sit down and organize this journal. These documents are hidden in magazines, among letters received from friends and supporters. They are used as bookmarks in some novels I'm sending home.

All my notes on Phil Kagan are there, in code, so that if they're discovered, no hack can decipher them. But there are names of inmates still under the jurisdiction of the BOP who have information about purchasing, about medical units, about the educational scam, food, etc. All of this and press material from *60 Minutes*. It's definitely not material I want the hacks to go through, because, if it's discovered as I'm walking out the door, they may not let me go.

Like other prisoners, I get to send personal papers and pictures to my home in a carton, but it must be inspected by my counselor and sealed by him and carried directly to the mail room. The timing is delicate. I have to get it to the mail room by noon, which is the hour when the mail room closes. I cannot leave the carton here, unattended. I can't take the chance a hack might go through it after I leave. There are too many articles that can be traced to individual inmates.

So, I'm watching for my counselor's car. It's going to be close. At 10:30 a.m., my counselor has not arrived. Ninety minutes to go. I'm sweating this one out. Finally, at 10:45 a.m., I spot his car and begin the search for him. I have one hour to get this done.

It is after 11:00 a.m. when I find him walking the corridor. He says he'll meet me in the mail room at noon. That's cutting it close. On the other hand, I can't take the chance in pressing him. The less time he has, the less time he'll take to inspect the package.

A few minutes before noon, we arrive at the mail room. My package is taken to a back room. I stand outside, sweating. The door opens. He approaches.

"Sign these," he says, and I look beyond him and see my package sealed with masking tape. It should be a breeze from here.

Tonight, it's my last supper. It's tough to imagine guys like Pat, who are looking at five more years, still making a fuss and a celebration over my departure.

On my last night, I celebrate. These are inmates with whom I've struggled, sweated, cursed, and laughed through this difficult chapter of my life. Out of nowhere (except prison ingenuity) someone produces a camera. They want pictures. We head to the arts room, where there is a proper background, and snapshots are taken of me with Coach, Paul, Mark, my cellmate, Bill, the Renegade Jew, and others.

By 10:00 p.m., most everyone has come and gone. I'm eager to climb into the rack for my last night here, but Coach and Paul have last-minute advice, instructions, suggestions, promises. It's as if they don't want the night to end. I think they don't want me to go.

When the lights finally go out, it will be a long time before I can fall asleep. I can't help wondering why, in the big picture, I ended up with these guys at this time. I wonder if I've helped them. I know it's helped me, and I'm grateful. In the dark, I reach for my rosary beads.

Wednesday, February 2, 1994

This morning, I'm awake before Camel. I see him coming. As quick as he arrives, he disappears. I guess Camel doesn't like good-byes either.

I didn't get much sleep. I kept seeing the faces of the guys who came by to say good-bye, including Shannon, the gay inmate, who has typed all my letters to the sentencing commission. I introduced him to inmates who otherwise would not have been seen talking to him, and he was grateful. It made him feel like a human being.

Even the group from Philly stopped by to say good-bye. When I saw them approach, I wasn't sure whether there was going to be a battle, and Paul said he wasn't, either.

The going-away party is something I'll never forget. With my cell-mate, Bill, having been fired from the kitchen, all the food that was stolen eventually will have to be replaced. In other words, repurchased from the commissary. While we were away taking pictures, other inmates were chilling salads and preparing crackers with pepperoni and cheese.

Countless others came by simply to say good-bye, and in their faces, I could see a flicker of hope that said, when this guy gets out, maybe he'll tell our story, and maybe someone will listen.

On this morning, Joe Timilty is walking on air. It feels strange to go through the normal routine of showering, shaving, dressing, and all the while knowing that it's the last time.

At breakfast, over an abomination of creamed turkey over biscuits, there is more swapping of addresses, phone numbers, and promises to get together. Maybe some of the promises will be kept, but probably not.

Here comes a big surprise, It's the leader of the African American community, who is six feet seven, who always has four henchmen with him, and with whom I haven't exchanged twelve words in 120 days because it was clear that he had no use for me.

I never took it personally. I knew he had no use for anybody who was white. Suddenly, however, he's standing over me like a skyscraper. He speaks in a towering voice.

"Just want to say that I and my group think you have handled yourself well. Never whined, did your time like a man. Some of the toughest guys here cry a lot. You didn't."

He shakes my hand and walks away. As quickly as he appeared, he goes back to his group.

My cellmate, Bill, starts a new job today, and I start a new life at a new home. He extends his hand and says the words that express how we feel about one another.

"You're a good cellmate."

I don't respond. I'm not supposed to.

Too late, anyway, for in an instant, he's gone. I watch him walk away. His limp is more noticeable, and I think it's because on these cold days he feels the pain. It occurs to me that he's been in prison for three years, and he'll be here for seven more. I have trouble absorbing the reality of that.

It's almost 8:00 p.m., and time for that last mile, that walk between my locker and the administration office. Paul and Louis, the Spanish Nightmare, walk it with me, as a sign of respect.

Inmates see these signs. They don't say anything. They don't acknowledge them. But nobody misses anything. You can't ask anyone to walk this leg with you. It doesn't work that way, but it is the last compliment that can be paid.

There are quiet embraces. I have to confess that the notion of men hugging one another makes us Irish pretty uncomfortable; we were brought up to be as cold as the waters off Killarney. Never show emotion.

As Paul, Louis, and I start walking those last steps through the administration building, there are inmates moving about. Some of them yell out encouragement.

"Good luck, Joe."

But for many of them, I no longer exist. I am gone already. Even my replacement in the latrine hardly looks up as I pass. I understand this perfectly. You can't let these departures bother you. They can cripple you mentally. As we go by the laundry, the Doc is standing in the doorway, waiting for me. We shake hands.

"Good luck, Joe."

"You too, Doc. I hope to see you someday under different circumstances."

I turn to go.

"Joe," he says, and I look back.

"Do yourself a favor. Forget this place. Erase all the memories from your mind."

I nod.

We pass the library. A large group of Latinos are waiting, the painters, TV watchers, workout enthusiasts, all Latinos, all of whom have turned out to say good-bye to an amigo, a sign of affection to one who has written their letters, read their mail, and given them respect. As we turn to go, one of them yells out, "Hasta luego, Rawhide…"

At last, the three of us arrive at the office. This is where they leave me. This is it.

Good-bye to Louis, the Spanish Nightmare, the best importer from Puerto Rico who still has five years to go. And good-bye to Paul, my friend from Boston, with six to go. Louis and I embrace. Paul and I embrace. With all this embracing, my Irish ancestors must be rolling in their graves, muttering to one another, where did we go wrong with young Joe?

This is the last stop. When I arrived, I came into this room, and I was stripped of street clothes. Now I am in the same room and about to be stripped of prison clothes. The hacks search my body cavities for contraband, and I am tempted to scream at them, "What in hell would I be taking out of here?"

Elaine sent clothes, a blue turtleneck, and a running suit from Rick Snyder's, blue in color and made for winter wear, and also a pair of running shoes. I put on the clothes Elaine has sent, and instantly I feel my personality change. My muscles become less tense. It's a strange feeling of looseness and liberation.

Back in the corridor, then down to the front office to pick up my airline ticket. The mood in the administration office is somber, almost as if they take no pleasure in seeing an inmate leave in civilian clothes, without cuffs, without leg irons. They return the money from my commissary account. I ask for copies of my final papers, and although it takes no more than thirty seconds, it incurs the displeasure of the staff.

Back out in the corridor and then, at long last, out through the door I entered 120 days ago. But this time, I open the door, and behind me, I hear a chorus of "See ya, Joe!" and "Good luck Joe!" and "Go get 'em, Rawhide."

I turn.

One last wave.

Then I turn again to look to the outdoors, to freedom, to the future.

I walk out of the building, and I watch, I feel, I hear, and I measure each footstep toward my liberty. Outside, the car that will bear me away from this awful place is at the curb, and I hear the sweet sound of its engine, idling.

It's cold out here, but beautiful. Nolan can't make it. He has a court appearance. So, he sends a car. I don't know the driver. I don't care. He looks great, and why? Because he doesn't have a badge. He's not carrying a club. In fact, surprise!—he's smiling. I say to myself, don't look back, Joe. Get in the car, close the door, sit back, relax.

The car makes its way down the driveway. I'm on my way home to Boston.

The driver asks if there's anything he can get for me. I ask for a large cup of store-bought coffee for the ninety-minute ride.

I'm in the back seat, watching the glorious Pennsylvania countryside sweep past, at peace, sipping coffee, struggling with my memories, savoring my dreams.

As we drive, I wonder whether people we pass realize that in my car, an ex-con is going home. And to what? What am I going home to? What happens now? I don't know.

The Doc said to forget Schuykill. That's probably the best advice, but I can't forget. It won't work. I saw too much. I know too much, and in good conscience, I cannot forget. I think what the Doc meant to say was this: "Forget what they did to you here, Joe, but don't forget those of us who are left here, rotting away."

The flight home this morning is an opportunity to reflect on how fortunate I am. Family and friends have stayed with me on this trip to hell and back, and now, I'm ready for the second day of the rest of my life. The plane wings over Providence, and then over the edge of the Atlantic Ocean and, finally, at long last, there it is, my hometown, Boston. No skyline ever looked better, no city ever looked more beautiful.

What a great feeling!

It is a lifetime since the day four months ago when I left Boston, and from up here in the plane, everything looks the same. But down there, it's never going to be the same, not for me, anyway. They have made sure of that.

Everyone in jail changes. But how have I changed, and how much? Time will tell.

EPILOGUE

B ack in his native Boston, the ironies and inanities merely continued. Joe was assigned to spend sixty days at a Coolidge House, a halfway house located near the YMCA on Huntington Avenue. It was a facility he had, ironically, been instrumental in establishing. Back in the early 1970s, he'd served on the Board of the YMCA and had supported creating the newly proposed halfway house in a nearby hotel, despite the objections raised by many local residents, who feared the kind of people such a facility might attract. Joe, committed to the use of halfway houses as a valuable alternative to prisons, had blocked efforts to convince the YMCA to oppose it.

Now, however, he was living there, and while his experience didn't change his mind about the potential value of such sentencing alternatives, it did dramatically reveal shortcomings that can arise from poor oversight and shoddy administration.

He was assigned to Room 310, a space smaller than his cell at Schuykill. His roommate, Larry, was serving five months at Coolidge House and had lost his home to foreclosure. Thus, he'd moved all his remaining worldly possessions into the tiny room. Joe, on the other hand, was not allowed to have sheets and blankets brought to him but instead was required to use the stained and worn items issued by the administration. Moreover, sharing was unnecessary because many rooms were empty.

Crowded conditions were only a minor problem, however. The building itself was old and seriously deficient. On days when the temperature outside was in the teens, the temperature inside was so high that it was difficult to breathe. Even with the windows open, wasting valuable energy, Coolidge House was uncomfortably hot. On the other hand, in the early morning, after the heat had been turned off for a few hours, the building would become too cold for residents to sleep. Furthermore, the windows were all barred (a major violation of Boston's building code) making escape in case of fire impossible.

Joe was accustomed to the kinds of problems old buildings posed, but he was appalled that a federal facility had made so little effort to retrofit the heating system and thus save the taxpayers thousands of dollars in heating bills. And the filth of the facility was a problem that could clearly have been avoided at little cost. Throughout his stay at Coolidge House he watched dozens of cockroaches roaming the dining area every evening. When he was assigned kitchen duty, he sent dozens scrambling each time he moved furniture around in order to mop. The endless parade of vermin, including rats, was stunning. Indeed, the attendant in the lobby complained that at night rats would come up the stairs from the cellar and had to be beaten back with a broom. As a former public official, Joe was appalled that the taxpayers were footing the bill for an institution that was grossly inefficient, wasteful, and disgracefully, unnecessarily filthy.

But wasted energy and unsanitary conditions were merely the most obvious of Coolidge House's inefficiencies. The administration was in every way unbelievably lax. Instead of serving as a halfway place for felons being reintroduced into society, instead of helping those people to bridge the gap between incarceration and independence, Coolidge House was a sleazy training ground for crime. Drug deals were commonly transacted on the sidewalk of the building—just what local residents had once feared. At the rear was a large bathroom used on occasion for sexual trysts, conducted with maximum sound effects, while halfway-house residents sat watching TV in the adjoining lobby. And although alcohol was strictly forbidden, the regulations were so badly enforced that inmates regularly brought liquor in through the front door and up to their rooms.

From time to time, the administration conducted "surprise" drug tests that were pathetic. Everyone was given a paper cup and asked to supply a urine sample. But those residents who were not drug-free simply hassled those who were to provide samples for them.

For Joe, the entire experience was a valuable reminder of the need for scrupulous and honest administration of valuable policies and programs that could not survive without such careful implementation. An honest, dedicated administrator, and a Congress willing to spend money on alternatives to prison, could transform Coolidge House from a disgrace to a valuable experience for men who would soon be rejoining society.

Each resident was granted one hour a day to exercise at the nearby YMCA and one hour on Saturday or Sunday for religious purposes. Some inmates were also granted extra free time, and some even got furloughs to go home from Friday afternoon to Sunday night. Joe was treated differently at Coolidge House from his arrival. He eventually saw this as part of a tacit conspiracy between the executive director of Coolidge House and the Justice Department, an obvious effort to induce him to break a rule, any rule, for which they could then discipline him.

Of particular concern to the executive director was the prospect that Joe's residency at the halfway house would be covered by the press.

"Now, let's talk about the media," he said to Joe at their first meeting. "I don't want a lot of publicity surrounding your stay here."

Joe answered with measured anger.

"I won't solicit the news media, but if a reporter puts a microphone in front of me and asks me a question, I will answer it. The right of free speech has not, so far as I know, been taken from me."

Still, life at the halfway house was certainly easier than it had been in prison. Every morning at nine, Joe left for work, alone, without handcuffs, and without being followed. He worked at a local restaurant company and returned from work every evening by nine. At first, he was also allowed to go to the nearby YMCA to work out for two hours a day, but that was soon reduced to one. He was happy to work within the rules, but the rules, as far as they applied to him, seemed to change frequently. At one point, for example, Joe was invited to testify before the US Sentencing Commission in Washington, DC, a body established by Congress to develop sentencing guidelines for federal inmates. His testifying was approved by the federal court, but the probation department extended his sentence at the halfway house one day to compensate for the time spent testifying.

Slowly, Joe reentered the world and picked up the pieces of his life. In many ways, his family emerged stronger than ever from the nightmare of his arrest, trial, and imprisonment. He and Elaine had feared that their children might lose all respect for the judicial system, as a result of Joe's experience, and they worked hard to convince their kids that Joe's case was not the norm and that most of the time the system does work. They also stressed that when the system doesn't work, it's usually not a failure of the system itself but of the people who run it, and they emphasized that we all have a responsibility to improve our government and our society.

Today, Joe works as a lobbyist, representing clients at the Massachusetts State House. Three of his children work in the public sector; two are in business, and two are successfully completing their education.

The US Attorney at the time of Joe's case, A. John Pappalardo, after a failed attempt to gain a state judgeship, has joined a Boston law firm that represents clients being prosecuted by the Boston US Attorney's office. James De Cotis is seriously ill. Monte Marrocco and Joe Benoit are still in real estate, despite their many violations of the law. Michael D'Avolio never served a day in jail. Michael Lo Presti is practicing law in Massachusetts and was never charged with any wrongdoing in connection with the gumball factory, since he'd never committed a crime. And John Parigian is under indictment in a criminal case.

The family of Phil Kagan has filed a $15 million lawsuit against the Bureau of Prisons in connection with Phil's death. Billy, Joe's cellmate at Schuykill, whom he saw in the visitor's room playing with his little boy, was found dead, hanging in his cell, under what the family claims are mysterious circumstances.

In the months after his release, Joe struggled seriously to identify any good that had been accomplished by his incarceration. Was society any safer now, he wondered, because he had spent four months at Schuykill? He didn't think so. His job as Permanent Latrine Orderly certainly didn't provide him with any skills that were usable on his reintegration to society. The system made no effort to "rehabilitate" him or to use his skills to help at the prison or in the surrounding community. Rather, his time was spent fighting a combination of boredom and bureaucratic and inmate insanity.

He did, however, receive an education of sorts. He learned that the prison system is corrupt, ineffectual, and largely meaningless and that it makes absolutely no sense for most nonviolent, first-time offenders. Millions of dollars of taxpayer money are wasted annually to incarcerate people who don't belong in prison, or who are lost as a result of mismanagement or corruption. More important, he learned that the system cries out for complicated, painful reform measures.

Thinking back on his experiences, Joe worked to formulate policies and recommendations that might improve the prison system, seeking a balance between stringency and fairness, a mix that would both punish dangerous criminals and protect society from violence, while seeking to redress wrongs in creative ways, moving beyond the warehousing of nonviolent offenders to healing social and community wounds. They are as follows:

1. Flexible Sentencing
Mandatory sentencing robs judges of their essential discretionary power and blurs the important constitutional distinction between legislative

and judicial branches of government. Pandering shamelessly to public fears about crime, legislators have passed simplistic and often impractical requirements for mandatory sentences. Yet these new laws do not touch the root causes of crime, they merely calcify the judicial system, so that many nonviolent, first-time offenders are sent to prison for years, at taxpayer expense, rather than providing community restoration. Testifying before the United States Sentencing Commission in 1994, Joe said, "There is no sense having judges on the bench if they cannot use the discretion that their years of experience have given them."

Sometimes, of course, long mandatory sentences for nonviolent offenders are necessary to set an example or to protect society from a serious predator. Other times, however, such sentences are simply wasteful, or worse, cruel and unnecessary. In the case of Sam the Colostomy Man, for example, life in prison constituted a hellish punishment well beyond what the law could possibly have intended. He might have provided more significant restitution to his community had he been allowed to serve time outside prison. A thoughtful judge, with the discretion to sentence according to the specific needs of each case, might have sentenced Sam to a shorter term in prison and a longer term providing such restitution.

At the same time that judges are forced, by mandatory sentencing policies, to send first-time, nonviolent offenders to prison, law enforcement agencies complain that violent criminals are often given abbreviated sentences because prisons are overcrowded. The result is exactly the opposite of that intended by mandatory sentences. People who *could* function more productively on the outside are on the inside, and people who *should* be on the inside, to protect society, are on the outside. We need to allow judges to draw on their professional expertise in imposing sentences that more specifically suit the individual crimes.

2. Creative Sentencing
The majority of the inmates serving time in federal prisons around the country belong there. But just as obviously, we might productively

reexamine the cases of the 20 percent who are low-level criminals with no record of violence.

The cost of imprisoning an inmate in the federal prison system is at least $35,000 a year If 13,000 inmates identified by the Justice Department itself as low-level criminals were to be released and confined to home and work, strictly monitored by a leg bracelet, taxpayers would save $455 million *annually*. (The cost of a leg bracelet is $95 per month and is paid for by the prisoner out of his wages.)

The benefits of such creative approaches are clear. If nonviolent inmates could hold down jobs on the outside, while being monitored through their leg bracelets, they would be producing *for* society rather than being subsidized *by* society. They would be contributing to the tax base, rather than drawing on it, while their families might be less likely to apply for welfare, and their children would certainly be less traumatized (and less likely to become social or behavioral problems themselves).

Our judicial system ought to allow nonviolent, first-time offenders to serve their time on weekends, when they could be assigned to do productive work in their communities, turning in a portion of their incomes to the government. This way, the government would get taxes from these people, their victims might receive some restitution, and taxpayers would not be spending $35,000 a year to warehouse them.

3. Halfway Houses

This is a good idea, being destroyed by inadequate or corrupt implementation. In theory, halfway houses allow inmates to live closer to their families, working at jobs full time. In theory, inmates turn over 25 percent of their salary toward the cost of their incarceration. And in theory, halfway houses provide a necessary bridge between incarceration and freedom, especially in helping inmates adjust to the world outside prison and to rebuild their lives constructively.

However, if Coolidge House in Boston is an example of federally funded halfway houses, ineptitude, corruption, and mismanagement have allowed America's halfway houses to deteriorate into drug-ridden, vermin-infested embarrassments. If we really want to lower the recidivism rate among criminals, we need to provide more stringent oversight of such institutions and to ensure that they are more effectively and intelligently run, with more practical transition services for inmates as well as more stringent enforcement of drug laws.

4. Meaningful Work
We need to make serious changes to the kinds of work inmates do within the federal system. In a society moving to push people off welfare and to create workfare, while slashing countless social programs, we have both the opportunity and the urgent need to rethink the kind of work nonviolent inmates can do. It's not just that eight hours of cleaning toilets or picking up cigarette butts is not "meaningful" work—the problem is worse: we're not using prisons to achieve *any* social good, whether restitution or repair of the social fabric. Surely, federal inmates could be put to work restoring America's bridges and roads or working in woefully underfunded nursing homes and mental hospitals or cleaning up abandoned lots in the inner city. Many of these federal inmates, especially those who are nonviolent, have skills and abilities they might bring to their work, skills in accounting or teaching, gardening or coaching, administering or filing, finances or carpentry. Instead of warehousing these people, we need to tap into their resources to restore our social order and their connection with the larger community.

5. Meaningful Education
Most prison experts agree that illiteracy and crime are closely connected. Indeed, about 70 percent of those in prison have been shown to perform on the lowest two levels of literacy scales. In response, millions of dollars of federal and state taxes have been spent to provide "educational" programs for inmates. Unfortunately, the opportunity to get a high school education in federal prisons is, in most cases, a sham.

The United States Department of Education pays the Bureau of Prisons $2500 for each inmate without a high school degree who attends classes and passes an equivalency test. Yet teachers who served with Joe at Schuykill say the test is geared to only a ninth-grade level.

The Education Department needs to reexamine this program carefully. Perhaps the education of inmates could be entrusted to local school boards or community colleges, which could use the funding from the Department of Education to pay for local educational programs or to supplement college scholarship funds.

6. Meaningful Religion

There's something fundamentally wrong with a system in which the chaplains, Catholic and Protestant, are direct employees of the Bureau of Prisons. At Schuykill, Catholic inmates saw Father Dene more as a guard than a cleric. As a result, they were reluctant, indeed unwilling, to confide in him, and so they never went to confession, believing that any sins they admitted would be repeated to the prison administration.

This is a flagrant violation of the most fundamental religious and spiritual injunctions of both church and society. The confessional has traditionally been accorded the most sacred privacy possible. The fact that Catholic inmates distrusted the priest so much meant, in effect, that they had no religious resource to turn to, no one who might have helped them achieve a kind of spiritual replenishment.

By contrast, the rabbi who ministered to the Jewish population was independent of prison management and thus highly respected and well trusted by Jewish inmates.

We need to rethink the policy of putting religious personnel on the prison payroll. If priests and minister from the prison's surrounding area aren't willing to tend to prisoners within their community, without pay from the Bureau of Prisons local divinity school students might be asked to do volunteer work in prisons; even those who couldn't administer the sacraments could still provide some religious consolation, without losing the trust of their charges.

7. Congressional Oversight

Busily cutting welfare and slashing social programs, the Republican Congress has paid little attention to the crisis in America's prisons. Unwilling to address complex social issues that don't lend themselves to glib, bumper sticker-like "solutions," Congress has postured dramatically in recent years on the issues of reducing the deficit and preventing crime. Yet it has done virtually nothing to ensure that federal prisons are run efficiently and intelligently.

Consider Schuykill's Wellness Center, the state-of-the-art health facility for guards. It is an outrageous waste of taxpayer money. Multiply this by sixty-six federal institutions, and you get a sense of the scope of waste and inefficiency in the implementation of federal prisons. How does the Bureau of Prisons get away with this unconscionable waste of public money in a time of federal cutbacks for the poor, the elderly, students, and others? Because both Congress and the Federal Office of the Budget lack the resources, the energy, and the will to expose a charade like the Wellness Center. And because any and all money spent on prisons is accepted, without examination, as "anti-crime" and therefore politically expedient.

8. Purchasing

It's not a glamorous issue, and it doesn't make for great political rhetoric, but the waste in prison purchasing processes costs the taxpayers an incalculable amount of money. At Schuykill, inmates with experience in the restaurant business told Joe that the Bureau of Prisons was paying top dollar for food of the lowest possible quality: apples, for example, so small and wormy that they would not ever be displayed at a regular market. Fish is weighed *with* the ice that keeps it fresh, jacking up the cost significantly.

The American public might not much care that prisoners aren't eating well. But the taxpayers certainly shouldn't be paying more for food than it's really worth. Furthermore, controlling such expenditures isn't very complicated. Effective management in the form of cost control and improved security would upgrade the quality of the food while saving the taxpayers thousands of dollars.

At institutions such as Schuykill, inventories are, of course, conducted regularly, but they are just as regularly inaccurate. For example, last year's inventory at Schuykill might have reflected thirty-six washing machines, but since guards have already stolen ten there may be only twenty-six this year. Nevertheless, inmates conducting the inventories are instructed to record thirty-six machines.

We need a stringent new system of purchasing control and accountability preferably conducted by a private, outside company with no connections to the prison administration.

9. Prosecutorial Misconduct

We need to rethink the prevailing prosecutorial policy of building investigations and cases solely on the evidence squeezed from one or two defendants, evidence given in exchange for immunity or special sentences. Granted, the government has been able to make some important cases, including Watergate, only through the use of this method. And at times, reliance on the testimony *has* allowed the government to go after more serious offenders.

Yet in recent years, especially since the onslaught of high-profile political corruption and drug cases in the 1980s, such practices have become the norm, even when they may not be necessary. At the very least, the practice of relying on informers and people turning state's evidence against former colleagues erodes public confidence in the justice system, turning it into a game of trade-offs and bartering rather than the judicial and judicious of community values to ensure the social good. At worst, as in Joe's case, it rewards the sleazy and corrupt while punishing those whose code of honor opposes naming names and violating trust.

Most of these issues, of course, are no longer even debated in our country. Politicians are fearful of introducing any proposal that might remotely be interpreted as sympathetic to criminals, while once-valuable alternative policies have fallen victim to the rush for simplistic and draconian solutions. Consider the furlough program, an honorable and progressive step in prison reform in the United States. During the 1988 presidential election, George Bush's cynical and profoundly racist use of the Willie Horton case to embarrass Michael Dukakis was seared into the minds of politicians, who are now reluctant to take the lead in *any* kind of prison reform, lest it play badly in their home districts.

Furthermore, in a country that incarcerates a larger percentage of its population than any nation on earth, prisons have become a big business. Although no one wants to live next door to a prison, a number of states, including Texas, Florida, and Pennsylvania regularly bid for prisons to be located within their borders, because the construction and the administration of these facilities provide jobs and a boost to the local economy. We risk getting locked into a cycle in which we build prisons because we want the jobs, not because we truly need the space. Why not put the same labor and money into building housing? Daycare centers? Assisted-living facilities?

In the process of filling these federal prisons, a central role is played by the US Attorney's Offices. Unfortunately, politically appointed US Attorneys often practice selective political prosecution, seeking high-profile cases that are likely to attract media attention and enhance their plea-bargaining negotiations. Justice, all too often, falls victim to the quest to win at any cost.

If Americans thought about these issues, or if our political leaders had the courage to discuss them, most of us would agree that something is seriously wrong when the United States imprisons so many of its people. And something is even more awry when that incarceration merely holds people in detention, rather than rehabilitating criminals or providing meaningful restitution to the community.

Made in the USA
Middletown, DE
03 May 2015